RURAL POLITICS IN NORTHERN IRELAND

For Monica with thanks

Rural Politics in Northern Ireland

Policy Networks and Agricultural Development Since Partition

ALAN GREER
School of Politics
University of the West of England

Avebury

Aldershot · Brookfield USA · Hong Kong · Singapore · Sydney

Published by
Avebury
Ashgate Publishing Ltd
Gower House
Croft Road
Aldershot
Hants GU11 3HR
England

Ashgate Publishing Company
Old Post Road
Brookfield
Vermont 05036
USA

British Library Cataloguing in Publication Data

Greer, Alan
     Rural Politics in Northern Ireland:
     Policy Networks and Agricultural
     Development Since Partition
     I. Title
     338.18416

     ISBN 1 85972 064 1

Library of Congress Catalog Card Number: 95-83289

Printed in Great Britain by Ipswich Book Co. Ltd., Ipswich, Suffolk.

Contents

List of tables

Acknowledgements

I would like to thank all those who have helped me to write this book. In particular I would like to acknowledge the assistance of the staff of the Public Records Office of Northern Ireland and of the library at The Queen's University of Belfast who helped me find my way through the myriad collections of official and other sources on which the book is largely based.

Also thanks to all those at Queen's University, the University of Manchester and the University of the West of England who helped me develop and shape my ideas. Patrick Buckland, Sydney Elliott, Edward Moxon-Browne and Rick Wilford provided invaluable guidance. Sue Hatt read the draft chapters and provided many useful comments.

Finally I owe a special debt of gratitude to Monica and my parents without whose help and understanding this book would never have been written.

Abbreviations

BMB	Bacon Marketing Board
CAP	Common Agricultural Policy
DANI	Department of Agriculture for Northern Ireland
DATII	Department of Agriculture and Technical Instruction for Ireland
DUP	Democratic Unionist Party
EC	European Community
FUW	Farmers' Union of Wales
GDP	Gross Domestic Product
ICOS	Irish Co-operative Organisation Society
IFA	Irish Farmers' Association
LFA	Less Favoured Areas
MAF	Ministry of Agriculture and Fisheries (England and Wales)
MAFF	Ministry of Agriculture, Fisheries and Food (England and Wales)
MANI	Ministry of Agriculture for Northern Ireland
MMB	Milk Marketing Board
NFU	National Farmers' Union
NFUS	National Farmers' Union of Scotland
NIAPA	Northern Ireland Agricultural Producers' Association
NILAA	Northern Ireland Livestock Auctioneers' Association
NIO	Northern Ireland Office
PMB	Pigs Marketing Board
SDLP	Social Democratic and Labour Party
SPMB	Seed Potato Marketing Board
UAOS	Ulster Agricultural Organisation Society
UFU	Ulster Farmers' Union

Introduction

Until the 1980s the unchallenged assumption that "rural means agricultural" informed the evolution of rural politics in Northern Ireland. Historically, the dominant approach to rural development has reflected an overriding concern with agricultural issues and the 'correlation of the "rural" with agriculture...relegated other dimensions of the wider rural economy to the sidelines of inquiry and policy formation' (Greer and Murray, 1993, pp. 3-4). Key issues such as rural electrification and housing were politically controversial during the Stormont period, for example, but policy was conceptualized within an agricultural perspective rather than a holistic view of rural society. In this context an analysis of the nature of rural politics must be primarily concerned with the agricultural sector. Political factors in turn are central to an explanation of agricultural development in Northern Ireland. Farmers collectively constituted a central influence on the political system. Governments were intimately concerned with agricultural policy which has always been of fundamental importance to political life in Northern Ireland.

This book provides the first comprehensive account of rural politics and policy in Northern Ireland since 1920. Developments are related to wider political and theoretical debates about the policy making process and about the nature of politics in Northern Ireland. Three key arguments are central to the analysis. The most significant influence on rural politics has been the relationship between Northern Ireland and Great Britain. Policy has been the result of a tension between 'parity' and 'particularity'. Parity refers to the demand that the farmers of Northern Ireland be treated as integral to the United Kingdom, especially in respect of financial assistance; particularity to the extent to which a distinctive regional policy was developed to suit *sui generis* regional conditions. Despite devolution between 1921-72 agricultural policy was rooted in a parity imperative. The fundamentals of agricultural policy for Northern Ireland were set in London and a policy for the United Kingdom as a whole emerged, especially after 1939. Consequently the autonomy of the regional Parliament was gradually attenuated. Nationalist demands for the formulation of a policy more in tune with the nature of rural life in Ireland were rejected and the powers granted under the 1920 Government of Ireland Act were not used to formulate a distinctive policy suited to regional needs.

Secondly, the Belfast-London nexus was underpinned by an ideological consensus between the Northern Ireland Government and the majority of farmers. A close relationship developed between the Ministry of Agriculture (MANI) and the Ulster Farmers' Union (UFU) which was essentially grounded in the prevailing ethnic conflict and the ethos of discrimination against Nationalists. A shared ideological commitment to Unionism was embodied in the demand for equality of treatment for farmers throughout the United Kingdom. The creation of a monopolistic consultative relationship between the Ministry and Union was rooted in overlapping political and rural elites. For example there were significant kinship ties between the UFU and the Ulster Unionist Party and membership of the Union was a *de facto* requirement for the post of Minister of Agriculture. This was reinforced by the predominantly Protestant character of the Ulster Farmers' Union, its unwillingness or inability to appeal to Catholic farmers, and its orientation towards British farmers' unions rather than those in the south of Ireland.

Thirdly, developments since 1972 have weakened both the Belfast-London nexus and the monopolistic relationship between the state and the Ulster Farmers' Union. The combination of political instability, the collapse of the Stormont system, the imposition of direct rule, and entry into the European Community (EC) has resulted in a new configuration of relationships. The Belfast-London nexus increasingly has been replaced by one centred on Brussels. The agricultural policy network fragmented after 1972 with the formation of an organisation concerned primarily with the interests of small farmers but with a largely Catholic membership. Finally the Anglo-Irish approach to general political and constitutional issues instituted in the 1980s has also contributed to an increasing recognition of the need to improve and extend cross-border cooperation in agriculture and rural development.

The starting point for the analysis is a scene setting account of the political and economic importance of agriculture and rural society in Northern Ireland. This is considered in both the historical and territorial context, including the importance of national and international developments. Themes explored include major trends in the regional agricultural economy in areas such as land utilisation, farm structure, the nature of production, contribution to gross domestic product, rural employment and mechanization.

Chapter Two summarises the limitations on the autonomy of the Northern Ireland Parliament in respect of agriculture and rural policy. These were constitutional, ideological, financial and political. The institutional and administrative structures established are situated within the overall perspective of national and international political economy. Policy developments in Northern Ireland were influenced by wider considerations of economic and trade policy including laissez-faire, protection and EC entry.

In Chapter Three the book charts the development of marketing policy since

1920, including the movement away from compulsory marketing schemes to voluntary cooperatives after EC entry. Underlying the analysis is the friction between the Ministry and the UFU on the issue of producer control of marketing boards.

Chapter Four deals with the development of price and production policy during and after the Second World War. Northern Ireland was included in a post war agricultural policy for the United Kingdom as a whole. Guaranteed prices and assured markets were provided for farmers throughout the United Kingdom under the 1947 Agriculture Act. Central to the discussion are the issues of remoteness from British markets and price parity. The impact on Northern Ireland of the changes to the system of agricultural support after EC entry are also outlined.

The concepts of 'parity' and 'particularity' are developed in Chapter Five to explain the nature of the relationship between Northern Ireland and Great Britain. The Belfast-London nexus is scrutinised in the context of general political and constitutional disputes between Unionists and Nationalists. In practice the formal autonomy of the regional Parliament on rural issues was restricted by the parity imperative. A combination of political priorities and financial dependence on Westminster dictated an approach which stressed the position of Northern Ireland as an integral part of the United Kingdom. This in turn severely emasculated the extent to which the Northern Ireland Parliament could formulate distinctive policies to meet the particular needs of regional agriculture.

Chapter Six applies the idea of a policy network to the relationship between the 'state' and the farmer in Northern Ireland. The period of devolution 1921-72 was characterised by a monopolistic consultative relationship between the Ulster Farmers' Union and the Ministry of Agriculture. Although theories of policy community and meso corporatism have some explanatory value, the notion of parentela is central to a proper understanding of the essential nature of the farmer-state relationship in Northern Ireland.

Policy changes stimulated by the congruence of the collapse of the Stormont regime and EC entry are outlined in Chapter Seven. Key policy developments since 1972, notably the milk quota controversy of the mid 1980s, are considered in the context of parity and particularity. The agricultural policy network also fragmented with emergence of a rival to the UFU in the shape of the Northern Ireland Agricultural Producers' Association.

The book concludes with an assessment of north-south relations in the agricultural sphere since 1920. Future prospects for agriculture are discussed in the context of more general pressures for constitutional change. In particular demands for an all Ireland CAP regime and the dynamic towards formalised cross-border cooperation effectively signifies the end of the parity dynamic in the context of the United Kingdom. The peace process and the framework documents, with their proposals for cross-border executive agencies, indicate clearly that the future development of agriculture in Northern Ireland will be conceived in all Ireland terms.

1 Agriculture, economy and rural society

Agriculture in the Northern Ireland economy

Many salient economic, social, cultural and historical factors have combined to create the distinctive characteristics of rural politics in Northern Ireland. The nature of economic development, particularly of the agricultural industry, is central to any understanding of political life in the rural context. Of fundamental importance has been the position of Northern Ireland as a region within the United Kingdom and its economic relationship with Great Britain. Regional economic performance has been largely determined by that of the United Kingdom as a whole and by wider considerations of international finance and trade including membership of the European Community. Even during the devolution period between 1921-72, the key levers of economic policy, including major taxes and the regulation of international trade, were retained in London and the economy of Northern Ireland was inextricably bound to that of Britain.

Trading ties with Britain were vital to the health of the Northern Ireland agricultural industry because it was essentially "export" oriented although there was also high dependence on imported inputs such as cereals for use as animal feed. Historically Britain has been both the chief source of raw materials and the major market for the two thirds or so of total agricultural output which was sent out of Northern Ireland, particularly livestock and livestock products which in 1991 accounted for some 87 per cent of the farmgate value of agricultural exports. In 1972 four fifths of exports and three quarters of imports passed through Great Britain, including goods in transit to or from foreign countries (Northern Ireland Digest of Statistics, March 1974, p. 77). At the beginning of the 1990s the Northern Ireland agri-business sector contributed some 33 per cent of total net exports and at least 60 per cent of agricultural output was still exported, mainly to Britain but increasingly to the rest of Europe and other countries (Department of Agriculture, 1993, p. 14).

On the other hand the export of surplus agricultural produce from Northern Ireland represented only a very small proportion of total United Kingdom food

4

production and consumption. For example, in 1937-38 Northern Ireland's share of total United Kingdom agricultural output was just over five per cent and in 1971-72 the proportion was just under seven per cent. For certain commodities, notably cattle, beef, pigs and eggs, the Northern Ireland share of total gross output was much higher at around 12 per cent each in 1971-72. In terms of food consumption the contribution of Northern Ireland was smaller as the United Kingdom was very much a net food importer with only 54 per cent of total consumption being met from home agriculture in 1971-72 (c.f. Reports on the Agricultural Statistics of Northern Ireland; United Kingdom Annual Abstracts of Statistics).

Economic development in Northern Ireland has been hindered by natural disadvantages. Geographic remoteness and the lack of natural resources, for example, imposed additional costs on industries such as agriculture which were export oriented. The regional economy has also suffered from the adverse effects of the concentration of employment in agriculture, shipbuilding, engineering, construction, linen and textiles. Although the importance of agriculture in the economy has been in long term relative decline it remains 'one of Northern Ireland's largest single production or service sectors' (Stainer, 1985, p. 4). Agriculture, forestry and fishing has provided the largest single source of civil employment and Gross Domestic Product (GDP) and makes a proportionately greater contribution to the Northern Ireland economy than for the United Kingdom as a whole (see Table 1.1). In 1988 agriculture, forestry and fishing accounted for nearly five per cent of total Northern Ireland GDP compared with around eight per cent in 1970 and 18 per cent in 1950. In terms of total workforce the sector accounted for nearly eight per cent in 1989 compared with 11.2 per cent in 1970 and 19 per cent in 1948 (Department of Agriculture, 1992b; Stainer, 1985, p. 4; Northern Ireland Digest of Statistics, September 1958, p. 7, March 1974, p. 82; Department of Manpower Services Gazette, No. 3, 1979, Table 6; Cmd 479, 1965, p. 144).

Although less important than in the Republic of Ireland the relative contribution to employment of the agricultural sector in Northern Ireland is much more significant than in the United Kingdom as a whole and 'is the highest of all UK regions, while only in East Anglia does agriculture contribute a greater share of regional GDP' (Department of Agriculture, 1993, p. 13). Primary production has also stimulated a whole range of ancillary industries such as food processing, feed milling, and machinery supply. The agri-food industry as a whole accounted for seven per cent of Northern Ireland's GDP and ten per cent of civil employment in 1992. Moreover the food and drink industry was worth some £1,600 million and the farm sector provided the inputs for around 250 food processing firms with an output value of some £1,300 million (Department of Agriculture, 1993, pp. 12-13). Thus the agri-business sector made 'a very important contribution to the manufacturing and production base. Farming, food processing and input supply account for around one-quarter of the combined GDP of agriculture and the production industries' (Department of Agriculture, 1993, p. 13).

Table 1.1
GDP and employment

	GDP (1988)	Workforce (1989)
Northern Ireland	4.6	7.5
United Kingdom	1.4	2.2
Republic of Ireland	10.9	15.1
EC12	3.0	7.0

Source: Department of Agriculture (1992b), p. 1.

Trends in agricultural structure and production

The nature of land utilization and agricultural production in Northern Ireland has been moulded by the physical environment, including the nature of the soil, topography and temperate climate (Cruickshank and Wilcock, 1982). As a result prevailing conditions in Northern Ireland have been more suited to pasture based livestock than arable farming. Besides general economic trends in the contribution which agriculture makes to overall GDP and employment there have also been significant structural changes within the Northern Ireland agricultural industry in the period since 1920. These have occurred in six main areas: land use, crop production, the livestock sector, farm structure, agricultural employment, and trends in product and income.

Land use

The total area of Northern Ireland devoted to agriculture fell from 88 per cent in 1923 to 78 per cent in 1991, largely as a result of urban sprawl and development. More significant was the trend away from tillage towards livestock production within the agricultural sector itself which continued uninterrupted after 1921, except during the abnormal conditions of the Second World War. By 1991 the area devoted to agricultural crops was just under eight per cent of the total area under crops and grass (six per cent of the total area farmed) compared with 26 per cent in 1923 and over 40 per cent in 1860. Conversely the grassland area increased steadily from 74 per cent of the total area under crops and grass in 1923 to 92 per cent in 1991. Over 70 per cent of agricultural land in Northern Ireland is also designated as 'Less Favoured Area' (LFA) by the EC under which land suffering from particular handicap is eligible for special assistance. LFA holdings, however, represent only 36 per cent of the cropped area and are even more heavily dependent on grass based enterprises (Department of Agriculture, 1992b, p. 30).

Crops

There have been significant relative changes within the context of a continuous decline of crop cultivation in Northern Ireland since the late nineteenth century. Production of the traditional field crops in Ulster declined dramatically, particularly after the Second World War. Potato acreage, for example, fell from over 160,000 in 1923 to a low point of about 27,000 (11,000 hectares) in 1991 although the peak was reached in 1948 when 210,000 acres were planted in response to the Agricultural Expansion Programme. Production fell less rapidly because of increased yields but nevertheless the estimated yield of potatoes was 237,000 tons in 1991 compared with 917,000 tons in 1923. Flax also suffered a general decline except for the boost given by the Second World War. About 125,000 acres of flax were planted in 1944 but commercial cultivation quickly plummeted until production had all but ceased by the early 1960s.

Cereal production has been much less important in Northern Ireland than in many other parts of the British Isles because climatic conditions, land quality, and farm structure are unfavourable. Only six per cent of the total crops and grass area in Northern Ireland was under cereals in 1991, accounting for under two per cent of gross output and under five per cent of aggregate gross margin. Even in 1923, however, cereals represented only 15 per cent of the total acreage. Within this general decline the traditional cereal crop, oats, was gradually replaced by barley. Whereas barley production was negligible and oats covered 55 per cent of the cropped land in 1923, by 1991 the positions were reversed at under five per cent for oats and 56 per cent for barley.

The other notable development was the increasing importance of horticulture, including fruit, vegetables, flowers and mushrooms which in 1991 contributed four per cent of gross agricultural output. Overall crops and horticultural production accounted for just eight per cent of gross output of Northern Ireland agriculture in 1991.

Livestock

If prevailing conditions militated against crop production the 'outstanding fact is that the climate favours grassland farming and that Ulster's specialisation in livestock and their products is a logical consequence' (Symons, 1963, p. 22). As arable farming diminished in importance so the livestock sector became more and more dominant in the agricultural industry, under the direct encouragement of the Northern Ireland Government. In 1991 livestock and livestock products accounted for nearly 90 per cent of the estimated gross output of Northern Ireland agriculture. Furthermore the numbers of cattle, sheep, pigs and poultry increased significantly, particularly in the period between 1945 and EC entry.

The total number of cattle almost doubled to over 1.5 million between 1922 and 1991. Dairying historically was dominant. Policy decisions to discourage milk production, for example in the 1960s and 1980s, and to encourage the beef sector contributed to a balance in herd numbers by 1991 when 52 per cent of cows were of dairy type and 48 per cent beef. Herd numbers fluctuated, however. The dairy cow herd increased steadily between 1972 and 1984 but fell thereafter under the pressure of EC measures to reduce milk production; the number of beef cows rose in the early 1970s then suffered a significant reduction after 1974 but recovered again in the late 1980s.

Receipts from cattle production form the largest single source of revenue for farmers in Northern Ireland. In 1991, for example, fat cattle was the most valuable enterprise accounting for 34 per cent of gross output. Milk production contributed a further 26 per cent but the dairy sector was slightly more important in terms of its contribution to gross margin. The cattle sector as a whole accounted for 60 per cent of the total value of the Northern Ireland agricultural industry. Moreover around 70 per cent of beef output went for export and accounted for some 37 per cent of the farmgate value of agricultural exports. Milk and milk products accounted for a further 30 per cent.

Sheep farming, either for wool or meat, contributed just three per cent of gross output by value in 1972 but subsequent expansion pushed this figure to ten per cent by 1991. Although also subject to fluctuation, the sheep flock numbered 425,000 in 1922 and rose to over 2.5 million by 1991 with a particularly rapid expansion from the late 1970s when Irish producers gained access to the French market and the EC introduced a common sheepmeat regime.

The small and owner occupied farm structure in Northern Ireland favoured a mixed farming system and pigs and poultry production historically was an integral component of the agricultural industry. Production became intensive in the post war period, partly because the sector was a means of increasing farm business size without having to acquire more land, and partly because of the availability of relatively cheap imported feed. In 1953-54 intensive livestock production accounted for over 50 per cent of total output by value but by 1991 this figure had fallen to 19 per cent.

In the inter war period the number of pigs rose dramatically from 118,000 in 1922 to 627,000 in 1939, especially under the impetus of organized marketing and import regulation in the 1930s. Indeed for most of the period up to 1972 pig production was easily the most important single branch of the Northern Ireland agricultural industry accounting for 30 per cent of the total estimated value of output sold off farms in 1962-63. After wartime contraction pig numbers rose steadily to a peak of 1.248 million in 1965 but governments actively discouraged expansion from the 1950s as production went into surplus. The effects of EC entry were especially adverse for the pig sector because it cut off supplies of relatively cheap imported feed stuffs. By 1991 the number of pigs had declined to 588,000 with fat pigs accounting for just eight per cent of the total value of agricultural output and nine per cent of the value of agricultural exports. Moreover high dependence on imported inputs meant that the pig sector's contribution to value added was even lower at five per cent of aggregate gross margin.

Poultry meat and egg production have been the most concentrated agricultural enterprises in Northern Ireland with 99 per cent of laying hens located on fewer than 300 farms (Department of Agriculture, 1993, p. 19). There was a spectacular rise in poultry numbers after 1923, reaching over 24 million in 1949, but the trend was subsequently downwards to just over 11 million in 1991. Eggs and poultry meat were by far the most valuable sector of the Northern Ireland agricultural industry throughout the period of wartime control providing over 38 per cent of the total value of gross output in 1947-48. By 1991, however, this figure had fallen to around ten per cent, just six per cent of gross margin because of low margins over feed costs.

Egg production traditionally was the dominant enterprise within the poultry sector. In 1953-54 eggs contributed 86 per cent of the value of the sector and made up 26 per cent of the value of all agricultural exports in 1957. After this, however, a gradual decline set in, consistent with government efforts to stem over production. By 1991 eggs represented under four per cent of agricultural exports in terms of value. On the other hand poultry meat production increased in importance, particularly from the 1960s, and accounted for over 60 per cent of the gross output of the eggs and poultry sector in 1991, with exports worth nearly seven per cent by value.

Farm structure

In the nineteenth century the land in Ireland was owned in large estates and the landlord-tenant system predominated. As a result of political agitation a series of Land Purchase Acts, culminating in the Northern Ireland Land Act 1925, transformed the system into one characterized by owner occupation of relatively small family farms. Paradoxically this development went against the general economic trend evident throughout western Europe for the amalgamation of holdings into fewer agricultural units. So whereas in 1923 the agricultural census returns enumerated almost 105,000 holdings over one acre, by 1991 the total number of holdings defined as statistically significant had fallen to just over 41,000. The trend was to larger holdings. In 1923, 70 per cent of significant holdings were under 30 acres and 26 per cent between 30 and 100 acres. By 1991 the average area per holding was over 63 acres (25.6 hectares) and some 43 per cent of all holdings were over 50 acres (20 hectares).

Because of the practice of conacre (a traditional system of short term land letting) the number of holdings has been an unsatisfactory indicator of the number of farms. In 1991, for instance, conacre lettings accounted for almost 20 per cent of the total land farmed in Northern Ireland. A distinction must therefore be drawn between a land "holding" and a "farm business" which includes conacre letting.

9

There were 29,363 farms with an average size of 85 acres (34.4 hectares) in 1991 and for the first time more than 80 per cent of the land growing crops and grass was farmed by units with at least 50 acres (Department of Agriculture, 1992b, p. 35). However although quite high by EC standards this figure is low in comparison with most other regions of the United Kingdom.

Since large intensive farm businesses can operate on small areas of land Standard Gross Margins (SGM) were developed as an indicator of farm business size. In 1991 the business size of more than half of the farms in Northern Ireland (16,100) was deemed to be 'very small' with less than 50 acres of crops and grass, 9,900 were classified as 'small', and 3,300 as 'medium' or 'large' (11 per cent of the total). On 'very small' farms which cannot provide full time employment or adequate income from farming activities, pluriactivity and non farming enterprises have developed. Over 70 per cent of 'very small' and 'small' farm businesses were located in LFA's compared with 43 per cent of 'large'. In addition 87 per cent of SGM was contributed by 'small', 'medium' and 'large' businesses, with 46 per cent of agricultural value added being contributed by 'medium' and 'large' farms (Statistical Review, 1991, pp. 35-6).

Specialization in individual enterprises has also increased at the expense of traditional mixed farming. Although there was a significant decline after 1987, specialist diary and mainly dairy farms still accounted for 27 per cent of all classified farms in 1991 but for just five per cent of 'very small' businesses compared with over 60 per cent of 'large' and 'medium' businesses. Over half of all classified farms depend on beef cattle and/or sheep; some 82 per cent of 'small' businesses rely on beef cattle and/or sheep but just seven per cent of 'large'.

The dominant trend in farm structure in Northern Ireland after 1921, therefore, was towards a specialization of production in fewer and larger units, facilitated by the conacre system which permitted expansion without the expense of land purchase. Despite this, however, the structure of agriculture in Northern Ireland remained characterized by relatively small, family oriented, farm businesses.

Agricultural employment

Northern Ireland has also experienced the long term decline in the number of persons employed in agriculture characteristic of developed economies. Whereas in 1924 nearly 218,000 people were enumerated as engaged in agriculture by 1992 this total had fallen to 56,500, including working spouses and female family workers. The fall was particularly rapid after 1945. A further 18,000 were employed in the ancillary sector, the importance of which was recognized in 1986 when the Industrial Development Board (IDB) filled the vacuum left by the demise of the Northern Ireland Agricultural Trust by establishing a Food Division.

Because of the owner occupied nature of farms in Northern Ireland, most of the agricultural workforce has been composed of family labour. The largest single category within the family sector was that of farm owners (excluding wives)

10

which numbered 70,000 in 1936 and represented 41 per cent of the total workforce. By 1991 there were just 34,300 owners and 4,600 wives of owners, partners and directors which represented some 70 per cent of the total agricultural workforce. Those working full time amounted to less than half of the total workforce and there were just 22,300 full time owners of farms. Hired labour was less important than in Britain where the landlord-tenant relationship was much more prevalent. Even in 1924 just over 20 per cent of the total agricultural workforce was composed of regular hired workers and casual labour. By 1991, however, the number of regular full time hired workers was only 2,000, or 3.5 per cent of the total workforce, with a further 1,300 regular hired part time workers and 5,700 hired seasonal or casual workers.

Mechanization, increased efficiency of production, better utilization of labour, and greater opportunities for employment in other sectors of the economy all contributed to the reduction in the agricultural workforce. Indeed in the 1960s it was the declared policy of both the United Kingdom and Northern Ireland Governments to encourage the movement from the land by providing alternative employment in the towns. By providing incentives for people to give up their farms, governments aimed to provide a better standard of living for those who remained on the land.

In January 1939 mechanization had made relatively little headway and the 'outbreak of hostilities found Northern Ireland farms very deficient in the mechanical power necessary for the fulfilment of the formidable tasks created by the urgent need for greatly intensified food production' (Ministry of Agriculture, 1951, p. 17). In the late 1930s the Minister of Agriculture tried to persuade the Cabinet to adopt a policy of increased agricultural production to promote employment in farming and ancillary industries. For Brooke the inevitable alternative was a rapid quickening of the drift from the land, a concomitant decrease in the purchasing power of the rural community, and an increase in urban unemployment. The only practical long term solution to the agricultural price problem was to lower production costs and increase output through rural electrification and the mechanization of farms (CAB4/401). The response of the Cabinet was to establish an inter-departmental committee to consider the possibilities of mechanization and the contribution which it might make to increased industrial employment (CAB9E/134/1). The committee's report, submitted to Craig in September 1939, recommended that all electricity generation and supply be entrusted to one public authority, and that the agricultural loans schemes be extended to the purchase of machinery. However a Ministry of Finance official (Duggan) opposed the policy of mechanization in principle because it would promote larger farms and inevitably lead to the destruction of the traditional family farming system in Northern Ireland, the maintenance of which should be a priority of the Government (CAB9E/134/1).

The Ministry of Agriculture was able to exploit the outbreak of war to further farm mechanization which played a key role in the food production campaign. Distribution and prices of tractors, machinery and implements were controlled by the Ministry which also encouraged farmers to buy the equipment through a hire purchase scheme. The mechanization of farming was advanced to such an extent that by the end of the Second World War there were some 7,300 tractors in Northern Ireland compared with just 858 in 1939. With the promotion of greater efficiency after the war the number of tractors continued to rise steeply, doubling to over 15,000 by 1950 and again to nearly 32,000 by 1961 when the limit of mechanization was effectively reached.

Performance indicators

Indicators of agricultural of product and income have also been developed to assess the performance of the agricultural industry. For example, estimates of gross agricultural product (gross output minus material inputs) in constant prices were provided in the Ministry of Agriculture's Eighth Report on Agricultural Statistics. This showed that the net output of farming in Northern Ireland rose from £35 million in 1954-55 to £55.5 million in 1965-66 (Eighth Statistical Report, p. 43).

According to the Ninth Report on Agricultural Statistics estimated Net Product (value of gross product minus machinery depreciation) increased from 99 in 1964-65 to just 114 in 1971-72 (1964-65 to 1966-67 = 100), with most of the increase after 1969 (Ninth Statistical Report, p. 56). The value of net product of Northern Ireland agriculture increased throughout most of the period between 1970 and 1984, and again between 1986-89, but there was a substantial decline in 1985-86 and after 1989 (Stainer, 1985, ch. 3; Statistical Review 1991, ch. 2). In real terms net product was estimated at 88.8 in 1991 compared with 132.3 in the good year of 1984 (1985 = 100).

Indices of output and product indicate overall performance but farm income (net product minus wage costs and interest payments) has been the major indicator of the actual returns received by farmers. Net farming income increased in terms of current prices throughout most of the post war period although there was a steep decline after 1989. In real terms, however, the index figure in 1970 was 103.6 (1970-72 = 100) but only in 1973 did this exceed 100 with a low point of 11.4 in 1980 (Stainer, 1985, p. 69). Fluctuation also characterized farming income in the 1980s with a doubling to 181.7 in 1984 followed by a decline to 75.8 in 1986 and a further increase to 177 in 1989 (1985 = 100). The 1991 figure of 85.7 was the second lowest for a decade and represented a decline of some 17 per cent in real terms on 1990 (Statistical Review 1991, p. 10). Moreover although lower incomes were recorded for all farm types, the decline ranged from 12 per cent in LFA cattle and sheep to some 46 per cent for dairy enterprises (Statistical Review 1991, p. 10). The alternative indicator of Farm Business Income shows similar trends, rising in current prices from £39.9 million in 1970 to £162.6 million in 1984. In real terms, however, the index figure was 103.3 in 1970 and only in 1973 did this exceed 100, falling to a low of 37.5 in 1980 and standing at 87.4 in 1984 (1970-72 = 100).

Agriculture and rural society

An appreciation of the salient characteristics of the agricultural industry in Northern Ireland is essential for a proper understanding of the nature of rural politics, of policy decisions taken in the agricultural sector, and of the demands made of governments by farmers and rural interests. Structural and economic considerations, for example, were central to the policy of the expansion of the livestock sector adopted by the Northern Ireland Ministry of Agriculture. The expansion of milk production under national and EC encouragement, and the reaction to the introduction of quotas in 1984, reflected the grassland nature of Northern Ireland agriculture. Similarly the size and structure of farms was crucial to the formulation of a small farmer programme in the 1960s. Attitudes to state control were rooted not only in social and cultural processes but were shaped by the owner occupied structure of agriculture. The individualism of Ulster farmers also formed a cultural barrier to collective action in the interests of agriculture and rural life as a whole.

Policy outputs in the rural and agricultural sphere influenced and were also much influenced by wider economic and social considerations. Uneven industrialization, for example, resulted in a roughly equal division between the urban and rural populations. This forced the regional Government continuously to strike a balance between the urban core and rural hinterland, predominantly dependent on farming and related industries. Senior figures in the Unionist Party, including Prime Ministers such as Brooke and Chichester-Clark, had rural and land owning backgrounds. Even Stormont was chosen as the site of the new Parliament precisely because it was outside the boundaries of the City of Belfast.

The endogenous solution to the land question in Irish politics created an agricultural industry characterized by relatively small farms when exogenous economic pressures were working in exactly the opposite direction. This combined with the extension of voting rights and popular democracy to put significant political influence in the hands of the rural population. However, the exercise of such political power to advance the interests of the rural population was attenuated by at least two countervailing factors. Firstly the Nationalist-Unionist cleavage was the primary determinant of political allegiance and cut across class and economic interests. Secondly the demographic and economic consequences of Plantation, in which Catholics were pushed westwards into areas of poorer land, gave rural life a particular ethnic character which reinforced religious differences. Thus there was a clear correlation between Catholics and relatively small farms west of the Bann, primarily reliant on the beef sector, and between Protestants and generally larger and more specialized farms east of the Bann which concentrated on dairying.

2 Context of rural politics

Responsibility for agricultural policy was transferred to the newly established Northern Ireland Parliament under the Government of Ireland Act 1920. The Ministry of Agriculture for Northern Ireland was established as one of the six government departments in 1921 and there were just seven Ministers of Agriculture during the Stormont period. Long tenure characterized the terms in office of Archdale, Brooke, Moore and West but Glentoran, Chichester-Clark and Phelim O'Neill served for a total of just six years (see Table 2.1).

Table 2.1
Ministers of Agriculture 1921-72

1921-33	Edward Archdale	1960-67	Harry West
1933-41	Basil Brooke	1967-69	James Chichester-Clark
1941-43	Lord Glentoran	1969-71	Phelim O'Neill
1943-60	Robert Moore	1971-72	Harry West

Constitutional and financial provisions

There were no specific limitations placed on the powers of the regional Parliament in the agricultural sphere but policy development was shaped both by the general nature of the Government of Ireland Act and by the overall political and ideological climate. Certain matters withheld from the general transfer of power had important implications for agricultural policy. National security, for example,

14

was the sole responsibility of Westminster and the defence of the realm during the Second World War entailed 'a wholesale invasion of the peacetime area of administrative jurisdiction of the Northern Ireland Government' (Blake, 1956, pp. 16-17). The precedence of Westminster legislation was established by Swain vs the Producers Bacon Co. (Collin Glen) Ltd (1939) when the courts decided that pig prices fixed under a 'national' regulation superseded those fixed under existing Northern Ireland law. Administrative decentralization gave the regional authorities some scope for the sympathetic implementation of policy although formal responsibility for most agricultural matters rested in Whitehall. Control of the food production campaign, for example, was delegated back to the Ministry of Agriculture from the Home Office by orders made under the Defence Regulations.

Stormont MP's could request information from regional departments acting on behalf of those in Whitehall and table motions asking the Northern Ireland Government to make representations to the British authorities. They could not debate the policy of the United Kingdom Parliament which was ultimately responsible for the conduct of the war. This placed a premium on the development of consultative machinery with the British Government. Direct formal communication between the Cabinet Secretariat and the Home Office continued but was supplemented by other channels including the appointment of a Home Office minister to Cabinet Committees to look after the interests of Northern Ireland as well as the presence of civil servants on the officials' sub-committees. For example, George Scott Robertson, the Permanent Secretary of the Ministry of Agriculture, was more or less permanently based in London throughout the war where he attended meetings of the Food Policy Committee and kept in constant touch with the relevant departments. The attenuation of the normal powers of the regional Parliament on the whole was willingly accepted by Unionists in the national interest. One opposition MP, however, questioned the delegation of powers over agriculture to Whitehall civil servants and insisted that Stormont was 'the determining factor in regard to the land conditions in Northern Ireland' (NIHC Deb 22, c. 2036).

In peacetime conditions the most important constitutional limitations affecting agriculture and rural development were those relating to external trade, taxation, and land purchase which remained the responsibility of Westminster. The prohibition on interfering with trade out of Northern Ireland, for example, restricted the development of marketing policy during the inter war years. This led the regional Government to press for amendments to the Government of Ireland Act such as those made in 1928 and 1933. More significant were the limitations imposed on the regional Ministry of Agriculture by the Government of Ireland Act. The Act did not envisage British Exchequer subsidies for transferred services which in turn would not be specifically related to British standards. If the Northern Ireland Government wanted to devote additional spending to agriculture, therefore, this would be done simply by increasing existing transferred taxes or by devising new ones.

Transferred sources of finance produced no more than 20 per cent of total revenue. Although the Northern Ireland Parliament had considerable freedom to determine priorities, total expenditure depended on two factors outside its control: the level of the Imperial Contribution and the fiscal policy of the United Kingdom. Expenditure quickly outstripped revenue and the Northern Ireland Government, politically unwilling to reduce public spending, pressed for revision of the financial arrangements of the 1920 Act to avoid the embarrassment of failing to balance the books. A series of agreements with the British Treasury, including the 'Simon' agreement of 1938 and the acceptance of the 'leeway' principle in 1954, effectively resulted in an expenditure based financial arrangement which was the antithesis of the original intention of the Act. The Northern Ireland Government abandoned the pretence of financial autonomy in favour of financial support from the British Exchequer to maintain services at a standard similar to those in Great Britain. The collapse of the financial arrangements of the 1920 Act was of crucial importance for the development of agricultural policy. The result was a reduction in the regional Government's freedom 'to pursue independent policies on transferred matters, since financial adjustment was inevitably accompanied by a degree of United Kingdom Treasury control which was certainly not contemplated when the Act was passed' (Cmnd 5460, 1973, para. 171; c.f. Birrell and Murie, 1980; Lawrence, 1965; Buckland 1979).

Ideological and political climate

Equally crucial in setting the parameters for policy development were the constraints imposed by the orthodoxies of political economy. Agricultural policy was moulded by national and international influences on matters such as free trade, protection, state intervention and membership of the EC. Initial policy development took place in the context of the dominant laissez-faire tradition of economic policy and was thereafter crucially influenced by subsequent changes in this environment. British economic orthodoxy exerted a powerful influence. Policy makers throughout the British Isles shared beliefs, attitudes and prejudices about the proper role of the state which were inevitably reflected in policy formulation. Economic libertarianism permeated the whole apparatus of the regional administration in the early years and the Ministry of Finance shared Treasury ideology on financial administration. Pollock, for example, ruled out a scheme of cheap loans for farmers as not only 'reprehensible in itself but exceedingly improper as regards the interests of the general taxpayers...such a policy is quite out of harmony with prudence' (NIHC Deb 6, c. 1128; c.f. PRONI, CAB9E/47/1).

Agriculture was unique in that an administrative apparatus had been established prior to partition. Established in 1900, the Department of Agriculture and Technical Instruction for Ireland (DATII) perceived its role in classic orthodox terms as one of removing obstacles which hindered 'the due exercise of initiative in industrial matters, and to creating a state of things in which private enterprise can act with confidence and freedom' (Cd 838, 1901, p. 21). When the functions of DATII in the six counties were transferred in 1921 the Ministry of Agriculture inherited an ideology, policy, and officials. The first Permanent Secretary, J.S. Gordon, had been a high ranking official in DATII and a significant number of other senior officials came from Dublin, or were transferred or seconded from Whitehall. From the outset, therefore, the agricultural policy of the Northern Ireland Government was formulated within a framework consisting of both constitutional and economic limitations, and of the political and ideological constraints imposed by regional, national and international influences. These interlinked factors shaped five main periods of policy development: laissez-faire, protection, the Second World War, post war consensus, and EC membership.

The influence of laissez-faire

Despite state intervention in agriculture during the First World War, including the administration of a tillage campaign by the DATII, laissez-faire orthodoxy was quickly reasserted. The desire of sections of the British agricultural elite for continued state intervention in peace time to halt rural depopulation, reduce dependence on imports, and reverse the trend away from tillage through increased home food production was fleetingly embodied in the 1920 Agriculture Act. This Act provided guaranteed prices for cereals but its repeal just seven months after becoming law confirmed free trade as the guiding light of state action in the agricultural sector (Whetham, 1974). Throughout the 1920s an interventionist agricultural policy was regarded as abnormal, undesirable, and publicly unpopular because of the priority accorded to cheap food. British policy, outlined in a white paper in 1926, rejected state control. Farmers were encouraged to concentrate on the production of milk, meat, eggs and fresh vegetables for which there was a naturally sheltered market. The correct course was to

> proceed on the lines of education and encouragement rather than of coercion, to endeavour to create that confidence which is essential for progress, to stimulate the private enterprise of those engaged in the industry, to assist them to organise themselves on an economic basis, and to protect them from the dislocation of reversals of policy and from rash proposals which would impair progress and breed insecurity (Cmd 2581, 1926, para. 8).

When Ireland had been excluded from the scope of the 1920 Agriculture Act the Ulster Farmers' Union, which had lobbied unsuccessfully for the inclusion of Northern Ireland in the subsidy scheme, expressed the hope that devolution would enable farmers to get a policy more in tune with their needs, including guaranteed prices for agricultural produce such as flax and potatoes. Rural Unionists and Nationalists alike supported guaranteed prices. For the Nationalist MP Cahir Healy, even if the Government was unwilling to break from the imperial apron strings there was plenty of scope for independent action in the form of guaranteed prices to 'put the farmer in the position of knowing before he puts his crop in the minimum price at which he could harvest it' (NIHC Deb 12, c. 161). There was little likelihood of such a strategy being adopted by the regional Government. Shaped by the constitutional limitations of the Government of Ireland Act and political pressures to follow the British example, the initial agricultural policy of the Northern Ireland Government was strictly orthodox. Demands for guaranteed prices, reduced land annuities or other subsidies were rejected because they were ideologically unacceptable, because the Northern Ireland Government could not afford them, and because they would place an unjustifiable burden on taxpayers in general. Increased public expenditure was strenuously opposed by sections of the Unionist Party. R.J. Lynn for example urged the Minister of Finance to 'put his foot down very firmly and to insist, in regard to public expenditure, that there shall not be an unnecessary pound spent in Northern Ireland' (NIHC Deb 12, c. 27). Although the Ministry of Agriculture was somewhat more activist than its British counterparts policy was formulated within an ideological environment which was strongly influenced by classical orthodoxy. Help for farmers was limited to palliatives designed to ameliorate the worst effects of depression. Policy followed the British lead and was limited to encouraging better marketing, creating and maintaining a comprehensive scheme of research and education, protecting plants and animals from disease, and providing relief from local rates.

Protection

Throughout the 1920s the prices received by farmers in the United Kingdom were depressed by increased foreign competition, the collapse of world prices, and reduced purchasing power. Subsidized foreign imports were widely regarded as the principal cause of price depression. From the middle of 1928 the increasingly vocal concerns of farmers were expressed by the main agricultural associations, representatives of rural constituencies, and at mass meetings such as those held in Cambridge, Berwick and Belfast in March 1930. The UFU, for example, claimed that the United Kingdom was being 'snowed-under by importations of foreign bounty-fed cereals and other agricultural produce with the result that, no matter how skilful and industrious the Northern Ireland farmer has been, he cannot find a profitable market for his produce' (Farmers' Journal, November 1929, p. 3018).

Self interest was often disguised as moral indignation and the plight of farmers was blamed on the sweated labour of immoral political regimes. For example, as part of a propaganda campaign the UFU published a list of 33 'patriotic firms who refuse to purchase or deal in Russian Oats' (Farmers' Journal, November 1930, p. 3357). Soviet grain was the product of convict labour 'produced and sent to us under conditions of unspeakable hardship...This is the new method of trying to conquer the world for Bolshevism. No industry could compete against such a menace' (Farmers' Journal, November 1930, pp. 3354-5). Meaningful assistance, however, required not just a ban on Soviet grain which accounted for only a very small proportion of total imports, but a comprehensive policy of import restriction for the United Kingdom.

Farmers in Northern Ireland were exasperated by the fact that the regional Government was powerless to regulate imports which was the responsibility of Westminster under the 1920 Act. The problem, however, was not dumping on the local market but on the vital British market which absorbed most of the surplus of Northern Ireland agriculture. UFU policy, adopted by many local councils and County Committees of Agriculture, demanded protection for farmers throughout the United Kingdom. For the UFU the approach was two stranded. Direct lobbying of the British Government included a telegram sent to Ramsay MacDonald in October 1930 which called for action against Soviet grain imports. Indirect pressure was exerted on the regional Government to intercede with the British authorities on its behalf. This demand found a ready ear within the Northern Ireland Cabinet in which Craig, Pollock and Archdale were strong advocates of protection. Craig hoped that

> within a reasonable time it might be possible by some form of protection - and I have always been madly keen in favour of keeping out the foreign stuff - to give the farmers of Ulster a fair crack of the whip. I see no other policy on the horizon at the moment that will give aid to the agricultural industry or any of our activities. Nothing less, in my opinion, will do any good. The rest is really only fiddling with the matter (Northern Whig, 15 July 1930).

There was little that the regional Government could do but 'bring pressure on the British Government to give us a chance by putting a duty on potatoes, oats, and other articles that will put up the price to the farmers, and at any rate help them to earn an honest living and not be dependent on doles or any other artificial assistance from the Government' (Northern Whig, 15 July 1930). The only option available to agricultural interests in Northern Ireland was to influence the economic policy of the British Government. Craig assured a UFU deputation that the Government supported import control, was 'in whole hearted accord with the policy annunciated by the Ulster Farmers' Union' and would 'endeavour by all means in their power to influence the British Government to accept this policy' (CAB9E/69/1). The Government, however, was reluctant to make direct representations to London when there was little chance of success. For Pollock, in a depressingly accurate summary of the impotence of the regional Parliament, dependence on the British market meant that until the 'mentality of the British people changed we can have no hope whatever that we can raise the price of the articles raised by our farmers, or improve their position' (NIHC Deb 12, c. 34).

It was financial crisis and the formation of the Conservative dominated National Government in 1931 which eventually led to the rejection of economic orthodoxy. In agricultural policy the objective was to prevent floods of very cheap imports in the short term and to stimulate a long term revival of British farming. Policy was influenced by national considerations such as the political unacceptability of taxes on food, and international considerations including trade agreements with foreign and dominion countries. As a result most important agricultural products were exempted from general tariffs under the Import Duties Act and policy after 1931 consisted of measures 'heterogeneous in character, improvised to meet a succession of particular emergencies, and uninformed by any general principle' (Astor and Rowntree, 1939, p. 32). Combinations of quotas, subsidies, levies, and marketing schemes were developed for each product with the aim of giving the home producer priority in the British market but modified in line with the political and economic priorities of the Government. The Wheat Act 1932, for example, combined a levy-subsidy with a home production quota whereas for the livestock sector the largely voluntary quantitative restriction of imports was preferred, linked to a Treasury subsidy.

The interests of the regional agricultural economy depended on, and were affected by, wider national and international considerations. Decisions about external trade taken at Westminster for the United Kingdom as a whole could prejudice or assist the interests of Northern Ireland agriculture. The Northern Ireland Government and the UFU believed that the interests of regional agriculture would be best served by a grassland based livestock policy for the United Kingdom combined with the quantitative control of imports. For Archdale it was imperative that the strategy adopted recognized the 'predominant place which live stock and live stock products occupy in our agricultural economy. A cereal policy is quite definitely against our interests and I believe solely in the interest of farmers in East Anglia and a few other areas in Great Britain' (CAB9E/69/1). A livestock strategy depended on cheap and plentiful imports of feed stuffs and was vulnerable to the restrictions on cereal imports demanded by the influential British wheat growers. The decision of the British Government to impose tariffs on maize, for example, was greeted with horror in Northern Ireland which used around 30 per cent of the total United Kingdom maize meal imports. Both the UFU and the Ulster Curers' Association (UCA), plus the milling trades, demanded that the tariff on maize be withdrawn (Farmers' Journal, March 1932, pp. 3715-17). With the active support of Craig and the Government a concentrated lobbying campaign was mounted in Westminster and Whitehall by the Northern Ireland agricultural policy network which persuaded the British Government to place maize on the exempt list.

The romantic notion of Empire free trade also threatened the position of Northern Ireland agriculture in the British market. The series of agreements reached at the Ottawa Conference in July 1932, for example, ruled out direct tariffs on dominion produce and granted it preferential treatment in the British market. British farmers were convinced that their interests had been sacrificed to the dominions in the interests of the manufacturing sector (Richardson, 1936, p. 140). Moreover bilateral agreements between the United Kingdom and foreign countries such as Argentina and Denmark further limited the scope of agricultural protection and threatened the interests of farmers in Northern Ireland. In an attempt to protect the interests of regional agriculture at the Ottawa Conference the Northern Ireland Government sent an advisory delegation including Brooke and Scott Robertson. A memorandum prepared prior to the Conference reaffirmed the livestock strategy and the need for free importation of feed stuffs such as maize (AG16/11/2).

Protection was 'a critical instrument employed by the Government in its attempt to bring about the reorganization and rationalization of home industry and agriculture' (Beer, 1969, p. 279). The British Agricultural Marketing Acts of 1931 and 1933 provided for the creation of compulsory and producer controlled marketing boards which were intended to help improve producer prices whilst lowering those paid by the consumer. Farmers made little use of the 1931 Act but the initial hostility to collective marketing was overcome by the decision to abandon free trade which provided the incentive for marketing reorganization. Under the 1933 Act the Board of Trade, after consultation with the agricultural authorities for England and Wales, Scotland, and Northern Ireland, could regulate imports of agricultural produce into the United Kingdom provided that complementary marketing schemes were introduced. Regulation of imports was thus an instrument for the reorganization of British agriculture and the introduction of marketing schemes was the price farmers had to pay for protection. This also fostered emergent processes of group consultation and boosted the status of corporate sectional interests such as the National Farmers' Union (NFU). The state actively encouraged the formation of producers' associations which were then brought into regular contact with government (c.f. Smith, 1990, ch. 3; Winch, 1969, p. 213; Beer, 1969, ch. 10).

Theoretically the Northern Ireland Government could have rejected this approach in favour of a distinctive policy for its own agricultural industry. In practice such an independent option was impossible on political, economic, financial and constitutional grounds. Financial dependence on disguised Treasury subventions ruled out a regional policy based on price and production subsidies. The control of imports into Northern Ireland would not just be ineffective but was constitutionally forbidden. So when the British Government adopted protection this covered the United Kingdom as a whole and the Northern Ireland Government had no option but to accept the parameters of agricultural policy set for it in London. This was not a question of an unpopular policy being foisted upon an unwilling Government because protection was strongly favoured by the Northern Ireland Cabinet. The main lines of regional policy thus continued to mirror British policy with the emphasis on marketing reform, albeit with some significant differences in implementation.

Farmers quickly became disenchanted as prices failed to respond to marketing reform and quantitative restriction. By 1938 falling prices led the UFU to express 'grave anxiety and alarm' on the agricultural situation which had 'never been worse within living memory' despite the assistance given by the state (CAB9E/23/2). The prospect of war was also used to justify arguments for a substantial expansion of home production on national security grounds. For example with memories still fresh of food shortages during the First World War, the UFU believed that the 'troubled condition of Europe may prove helpful to the producer' (Farmers' Journal, May 1936, p. 660). The British Government, however, stuck to the doctrine of 'normal trade' which held that peacetime production should not be increased on purely defence grounds. Nevertheless disquiet about the impact of import control, both on the cost of living and the British agricultural industry, was reflected by the movement of influential opinion towards a policy of price insurance coupled with voluntary controls on imports. The 1937 Agriculture Act combined a limited storage programme with measures to increase soil fertility, including subsidies on lime and basic slag, and a price insurance scheme for oats and barley. Following a policy review involving the Agricultural Departments and the Farmers' Unions, the Agricultural Development Act 1939 extended price insurance to sheep, increased the rates of existing subsidies, introduced an acreage subsidy for ploughing up grassland, and created a reserve pool of agricultural machinery. So despite the refusal to put agriculture on a war footing the peacetime policy of the British Government in the late 1930s was influenced not just by the needs of domestic agriculture but by the wider international political situation. Measures to increase soil fertility, for example, were designed so that should an emergency arise the Government would be able 'immediately to take advantage of improved fertility but, should it not arise, we should be increasing the productivity of our land and stock by means which are consistent with, and not opposed to, the normal development of our agriculture on economic lines in time of peace' (HC Deb 324, c. 433). By 1939, therefore, there was in place a comprehensive, though largely uncoordinated, structure of financial assistance for farmers ranging from grants to encourage increased soil fertility to price insurance for staple commodities such as milk, fat cattle, sheep, bacon pigs, and cereals.

Agricultural policy after 1932 marked a radical departure from anything that had gone before. State intervention, albeit haphazard, was legitimized and despite hostility from farmers was clearly the price to be paid for state assistance. In the words of Astor and Rowntree there could be

> no return to the old conditions under which the prosperity or adversity of the different branches of agriculture was regarded as lying outside the proper functions of the State...the dethronement of laisser-faire is final, and there is no real possibility of a restoration. For the fundamental economic conditions which made laisser-faire a workable principle in the nineteenth century have passed away (Astor and Rowntree, 1939, p. 40).

The Second World War

After 1918 memories of how close the United Kingdom had come to running out of food during the war were 'too vivid to allow any illusions that what would be required of British farming in the event of war would be merely a continuation of peace-time practices or even at most an intensification of them' (Murray, 1955, p. 40). The thoroughness of preparation for war has been a matter of some dispute but there was general agreement that comprehensive state control and the tillage of grassland would be essential to provide both food for human consumption and animal feed stuffs. The wartime food production programme was implemented through a tripod of interlinked approaches: physical controls, financial incentives, and psychological exhortation. For example, the psychological 'confidence' of farmers in government policy tended to rise and fall in line with perceptions of the adequacy of financial incentives and the necessity for physical controls.

During the war the British Government controlled agricultural policy for the United Kingdom as a whole. The inclusion of Northern Ireland in the pre war ploughing up and fertilizer subsidies funded by the United Kingdom Exchequer reflected the importance of the surplus food production of Northern Ireland agriculture in wartime. The regional Ministry of Agriculture was stripped of its powers of independent policy formulation and simply implemented policy and programmes decided in London. Of course, the Ministry tried to fit schemes to prevailing regional conditions but the scope to do this was limited by considerations of constitutional formality and of the need for 'equity of sacrifice' throughout the United Kingdom. Responsibility for food production in Northern Ireland, for example, was formally vested in the Home Secretary but administration was delegated back to the Ministry of Agriculture. The regional Ministry could not re-delegate executive powers in order to create special local machinery for decentralization but took over the existing County Agricultural Committees for the duration of the war. The livestock strategy was cleverly linked to the tillage programme and the Ministry encouraged a large increase in home produced feed stuffs to compensate for the much lower level of imports. Every farmer had to realize that he was 'not growing corn crops which will go direct to feed the population, he is growing crops to preserve his own existence by producing stock and stock products' (CAB3A/116). Tillage orders required each farmer to cultivate a specific portion of his total arable area, although this was never more than half and varied according to prevailing conditions (see Table 2.2). Special concessions were granted to Fermanagh and south Antrim where the soil was less suited to intensive cultivation on a large scale and individuals could be exempted from compulsory tillage in very exceptional circumstances. At the peak of the war effort in 1943 a total of 851,000 acres of land was cropped in northern Ireland, an increase of over 80 per cent on the 1939 figure and only a little short of the peak acreage attained during the First World War (Murray, 1955, chs. XI and XII).

Whereas British farmers were given specific directions about which crops to grow in which fields, in Northern Ireland the Ministry of Agriculture fixed the overall quota and it was 'left to the good sense of farmers to decide the type of crops to be sown or planted and to choose what new land would be broken up' (Ministry of Agriculture, 1951, p. 3). Voluntary compliance was generally forthcoming. During the ten years of compulsory tillage 7,195 specific directions were issued, 320 farmers were prosecuted for the evasion of tillage orders, but only in four cases were farmers dispossessed of their land.

Table 2.2
Minimum tillage quotas 1940-49 (%)

	1940	-41	-42	-43	-44	-45	-46	-47	-48	-49
Armagh, Down, Derry, Tyrone & North Antrim	20	33.3	40	45	45	45	35	30	35	30
Fermanagh	20	33.3	40	45	30	30	25	20	20	20
South Antrim	20	33.3	40	40	40	30	25	20	20	20

Source: Ministry of Agriculture, 1951 (Cmd 295), p. 2.

The efficiency of the tillage campaign was inextricably linked to assurances of remunerative prices. Ulster farmers, according to the UFU, neither 'expect nor desire to make money through the national difficulty; they want to pull their weight in winning the war. They merely ask for an assurance that they will not be financially ruined as a result of their efforts in so doing' (Farmers' Journal, December 1939, p. 95). During the war farm prices were negotiated and fixed at a 'national' level and farmers in Northern Ireland received guaranteed prices and assured markets for their produce. Although there was discrimination between individual commodities there was little regional variation in the prices paid to producers throughout the United Kingdom for the same crop, irrespective of proximity to or remoteness from the main markets. Prices emerged from internal tussles about strategy. For example, the Ministry of Food and the Treasury wanted a reduction in livestock numbers and a differential price structure which favoured the production of potatoes, wheat, and milk at the expense of fat cattle, eggs, poultry and pigs (Hammond, 1951, p. 81). On the other hand the Agricultural Departments favoured an overall expansion of production allied to a general rise in prices to cover rising costs. It was the responsibility of the Government to create the conditions which would enable producers to deliver the goods. If the 'desired increase in home production is to be secured a higher level of prices will be necessary for agricultural products generally...a level of prices which will provide a reasonable return to the farmers and enable them to pay a fair wage to the worker' (HC Deb 355, c. 1389).

This tension was illustrated by a decision in August 1940 to increase the total sum available for farm prices but to reduce the price of oats, barley, fat cattle and fat pigs and increase those of milk and potatoes. For the three Farmers' Unions (NFU, NFUS, UFU) the Government had reneged on pledges given to the agricultural community on price policy and they established a special sub-committee to coordinate a common strategy. The UFU, for example, sent a resolution to both the Northern Ireland and British Governments which declared that Ulster farmers viewed 'with alarm and disgust this breach of faith with the industry which creates immediately a complete lack of confidence and faith in Government promises and pledges' (Farmers' Journal, October 1940, p. 43). The whole case had to be reconsidered as a matter of urgency 'if the farmer's heart is not to be broken, and if he is to give his best to the nation in its time of peril' (Farmers' Journal, October 1940, p. 43).

Arising from the furore the British Government moved to restore confidence by giving a pledge that fixed prices and assured markets would be guaranteed for the duration of hostilities and for at least one year thereafter. The Government acknowledged 'the importance of maintaining after the war a healthy and well balanced agriculture as an essential and permanent feature of national policy' (HC Deb 367, c. 92). By the end of 1940 both a rational price schedule embodying wartime priorities, albeit at the relative expense of certain sections of producers, and a mechanism for arriving at the prices themselves had been established.

The 'pledge' was open to different interpretations. The Farmers' Unions interpreted it as an automatic increase in all prices to compensate for any increase in costs whereas the Government held that the prices of individual products could be adjusted upwards or downwards according to the requirements of food policy (Smith, 1990, ch. 4). As the war progressed farmers increasingly interpreted price decisions as indicators of what they could expect in the post war period. By late 1943 the Farmers' Unions were profoundly uneasy at the unwillingness of the British Government to open discussions on post war policy. It was argued that this was damaging to the food production campaign because it was the primary cause of a rapid deterioration in 'confidence'. According to the UFU the decision not to increase prices in 1944 not only destroyed 'confidence' but was a sign that with the 'great improvement in our military position throughout the world the history of the last war is repeating itself and that the country's pledges and obligations to its farmers are once again to be dishonoured' (Farmers' Journal, January 1944, p. 116). An unprecedented UFU Council resolution called on the British Minister of Agriculture 'to resign and make room for someone who will honour and respect the pledge which has been made by the National Government. Farmers in Northern Ireland have lost faith in him completely and would not believe any promises which he might give to the industry in the future' (Farmers' Journal, February 1944, p. 145).

Post war consensus

The persistence of the main lines of wartime agricultural policy into the post war period, particularly the system of guaranteed prices and markets, had very important consequences for policy development in Northern Ireland after 1945. Post war policy was again influenced by wider ideological and political considerations. State intervention was further legitimated by the wartime experience. In 1943, for example, Churchill expressed the belief that the state

25

would have to shoulder a substantial financial burden if the expansion and improvement of agriculture, and a reasonable level of prices for producers, was to be maintained after the war (The Times, 22 March 1943). Neither could agriculture in the United Kingdom be insulated from the general pressures for change and reconstruction which built up during the war. Farmers tried to capitalize on the strengthened political position which agriculture had gained during the war because of the increased dependence on home products. Patriotic duty was often explicitly linked to post war rewards and the UFU, for example, urged farmers to meet their tillage obligations in the knowledge that in so doing they were 'not only helping to win the war, but paving the way to stability and security within the industry afterwards' (Farmers' Journal, February 1940, p. 138).

Agricultural policy was also crucially influenced by the reconstruction of the international political and economic system. The World Food Conference at Hot Springs, Virginia in the spring of 1943 led to the creation of the Food and Agriculture Organisation of the United Nations as a permanent international body. This Conference recommended an expansion of production of foods such as vegetables, milk, eggs and meat which best promoted improved diets and better health. Individual governments were urged to increase and improve food production by taking action in the areas of agricultural credit, cooperation, education and research, and animal health. The interdependence of nations and the importance of international cooperation to ensure that markets were available to absorb increased production was also emphasized. Although trade restrictions were condemned it was recognized that worldwide expansion of production required that producers received a fair return for their labour. As efficiency would be threatened by excessive short term price fluctuations, the Conference reluctantly admitted that international commodity regulation would probably be necessary, albeit with proper safeguards for the consumer.

The Hot Springs Conference provided the context for the development of national agricultural policies but the initial consideration of post war policy in the United Kingdom pre dated the Conference. The foundations of post war policy, the twin pillars of stability and efficiency, were laid down as early as July 1942 as a result of intra-governmental discussions and confidential consultations with a 'small number of persons of influence in the agricultural world' (Murray, 1955, p. 348). In Britain the Ministry of Agriculture (MAF) successfully promoted consensus on the basic principles of national policy. The plethora of policy statements and documents which emanated from agricultural organizations after 1943 exhibited a striking degree of unanimity on the essential principles of long term policy (Murray, 1955, p. 350; Self and Storing, 1962, p. 21). Although they approached the problem from different ideological perspectives, consensus also characterized the post war agricultural policies developed by the main British political parties. All focused on the need for increased home food production to underpin a prosperous and efficient agriculture, stable prices and a reasonable return for producers. Whilst the specific means of attaining this end differed, it was generally recognized that some state direction was necessary to promote improved efficiency. Thus the 1947 Agriculture Act was 'a product of the combined wisdom of all the different sections of the industry, and of the advertised views of the three major political parties' (HC Deb 432, c. 625).

In Northern Ireland the issue of post war reconstruction also assumed great political importance, highlighted by the incompetent management of the war effort and the failure of the gerontocratic regional Government to deal adequately with socio-economic problems. The muddled response was evident from the wrangling and territorial disputes within the Andrews Cabinet and conflicting institutional mechanisms were created to consider post war policy. The Minister of Agriculture was part of a group which successfully opposed plans to allow the Planning Advisory Board to create independent functional sub-committees. This ensured that consideration of post war policy was kept within government departments, coordinated by a Post-War Reconstruction Committee of the Cabinet formed by Brooke shortly after he became Prime Minister in May 1943 (CAB4/524; NIHC Deb 25, c. 2922).

The critical consideration was that the fundamentals of post war policy in important areas such as agriculture were determined in London. Despite the improved financial position during the war, it was certain that the maintenance of comprehensive social and economic programmes at the British level would require Treasury subsidy. Brooke insisted that little could be achieved until British policy was decided because it was 'most desirable that our plans should fit in with those likely to be adopted in Great Britain' (CAB4/513). Pleas by Spender and others 'to avoid the "rubber stamp" policy of doing something merely because it is being done in Great Britain' fell on deaf ears (Ditch, 1988, p. 87). The freedom of action of the regional Government was limited by Brooke's insistence that because of the 'declared policy of the Unionist Party that our working classes should not suffer by the grant of self-government to Northern Ireland' there could 'be no deviation from the policy of maintaining equality of social services between Northern Ireland and the rest of the United Kingdom' (CAB4/735). The regional machinery for post war reconstruction, therefore, was not 'especially constructive in its contribution to the alleviation of the problems associated with the transition from war to peace' and the lead came from the British Government with varying degrees of input from the local administration (Ditch, 1988, p. 88).

In April 1943 the Ministry of Agriculture set up the Babington Committee to 'enquire into and report upon the future of Agriculture in Northern Ireland and to advise upon the steps necessary to effect its maximum development and improvement' (Cmd 249, 1947, p. 7). The scope of the Babington Committee was limited, however, by the assumption that its recommendations would be integrated into the fundamental elements of post war agricultural policy for the United Kingdom. Circumstances dictated that no specific pledges about regional agricultural development could be made until the essentials of price and production policy had been agreed at a national level. As a result of the step-by-step policy in the inter war period and the emergence of an integrated national policy during the war, decisions taken in London set the parameters of local policy development. A combination of domestic pressure from farmers and the Ministry in Northern Ireland, the contribution made by regional agriculture to winning the war, and the strategic importance of increased food production after the war, helped to ensure that the principles of post war agricultural policy would be formulated and applied on a United Kingdom basis.

Post war policy emerged from two interdependent sets of negotiations - one at the United Kingdom level involving the Agricultural Departments and the representative organizations of agriculture, and the other at the regional level encompassing the local policy network. So whilst the UFU welcomed the appointment of the Committee as an indication of the regional Government's commitment to agriculture it also stressed that Babington should not delve deeply into matters of high policy at the national level. The Ministry of Agriculture and the UFU continued bilateral discussions on matters within the scope of a secondary policy area where the regional Government retained independence and flexibility, including agricultural research and education, crop and animal improvement, forestry, and a whole range of ancillary services such as processing, drainage and rural housing. Within this context the Babington Report was anything but revolutionary and reinforced existing policy. The Ministry accepted many of the specific recommendations, for example on breeding and education, and some of these were incorporated into the 1949 Agriculture Bill.

Much more important were the consultations at national level on the fundamentals of post war policy between the institutions of the state and the representatives of the agricultural industry. The Ministry of Agriculture and the UFU helped to formulate the national policy with their British counterparts. The programme issued by the UFU in February 1943 was firmly situated within the evolving policy consensus. As such the promotion of a 'healthy and well-balanced agriculture' should enable the farmer to do four things: provide a respectable standard of living for himself and his family, pay a comparable wage to his worker, keep his land in good fertility, and keep his property in repair (Farmers' Journal, May 1943, p. 199). The central demand was for guaranteed prices and assured markets allied to import control. As the policy could only be delivered by the British Government as part of a national programme the UFU intended to 'bring the proposals to a stage where they might be safely merged within the framework of a wider arrangement that would represent the considered views of all similar responsible and authoritative organisations in the United Kingdom' (Farmers' Journal, May 1943, p. 203).

Drawing on the general policy consensus, the objective of post war policy was to 'promote a healthy and efficient agriculture, capable of producing that part of the nation's food which is required from home sources at the lowest price consistent with the provision of adequate remuneration and decent living conditions for farmers and workers, with a reasonable return on capital invested' (HC Deb 415, c. 2334). This was welcomed by the UFU for at long last placing food production 'above the arena of party politics' and was 'likely to eliminate the industry from the position of being the national Cinderella. Here, at last, then, we have got something on which political parties substantially are agreed and which provides that element of stability and continuity of policy which is so necessary to establish confidence' (Farmers' Journal, December 1945, p. 111).

The 1947 Agriculture Act represented the acceptance of responsibility by the state for the provision of a reasonable income to farmers and was built around the twin pillars of 'stability' and 'efficiency' (Self and Storing, 1962; Smith, 1990, ch. 4). Stability was provided through the provision of guaranteed prices and assured markets for all the principal agricultural products. The legislation specified which commodities were to qualify for state support (fat cattle, sheep and pigs, milk, eggs, wheat, barley, oats, rye, potatoes and sugar beet - wool was added later) but was deliberately vague on the question of what constituted proper remuneration for those engaged in the agricultural industry. This was intended to be reconciled through cooperation and partnership between the state (the Agricultural Departments) and the representatives of producers (the three United Kingdom Farmers' Unions) under the auspices of an Annual Price Review. As the interests of farmers had to be balanced against other competing demands made on the economy, departments such as the Treasury, the Board of Trade, and the Ministry of Food also played an important role in intra-governmental discussions prior to the Review. In return farmers reluctantly accepted state control and direction to ensure the efficient management and husbandry of the land as the price to be paid for guaranteed prices and markets. To achieve the parallel goal of efficiency the British Government took supervisory powers, with dispossession as the ultimate sanction, to ensure that all agricultural land was efficiently managed and farmed according to specified 'rules of good husbandry' and 'rules of good estate management'. Part I of the Act concerning guaranteed prices applied to the United Kingdom as a whole but the efficiency and sanctions provisions in Part II were the subject of separate legislation in Scotland and Northern Ireland: the Agriculture (Scotland) Act 1948 and the Agriculture Act (Northern Ireland) 1949.

Until EC entry in 1973 the 1947 Act formed the cornerstone of agricultural policy in the United Kingdom. Support for farmers, in the context of international trade considerations and the cheap food policy, was provided through Exchequer funded price guarantees and production incentives rather than levies on imports. All governments, however, grew increasingly concerned about the level of state subsidy and manipulated the Annual Review machinery to plan output, limit Exchequer liability, tackle over production and encourage improved efficiency. Decontrol and the introduction of deficiency payments in the 1950s, for example, was intended to make agriculture more responsive to market forces; in the 1960s standard quantities were introduced and policy shifted in the direction of import restriction, although this was limited in scope and based on voluntary international agreements. On the other hand significant political constraints limited governments' freedom radically to alter policy direction. Continuity of policy was promoted by the close relations and shared ideological consensus between the Farmers' Unions and the Agricultural Departments. Indeed the significant feature of those fundamental decisions which changed the direction of agricultural policy, including the adoption of deficiency payments, was that they were generally forced on a reluctant agricultural policy network by other interests in the government.

Agriculture and European Community membership

Attitudes to EC membership in Northern Ireland were conditioned by general political factors which reflected fears and hopes about the impact on the constitutional position. The political and agricultural communities in Northern Ireland were equivocal about EC membership and attitudes ranged, even within parties, from reluctant acceptance to outright hostility. Whereas Unionist suspicions were reinforced, however, Nationalists became increasingly enthusiastic as it dawned that EC membership provided a useful conduit to pursue their political aims. Within this general framework the impact of EC membership on regional agriculture was a central concern. Despite extensive support for farmers in Northern Ireland through the Common Agricultural Policy (CAP), and the willingness of all politicians to strive to extract the maximum benefit, political attitudes were replicated in the agricultural context. Paisley, for example, claimed that because the United Kingdom was a net contributor to EC funds, membership meant an effective transfer of resources from Northern Ireland farmers to those in the Irish Republic and also virtually wiped out the intensive sector by cutting off supplies of cheap cereals (Belfast Telegraph, 30 May 1984). Sceptical Ulster Unionists also claimed that EC membership had damaged regional agriculture. John Taylor, for example, alleged that the Northern Ireland consumer subsidized Éire producers and that the 'crisis of Ulster agriculture today is the direct result of EEC membership' (Belfast Telegraph, 6 April 1984). On the other hand the Alliance Party and the Social Democratic and Labour Party (SDLP) pointed to the advantages of Community membership. For Alliance, Addie Morrow stated that the 'much maligned EEC has shown much more sympathy for Northern Ireland agriculture than our Westminster Government and, in fact, we would be much worse off if we were left to the tender mercies of Margaret Thatcher' (Belfast Telegraph, 13 April 1985). John Hume believed that those in favour of withdrawal had to explain how Northern Ireland farming would survive the removal of EC support and isolation from the main world consumer market. EC membership also had political advantages because 'inside the framework of the EEC we can break away from dependence on Britain and improve the standards of our people' (Belfast Telegraph, 9 June 1984). Even Sinn Féin's Danny Morrison saw the EC not only as a platform to harangue the United Kingdom over its presence in Northern Ireland but as a forum to help 'preserve and defend the existing grants and measures for farmers' (Belfast Telegraph, 23 May 1984).

The Northern Ireland administration was unable to adopt a public stance, either critical or supportive, because EC entry was the constitutional responsibility of the Westminster Parliament. Before 1972 for example, all the regional Government could do was try to make the British Government aware of the importance of the 'vital interests of Northern Ireland in maintaining a prosperous agricultural industry and in the preservation and expansion of industrial employment' (NIHC Deb 49, c. 158). In return the Home Secretary gave frequent assurances that the Northern Ireland position was kept fully in mind and that the views of the regional Government on relevant matters would be canvassed as negotiations progressed. At the departmental level during the period leading up to EC entry close cooperation was maintained the between the regional Ministry and 'the other United Kingdom Agricultural Departments and in Brussels, while Northern Ireland had representation on the United Kingdom negotiating team. These meetings and consultations ensured that Northern Ireland's special requirements were not overlooked during the EEC negotiations' (Department of Agriculture, 1973, p. 11). Expressions of confidence that Whitehall would not overlook the representations of the Northern Ireland Government in negotiations on EC entry were criticized by some opposition members as an abdication of responsibility. It was believed that because of the relative insignificance of Northern Ireland within the United Kingdom it was dangerous to leave important policy to the Westminster Government which would likely sacrifice the interests of agriculture to those of the industrial and urban community.

The Ministry of Agriculture convened a series of meetings in 1970 with the other components of the agricultural policy network including the UFU, marketing boards and trade interests which discussed the prospects for the major commodities. The UFU and marketing boards established a joint liaison group to coordinate assessments of the impact of EC entry. There was particular concern about the adverse repercussions on the intensive sector of high cereal prices under the CAP regime and about the prospects for production grants which were of great importance to Northern Ireland agriculture. For the UFU it was 'imperative to retain those aids which, because of our remoteness, are essential to the viability of our industry and to pay due regard to our special needs in the development of regional policy within the E.E.C.' (Farmweek, 12 October 1971). Perhaps the chief concern for the Ministry of Agriculture, however, was the protection of Northern Ireland's disease free status in the context of the free movement of animals within the EC. In the negotiations on entry the United Kingdom Government secured derogations which allowed the Ministry to continue its animal health programme, particularly in respect of foot and mouth disease. After a review in 1977 such derogations continued into the 1980s but were finally ended at the end of 1984.

Although often regarded as hostile, the United Kingdom Farmers' Unions never opposed EC entry and gradually became convinced of the benefits of Community membership. There was initial concern about the effects of EC entry on domestic agriculture because the three Farmers' Unions were unconvinced that the EC's import levy system of agricultural support could maintain a prosperous and efficient agricultural industry. The Farmers' Unions made it clear to the Government that they would strenuously oppose EC entry if it undermined the principles enshrined in the Agriculture Acts. For farmers the paramount consideration was whether any new support arrangements would provide as much assistance as the British system and also continue to provide cheap food for the consumer. The UFU, for example, would 'resist attempts to dismantle tried and proved systems of support unless it was convinced that these would be replaced by systems which were equally effective' (Farmers' Journal, 1 September 1961, p. 13). At Stormont MP's urged the Northern Ireland Government to press Westminster to maintain the British agricultural support system as the alternatives were unsuitable for both producers and consumers.

By the time of the ultimately successful negotiations in the early 1970s United Kingdom farmers were more willing to embrace the CAP as pressure increased on the domestic deficiency payments system. The UFU saw little point in giving a yes or no opinion which would count for little in the general United Kingdom context and the Farmers' Unions concentrated on getting the best possible deal and transitional arrangements into the CAP for United Kingdom agriculture. An examination by the UFU of the likely impact of EC membership concluded that it was 'unlikely to undermine agriculture in Northern Ireland. It is, however, likely to accelerate certain fundamental trends in structure and choice of product which are already underway' (Farmweek, 12 October 1971). During the 1975 referendum campaign the three Farmers' Unions actively urged a vote for continued membership. The UFU believed, with some reservations, that it would be 'in the best interests of Northern Ireland farmers for the U.K. to stay in Europe' and it welcomed the decision of the British people to remain in the EC (Farmweek, 20 May 1975).

When the United Kingdom joined the EC in 1973 'agricultural policy was totally transformed' as the system of deficiency payments was replaced by import levies and intervention buying to maintain the market price (Smith, 1990, p. 147). This transferred the cost of agricultural support from the taxpayer to the consumer whilst maintaining overall expansion. The move towards import levies began in the 1960s as the state grew increasingly concerned about the cost of agricultural support. Following the breakdown of the Common Market negotiations in January 1963, for example, the system of agricultural support was reviewed to find ways to bring the cost to the Exchequer under more effective control. The result was a series of voluntary agreements on the regulation of imports and the Agriculture and Horticulture Act, 1964 which permitted the introduction of minimum prices and levies on imports. The aim was to inject a greater degree of stability into the market and 'not to raise market prices generally by restricting supplies but to ensure that the support system is not undermined by excessively low market prices leading to heavy demands on the Exchequer' (Cmnd 2315, 1964, para. 3).

In 1970 the decision to raise minimum import prices of cereals and introduce import levies further confirmed the direction in which agricultural policy was moving. Increased production was also regarded as an important element in the preparation for EC entry. To help ensure that United Kingdom agriculture was in a position to take advantage of the opportunities provided by the EC after the transitional period, production was expanded and the 1972 Annual Review was the most expansionist since 1948. By the point of EC entry in 1973, therefore, the United Kingdom had already moved some way towards the CAP principles of agricultural support. Widespread unease about the CAP, especially overproduction and high consumer prices, was reflected in the Labour Party's demand for renegotiation of the terms of entry. Nevertheless, for the first decade after EC entry all United Kingdom governments maintained an expansionist policy to reduce dependence on imported food and there was little opposition to the dominant agenda of high support and high production. Moreover agricultural interests were strengthened by EC entry as policy 'continued to be made amongst a small group of institutions which favoured farmers and excluded non-agricultural interests' (Smith, 1990, p. 168). The expansionist policy followed in the 1970s was embodied the White Paper 'Food From Our Own Resources' (Cmnd 6020, 1975), updated by 'Farming and the Nation' (Cmnd 7458, 1979). In 1976, when Britain was calling for a reduction in Community milk production, the price of milk to British farmers was actually increased on the grounds that although the Community was self sufficient the United Kingdom was not (Smith, 1990, p. 171). Moreover one of the first actions of the new Conservative Government in 1979 was to devalue the green pound which increased the prices received by British farmers and boosted production.

The seeds of policy change, however, were contained in the very success of the CAP. Encouraged by high prices and technological advances most of the major agricultural commodities were in surplus by the early 1980s. Overproduction and food surpluses, the increasing cost of the CAP, and international criticism built up an inexorable pressure for CAP reform. There was also pressure from consumers and environmentalists prompted by concern for human, animal and environmental health. By late 1983 there had been 'a major change in attitude towards agricultural policy. On two fronts the agenda was being questioned. Firstly, over the cost of the policy and secondly, over the effect on the environment' (Smith, 1990, p. 178). This shift in policy marked the end of agricultural expansion and recognized the political and economic unacceptability of increasing surpluses. The policy response at the EC level included a variety of methods of controlling production including price restrictions, levies, quotas, stabilizers and set aside as well as moves to more environmentally sensitive farming. Nonetheless, Smith has questioned the extent to which there has been a radical change in agricultural policy. At most production has been constrained to reduce surpluses but there has been no reversal from high input/high output, technology based, intensive farming. Reform has been designed not to undermine but to safeguard the principles of the CAP which are still widely supported in agricultural circles throughout the EC.

3   The politics of marketing

Marketing was a central pillar of the agricultural strategy followed in Northern Ireland after 1920. The overall aim was to improve the quality of agricultural output and to promote efficient marketing. The key influence on policy was dependence on the British market where local commodities competed with high quality and well marketed overseas produce, and also the relative disadvantage of remoteness and high transport costs. Northern Ireland farmers paid scant attention to marketing and during the First World War, for example, the sale of poor quality products at inflated prices on the British market badly damaged the reputation of Ulster produce. The importance of improved marketing was emphasized from the outset and one of the most pressing needs was to restore the reputation of Ulster products in Britain. Marketing was integrated with the other elements of Ministry strategy such as agricultural research and education in an effort to improve both marketing and the production of better quality commodities.

Initially the new Ministry of Agriculture adopted a cautious approach which embodied contemporary attitudes to agricultural development. As in Britain the intention was to promote the conditions in which individual initiative could flourish. The prevailing orthodoxy as expressed by Pollock in his 1927 budget speech was that the 'distribution of large sums of money among our farmers, the vast mass of whom only get a few shillings each, and others a pound or two, has no good effects whatever, and is simply squander-mania...the agricultural industry will never be brought into a state of prosperity by a system of pauperization' (NIHC Deb 8, c. 1321). With comprehensive financial subsidies ruled out, policy innovation was restricted to the traditional areas of concern including education and research, breeding and marketing, promoting cooperation, and rate relief.

Education was integral to agricultural improvement because farmers had to be persuaded to adopt new marketing and breeding methods and initially the Ministry 'largely confined itself to the policy of educational activity, which the Department of Agriculture and Technical Instruction had been carrying out for all Ireland' (Harkness, 1935, p. xiv). For the Ministry of Agriculture education was closely linked to research because the permanent amelioration of agricultural depression

34

lay 'in the wider dissemination of a knowledge of those principles of improved farming practice which scientific research makes available' (Ministry of Agriculture, 1930, p. 5). The Ministry established research divisions but the most important innovation was the collaboration with Queen's University in the foundation in 1924 of the Faculty of Agriculture. The University provided the land on condition that the Government meet most of the capital outlay and the costs of administration. The result was a situation in which Faculty staff were civil servants paid directly by the state but who taught for the University on a part time basis. In later years this arrangement was the subject of some criticism on the grounds that it hampered the free and independent provision of policy advice.

The problem was that the innate conservatism of Ulster farmers bred a resistance to new methods and a scepticism about the benefits of research and education. Some MP's such as George Leeke accused the Ministry of 'throwing money away on senseless policies of research, which are not going to be beneficial to the farmer' (NIHC Deb 8, c. 2390). Others like Rowley Elliott insisted that 'all the available money that can be conserved for agriculture should not go so much for research as in the alleviation of the unbearable burden of rates' (NIHC Deb 8, c. 216). Progressive elements in the leadership of the UFU, however, recognized that the Union had increasingly to 'direct its efforts along educational lines, such as the dissemination of information on agricultural subjects, including the results of scientific experiment and research' (Farmers' Journal, May 1925, p. 1889). Indeed one of the objectives of the Union was to bring farmers up-to-date with developments in agricultural practice, particularly through branch meetings and the pages of its official mouthpiece, 'The Farmers' Journal'.

A UFU initiative led to the establishment of the Agricultural Research Station at Hillsborough in 1928. The UFU proposed that the experimental farm be financed by an endowment fund drawn from money granted for rate relief and a matching amount from the Ministry of Finance. Day to day control would be in the hands of a board of trustees composed of farmers because independence from government control was essential to secure the cooperation of the agricultural community. This would also encourage farmers 'to keep pace with modern scientific developments and thereby provide themselves with the most effective means of protecting themselves and their markets from the persistent and increasing competition to which we are being subjected' (CAB9E/34/1). The Minister of Agriculture strongly supported the proposal because it involved the active participation of farmers in agricultural development and marked a recognition of the importance of research, particularly given earlier reluctance to the funding of development schemes from money earmarked for rate relief (Buckland, 1979, p. 132). The fact that farmers were prepared to sanction substantial investment in an experimental farm

> entailing as it does a sacrifice on their part at a time when their industry is in a serious condition, is worth more to this Ministry than a substantial grant from Government sources which involved no active participation or sacrifice

by the farmers themselves...Hitherto the Ministry has been literally driving the farming community along the road of scientific development - driving them so to speak in a badly scattered mass - and now we have a unique offer by the farmers themselves to travel along the road of their own accord and, what is more, to help to pull the machine and at a more rapid rate (CAB9E/34/1).

Although the Cabinet liked the idea in principle, Craig and Pollock wanted control to be vested in the regional Parliament, a suggestion completely unacceptable to the UFU which would only support the use of the rate relief grant if it was recognized as 'a gift from the farmers and that this recognition is consummated by conceding to them a share in the direct control and management of the Experimental Farm' (CAB9E/34/1). After lengthy discussions, Archdale persuaded the Cabinet to accept the UFU scheme, satisfied that 'any criticism regarding the diversion of part of the Supplemental Agricultural Grant will have no serious support within the agricultural population' (CAB9E/34/1).

Agricultural marketing: licensing and grading

The reluctance of farmers voluntarily to embrace new methods led the Ministry of Agriculture to adopt a strategy for the compulsory inspection and grading of all farm produce sent out of Northern Ireland, complemented by legislation to improve the quality of livestock such as the Livestock Breeding Act 1922 (Ministry of Agriculture, 1924, p. 26). Policy development was necessarily incremental, however, because of resistance to new methods amongst farmers and the limitations of the Government of Ireland Act.

Before 1928 the Government of Ireland Act prevented the regional Parliament from legislating in respect of trade out of Northern Ireland. In the case of the Marketing of Eggs Act 1924, for example, this limitation was overcome by licensing all egg dealers whether involved in the export trade or not. However a clause included in the Northern Ireland (Miscellaneous Provisions) Act 1928 made it clear that Parliament was not prevented from making laws to regulate the quality of livestock and agricultural produce sent to Great Britain, the Isle of Man, or the Irish Free State.

The main constraints on policy were imposed by the conservatism of Northern Ireland farmers and their hostility to state intervention. Spender, for example, pointed out that Archdale sympathized with the need for a radical policy of state directed marketing but 'no one could appreciate the inertia and, in fact, active obstruction which met every proposal for better methods. He was doing his best to make improvements but found that if he made his changes too violently they were actively obstructed' (CAB9E/23/1). There was constant criticism of the Ministry of Agriculture's penchant for state direction. Rowley Elliott, for example, complained of an 'overdose of legislation and an overdose of inspectors' which made it practically making it impossible for farmers to carry on their business (NIHC Deb 7, c. 1571).

Given this distrust of state regulation the Ministry of Agriculture placed great reliance on consultation to secure the widest possible measure of agreement in advance of legislation. The Ministry was also able to draw on an emergent elite consensus. Representative bodies such as the UFU, although temperamentally opposed to state control, accepted that state action was essential to guarantee the quality of exported produce. This was underpinned by the creation of a network of expert advisory committees which covered the main agricultural sectors. Such a strategy helped to neutralize opposition to controversial aspects of policy but the Ministry was nonetheless willing to override vocal sectional opposition to the extension of state supervision, for example the hostility of Armagh apple growers to the 1931 Marketing of Fruit Act (CAB9E/75/1-2; Buckland, 1979, pp. 137-139).

In the inter war period much agricultural legislation was based on the recommendations of independent committees. The Marketing of Eggs Act 1924, for example, was grounded in the Charlemont Report and the Marketing of Potatoes Act 1928 was suggested in the Mark Report (Cmd 27, 1924; Cmd 75, 1927). The Mark Committee (known after its chairman, a Unionist MP and leading member of the UFU) was established in 1927 as a typically populist response by Craig to the rural unrest he encountered on his tour of the province in late 1926. The Committee supported the policy of compulsory grading and inspection but also advocated increased cooperation amongst producers, promoted by a government programme of education. More significantly, the incremental strategy of the Ministry of Agriculture was endorsed. Every step needed to be subject to consultation between the Ministry and affected interests and

> no attempt should be made at once to establish a system of inspection for every class of farm produce. We are convinced that the safest course to pursue would be to select a particular branch of our export trade in regard to which the need for improved grading, packing and preparation for market generally is clearly pressing; to legislate specifically for that particular trade; and then, in the light of the experience of the operation of that legislation, to bring other branches within the inspection system (Cmd 75, 1927, para. 32).

As a result the gradual introduction of a series of Acts laid down marketing standards for all agricultural produce sent to Britain, including the Marketing of Potatoes Act (1928), the Marketing of Dairy Produce Act (1929), the Agricultural Produce (Meat Regulation) Act (1930), and the Marketing of Fruit Act (1931). The changed national conditions after 1932, however, provided the opportunity for a more far reaching reform of agricultural marketing.

Agricultural marketing in the 1930s

After 1932 agricultural marketing was synonymous with commodity marketing boards. The guiding principle, elucidated by the Mark Committee and the Linlithgow Commission in Britain, was that the main problem faced by farmers was the wide disparity between producer and consumer prices for which poor marketing was largely to blame. The suggested solution was the creation of organizations to control the output and marketing of agricultural produce. In Britain the Agricultural Marketing Acts of 1931 and 1933 provided for the creation of marketing boards as the main vehicle for the reorganization of marketing. During the 1930s producer controlled marketing boards were established in Britain for commodities such as pigs, bacon, milk, and potatoes. The limitations of producer controlled marketing, however, were acknowledged by the different approaches taken for wheat, sugar and livestock. The lack of protection for the consumer was also a concern and the Lucas Report in 1947 recommended the creation of commodity commissions whose members would be appointed by the government as the 'business executives of the tax-payer'. Disagreements within government and the vehement opposition of the Farmers' Unions ensured that the Lucas proposals were shelved in favour of a limited amendment to the Agricultural Marketing Acts to make producer marketing boards more responsive to the public interest.

Because import controls could limit the outlet for Northern Ireland produce in Britain, the regional Government was drawn into the formulation of British marketing policy. Although the extension of the British Marketing Acts to Northern Ireland was constitutionally undesirable, the regional Parliament was required to assure the British authorities that the marketing of Northern Ireland produce would be regulated (CAB9E/57/2). Indeed where a commodity was regulated in Britain it was compulsory for a complementary scheme to be framed for Northern Ireland. As a result the Agricultural Marketing Act (1933) paralleled the British legislation and facilitated the introduction of agricultural marketing schemes in Northern Ireland. However, whilst the regional marketing boards had trading powers similar to those in Britain there were significant differences in the nature and extent of government control. For example, whereas British marketing boards were largely controlled by producers themselves, the Ministry of Agriculture retained the right to appoint three members to the Northern Ireland equivalents. The Ministry of Agriculture also retained control over the preparation of schemes in contrast to Britain where producers had the power of initiative. Although Andrews argued in Cabinet for as much producer control as possible, the Ministry of Agriculture opposed any dilution of its supervisory powers. This was justified by the need to ensure coordination with parallel British schemes and by the claim that only it possessed the expertise necessary to frame complex schemes which were in the best interests of all producers. Moreover although schemes required initial parliamentary approval and reaffirmation after two years, Archdale refused to allow parliamentary amendment because this might undermine the extensive prior consultation with the agricultural community.

Pigs and bacon

Reorganization of the chaotic system of pigs marketing was a top priority (Ministry of Agriculture, 1937; Buckland, 1979, pp. 144-47). Although the Agricultural Produce (Meat Regulation) Act 1930 regulated the marketing of exports, producer opposition frustrated attempts to reorganize the whole domestic pig industry until the early 1930s. Following the British Government's decision to regulate bacon imports and the Lane-Fox Report on the reorganization of the pig industry in 1932, producer marketing boards for pigs and bacon were established in Britain, linked by a system of contracts. This required the formulation of complementary schemes in Northern Ireland. The remit of the Lane-Fox Commission was widened to include Northern Ireland and there was some tension between the Ministry of Agriculture and the Commission over the extent to which the schemes could be adapted to meet the special conditions of Northern Ireland. Worried about opposition to the scheme in Northern Ireland the Ministry arranged for the Lane-Fox Commission to visit Belfast to allay fears about the scheme and to demonstrate that the interests of Ulster farmers were being fully considered. However the Ministry also warned producers and curers that demands for further concessions would weaken the chances of its own suggestions being accepted by the Commission. The Ministry considered the British system of individual contracts to be completely unsuitable but Lane-Fox objected to its proposal for a quota system because it had insufficient safeguards for the consumer and would 'extend to the farmers and curers of Northern Ireland privileges not enjoyed by the farmers and curers of Great Britain' (AG16/11/4). Harkness, who sat on the Lane-Fox Committee as an observer, gave the standard reply that it was simply because of the 'different conditions of production for Northern Ireland' that different administrative arrangements were proposed (AG16/11/4). Agreement was eventually reached when the Ministry gave assurances that it would introduce administrative machinery to ensure that a definite quota would be fulfilled in Northern Ireland.

The Northern Ireland Pigs and Bacon Marketing Schemes became operable in October 1933. The Boards were composed of three Ministry appointees and eleven members elected by registered producers and curers. The Pigs Marketing Board (PMB) had the statutory right to buy and sell pigs, fix prices, and encourage cooperation amongst pig producers; the Bacon Marketing Board (BMB) regulated bacon sales and represented curers. The schemes experienced severe administrative problems in both Britain and Northern Ireland. In Britain the contract system failed to guarantee supplies to curers and the schemes were replaced under the Bacon Industry Act 1938 which combined a guaranteed price for Wiltshire bacon pigs with measures to rationalize curing establishments. The reorganization of the pig industry in Northern Ireland faced more fundamental problems. Increased domestic production encouraged by the PMB depressed bacon prices despite

39

import restriction and curers campaigned for an indemnity loan against losses. On the other hand, the Ministry was inundated by complaints from farmers about the attempts of curers to undermine the schemes. Clearly in sympathy with producers, Brooke accused the curers of trying to obstruct the Ministry's policy of developing Wiltshire cured bacon in Northern Ireland (AG16/13/15; Buckland, 1979, p. 147). Although an indemnity loan for curers was agreed in November 1934 the Ministry introduced policy changes which led to the demise of the BMB. The Agricultural Marketing (Pig Industry) Act 1934 established a Pig Industry Council to fix prices, composed of three representatives each from the Ministry, producers and curers. Increased regulatory powers for the Ministry, including the ability to license new bacon factories and prosecute curers who undercut fixed prices, left the BMB surplus to requirements and the bacon scheme was allowed to lapse. Predictably the BMB opposed the 'multiplication of boards, levies, quotas and paid officials, and...intensified bureaucratic control of the unfortunate curing industry' (AG16/13/15). For the Ministry of Agriculture, however, its policy was vindicated by the near trebling of both pig numbers and the total value of output in the 1930s which made pig production the most valuable branch of the livestock industry in Northern Ireland.

Following the introduction of the Bacon Industry Act in Britain in 1938 Brooke decided to introduce parallel legislation. This was delayed by financial haggling with the Treasury and the Ministry of Finance but eventually the Treasury reluctantly agreed to a deduction of up to a maximum of £400,000 per annum from the Imperial Contribution (CAB4/403). At the same time Brooke dissolved the PMB on the grounds of financial and administrative malpractice but also because it opposed the Bacon Industry Bill for being insufficiently sensitive of regional conditions. For Brooke, however, the issue was of

> crucial importance to Northern Ireland agriculture in establishing the principle that agriculture in Northern Ireland is entitled to the same measure of assistance as agriculture in Great Britain...and if we refuse a price insurance scheme for pigs it will be quite impossible to argue in the future that we participate in a price insurance scheme for other commodities (NIHC Deb 22, c. 1364-5).

Indeed contracts, rejected as unsuitable just a few years before, were now embraced in an attempt to gain acceptance of the principle of parity.

Milk

Milk production was also bedeviled by poor marketing. Indeed marketing problems in the milk sector encouraged cooperation amongst farmers and the UFU, for example, had its origins in attempts by milk producers to negotiate more effectively with retailers. In the 1920s voluntary price agreements were prone to break down because individual farmers undercut the agreed price. When certain retailers refused to discuss prices with the UFU in November 1931 the Union called a 'milk strike' in which barricades were erected and flying pickets roamed the countryside to milk the cows of producers outside the action to prevent supplies from reaching Belfast. The action was only called off when Craig summoned all parties to Stormont and arbitrated a settlement. The UFU regarded this as an important victory and a clear demonstration of the benefits of collective action (CAB9E/111/1).

Substantial imports of milk products, especially butter, influenced prices in the British market. Although the scope for protection was limited by trade agreements the regulation of imports from foreign countries and the Irish Free State necessitated the reorganization of marketing. Based on the recommendations of the Grigg Reorganisation Commission, marketing schemes were established in October 1933, one for England and Wales, one for the Isle of Man, and four for Scotland. In Northern Ireland the reorganization of marketing had to take account of important regional differences, particularly that only 30 per cent of milk production was consumed in liquid form compared with about 70 per cent in Britain. As a result the Ministry of Agriculture rejected the English approach in which producer prices were equalized through a pooling system because it would unfairly penalize producers of liquid milk in favour of creamery suppliers and because it wished to stimulate the consumption of high quality milk (Harkness, 1935, p. xxiii).

Lack of progress in the reform of milk marketing caused friction between the Ministry of Agriculture and the UFU which grew increasingly impatient as a draft scheme failed to appear. Ministry caution, administrative difficulties in tailoring the scheme to the specific conditions of Northern Ireland, and negotiations with the Treasury caused much of the delay. The Ministry proceeded with caution to ensure that the scheme was properly thought out, compatible with those in Britain, and to overcome potential producer opposition. Scott Robertson was adamant that to introduce a milk scheme before September 1934 would make the cure worse than the prevailing ailment and would 'land not only the Ministry but the Government into most serious difficulties' (CAB9E/122/1). To formulate a successful scheme for numerous and varied interests the Government needed to 'carry with us in our effort not only their goodwill but their active support' (CAB9E/122/1). Moreover the workload imposed on the Ministry by marketing reorganization was 'somewhat terrifying and we will quite clearly have to secure extra staff and create a marketing section within the ministry' (CAB9E/122/1).

Complex financial negotiations with the Treasury also contributed to delay. When the British Government introduced an emergency subsidy to prevent the collapse of the milk schemes the Ministry demanded equal financial benefits for Ulster producers. It was argued that because the British subsidy was in lieu of import control for which the Northern Ireland Government had no responsibility 'it would not be proper for Northern Ireland to assume financial responsibility for this transitional stage in the policy of the United Kingdom Government' (CAB9E/122/2).

Both the Treasury and MAF strongly opposed a British subsidy for Northern

Ireland milk producers. When it was discovered that MAF had argued that no financial help should be given to Northern Ireland, the Ministry of Finance complained that it was 'quite improper that questions of Northern Ireland finance...should be prejudiced in this way by one of the Imperial Government Ministries' (CAB9E/122/2). For the Treasury the case made by the regional Government implied only that 'the Northern Irish dairy farmer has a strong claim for help from his own Government, but does not appear to justify an appeal to the Imperial Exchequer as of right' (CAB9E/122/2). Indeed, if the British schemes were unsuited to Northern Ireland because of different regional conditions then 'just as the problems differ, so should the remedy' and 'no attempt should be made to apply, in the peculiar conditions obtaining in Northern Ireland, a method which was designed to suit the circumstances of the industry, and of the marketing schemes, in Great Britain' (CAB9E/122/2).

Restrictions on butter imports from southern Ireland, favoured by the Treasury, proved impractical because re-exports of Irish butter from Britain to Northern Ireland could not be prevented in line with the constitutional prohibition on interference with trade within the United Kingdom. Moreover the United Kingdom Market Supply Committee suggested that the best safeguard for Northern Ireland milk producers might be for the Northern Ireland Government to 'be in a position to extend to milk producers some form of temporary financial assistance similar to that given to the Milk Marketing Board in Great Britain' (CAB9E/122/2). A reluctant Treasury eventually made an emergency payment of £200,000 to meet the needs of Northern Ireland but insisted that no precedent had been set. When low milk prices required the continuation of the payment to British producers the Treasury was able to reduce the payment to Northern Ireland to £100,000 and insisted that the regional Government should provide any additional support from its own resources. The Ministry of Agriculture, however, reiterated the view that despite administrative differences between the milk schemes 'the real position is that the service is a United Kingdom service and our Ministry of Agriculture administer the service on lines approved by you as appropriate to our local conditions' (CAB9E/122/1). When the Treasury subsidy to milk producers was discontinued the Northern Ireland Government continued to assist creameries and Brooke made it clear that such payments would be 'recovered out of Northern Ireland's share of reserved taxation and will not therefore involve an additional charge on our taxpayers' (NIHC Deb 19, c. 1894-5).

The Northern Ireland milk marketing scheme was designed to insulate and protect the liquid milk market, assist producers of manufacturing milk, and ensure a better, safer, and affordable milk supply to the consumer (Ministry of Agriculture, 1937, p.19). For example, a fourfold grading system set quality standards, distributors and producers were subjected to Ministry inspection, and the Ministry also fixed differential licence fees and bonus payment scales to encourage the production of higher quality milk for liquid consumption. Despite its demands for marketing reform, however, the UFU was unhappy with the details of the scheme. Brooke resisted pressure to 'follow slavishly the precedent of the British Schemes over here' and the Northern Ireland scheme differed in several important respects from the British equivalents (CAB4/324). These variations were justified because of the different conditions prevailing in Northern Ireland, the lessons learnt from the British experience, and the need to protect consumers.

The most controversial departure from British practice was the refusal to establish a producer controlled scheme under the Agricultural Marketing Act but to introduce a separate Milk and Milk Products Act (1934). The UFU was horrified by the degree of state direction and was particularly dissatisfied with the Ministry's acceptance of the Grigg recommendation for a joint council (rejected in Britain) with the addition of consumer representatives. Just seven of the 17 members of the Joint Milk Council (JMC) were elected by producers whereas three including the chair were appointed by the Minister of Agriculture, three were appointed by the Minister of Home Affairs to represent consumers, and four were elected by distributors. For the UFU the Ministry of Agriculture had effective control because its appointees fixed prices in the absence of unanimity between the diverse interests on the Council. The UFU criticized the JMC as 'a farce, and only a means of throwing dust in the farmer's eyes and making him believe that he has some control of the scheme when, in reality, he is at the mercy of the Civil Servant' (Farmers' Journal, October 1934, p. 53). The rest of the 1930s witnessed periodic protests against the price determinations of the JMC. In October 1936, for example, a mass meeting of farmers expressed unanimous disapproval of the determinations of the JMC. Although the price of wholesale milk was increased in 1937 farmers remained disenchanted with the performance of the marketing scheme which they believed had increased government control but failed to do the same for producer prices.

Potatoes

Market fluctuation and price instability had always characterized the potato sector but it was British complaints about poor quality which prompted the first marketing reforms. The Marketing of Potatoes Act 1928 regulated and licensed the export trade to ensure proper grading. Although this was generally supported there were the usual complaints from farmers about excessive bureaucracy and state intervention.

The reorganization of domestic production to stabilize supply and demand was less easily achieved. Archdale even attributed stagnation of demand to the fact that 'young ladies in England like slim figures...it is the change in the fashion of the figure of young ladies that is responsible for the decline in the consumption of potatoes in England' (NIHC Deb 12, c. 134). Imports into the United Kingdom were regulated in the 1930s, accompanied by the introduction of a Potato Marketing Scheme in Britain (British Association, 1938, p. 172). This again required a parallel reorganization of the trade in Northern Ireland. Despite pressure from the UFU it was decided that the potato scheme could be most 'efficiently and economically operated if grafted on to the existing potato administration of the Ministry of Agriculture rather than by setting up a Statutory Board under the Marketing Act of 1933' (CAB9E/57/2). Because of the importance of potatoes as stock feed the Ministry of Agriculture was unwilling to limit production. All that was needed was broad regulatory powers to control shipments of potatoes in order to prevent surpluses undermining the British Potato Marketing Board and this was facilitated by a further amendment to the Government of Ireland Act in 1933. As a result the Ministry and the UFU agreed the maximum level of shipments of potatoes to Britain with the Potato Marketing Board and domestic legislation was amended to permit minimum grading standards for the home market.

A sectoral organization - the Northern Ireland Potato Marketing Association (NIPMA) - was set up in 1935 with the assistance of the Ministry of Agriculture. Composed of representatives of licensed merchants, producers and the Ministry, NIPMA was responsible for ensuring orderly marketing, could recommend prices, and played a key role in negotiations with the British Potato Marketing Board. In June 1936, for example, a "gentleman's agreement" was reached in which the latter recognized the principle that Northern Ireland was an integral part of the United Kingdom and had free access to the British market; in return NIPMA undertook voluntarily to limit shipments from Northern Ireland to Britain in years of surplus. The final piece in the inter war jigsaw was the Marketing of Potatoes Act 1938 which introduced a statutory Potato Marketing Scheme to permit cooperation with the British equivalent. The "gentleman's agreement" with the British Potato Marketing Board was recognized and the price fixing role of NIPMA was acknowledged. For Brooke, one main advantage of the scheme was that because it was financed through licence receipts and a levy on shipments no Exchequer funding was involved.

Post war marketing

After 1945 the Northern Ireland Government's approach to agricultural marketing was even more inextricably linked to that adopted by the British Government. The Ministry of Agriculture was directly involved in the Whitehall policy formulation process and helped to shape the general pattern of marketing in the post war years. A key factor was the need to coordinate the marketing arrangements for guaranteed commodities throughout the United Kingdom to facilitate the administration of the 1947 Agriculture Act. Particularly important was the Agricultural Marketing Act 1949 which permitted the creation of marketing schemes for the United Kingdom as a whole, for Scotland and Northern Ireland, or for England and Northern Ireland. Regional schemes continued to be promoted under the Agricultural Marketing Act 1933. The UFU pressed insistently for the inclusion of Northern Ireland in United Kingdom marketing schemes in an attempt to consolidate the wartime price parity in the face of a return to free market conditions. Harry West, for example, claimed that the 'operation of a scheme applicable to the whole of the United Kingdom and administered by the single board as provided by the Marketing Act of 1949, would have a greater chance of attaining parity of price, or as near as possible, than any other marketing system' (NIHC Deb 38, c. 2306). The Ministry, however, was wary of ceding transferred powers to organizations outside its control. The policy was to 'consider every case on its merits, always bearing in mind the constitutional responsibilities of the Government here with regard to the administration of Northern Ireland affairs, and also our desire to further the interests of Ulster producers' (CAB9E/57/4). As commodities were gradually decontrolled the diversity of post war marketing became apparent. No one system of marketing could cover adequately the different problems of individual products and what emerged in Northern Ireland was a hybrid of schemes operated under specific legislation of the Stormont Parliament (beef, potatoes, poultry, flax), and local (pigs, milk, herbage seeds, seed potatoes) and national (eggs, wool) producer controlled marketing schemes.

With the removal of wartime controls the Northern Ireland Pigs Marketing Board was restored as a permanent producer controlled organization but the restoration of the British Milk Marketing Boards posed more difficult problems. The Babington Committee rejected outright producer control but recommended that the pre war legislation be replaced by a milk marketing board representing producers and a milk commission to protect the interests of the public (Cmd 249, 1947, ch. XV). Following the decision to use marketing boards to implement price guarantees under the 1947 Act the Ministry of Agriculture decided to establish the Northern Ireland Milk Marketing Board (MMB) in 1955. This was hailed by the UFU as a major achievement after over twenty years of campaigning (Farmers' Journal, December 1954, p. 13).

Marketing reform was extended to other sectors after the war. For example, the Seed Potato Marketing Board (SPMB) was set up in July 1961 after a joint request from the UFU and the trade interests. Marketing boards were also established for wool, eggs, and herbage seeds. For wool and eggs the regional Ministry actually supported the UFU case for single boards for the United Kingdom. Indeed the proposal for a national wool marketing scheme had led to the inclusion of Northern Ireland in the British marketing legislation in 1949. In the case of wool the Ministry argued that a regional scheme would be 'futile and useless' because only 11 per cent of producers and three per cent of output was contributed from Northern Ireland and most production would be handled by a British board (NIHC Deb 34, c. 1426). In 1950, therefore, the British Wool Marketing Scheme became operable after approval by both the Westminster and Stormont Parliaments. For the UFU the wool scheme represented a definite sign of progress towards democracy in comparison with the 'state socialism' of the pre war period and Harry West was returned unopposed as the Northern Ireland representative on the British Wool Marketing Board in 1951 (Farmers' Journal, January 1951, p. 4).

Over 900 objections were lodged against the Farmers' Unions original proposals for a national egg marketing scheme and the lengthy public inquiry led to changes in the scheme (Self and Storing, 1962, pp. 100-102). These were reluctantly accepted by the Unions although the UFU continued to regard the scheme as a 'cause for rejoicing' and a 'milestone on the road towards better and more efficient marketing of home-produced farm produce' (Farmers' Journal, May 1957, pp. 13, 21). Moore's regrets about the abandonment of the Northern Ireland egg marketing legislation were outweighed by the decision to pool transport costs. This helped overcome the remoteness disadvantage faced by Northern Ireland producers and reduce the wide disparity in egg prices between Northern Ireland and Britain which emerged after decontrol (CAB9E/57/6). The scheme was approved by the Northern Ireland Parliament in November 1956 without a murmur about interference with its constitutional powers although one MP did object to interference with the individual liberty of the producer (NIHC Deb 40, c. 2657).

In the case of grass seed the Northern Ireland Government refused to agree to a United Kingdom marketing scheme in 1950. Although the Ministry promised to consider the creation of a regional board it decided to purchase seed at guaranteed prices under the Herbage Seeds Act 1955. In 1964, however, the Government and the UFU reached agreement on a producer controlled Herbage Seeds Marketing Board.

Fatstock marketing: a case study

Fatstock presented the most difficult and complex marketing problems of all the agricultural commodities. During the 1930s the recommendation of the Reorganisation Commission for Fatstock in England and Wales for a marketing scheme linked to import control had not been acted upon. Instead the British Government formulated a policy for the reorganization of marketing and slaughtering and provided a subsidy for producers under the Cattle Industry (Emergency Provisions) Act 1934. A Cattle Committee was set up to administer the subsidy for which the Ministry of Agriculture acted as agent in Northern Ireland. There was little debate about the extension of the temporary beef subsidy to Northern Ireland whose producers received an initial Treasury payment worth £250,000 and the improvement of marketing was left to the regional Government. For Scott Robertson this success was the result of the precedent set in the milk sector but also of his Ministry's efforts to enlist the help of Walter Elliott, the British Minister of Agriculture who was regarded as particularly sympathetic to Northern Ireland.

Post war proposals for fatstock marketing were strongly influenced by the experience of wartime state control. The Babington Committee, for example, contrasted the efficiency of controlled fatstock marketing with the pre war disorganization. It recommended the creation of a marketing board representing producers and a fatstock commission responsible for the purchase, central slaughtering and processing of all fat cattle and sheep in Northern Ireland (Cmd 249, 1947, p. 99). A joint Working Party of the three Farmers' Unions proposed a single United Kingdom producer controlled marketing board for all cattle, sheep, and pigs (Farmers' Journal, November 1952, pp. 5-9). In his maiden speech at Stormont, Harry West accepted the reconstitution of the PMB only on the understanding that it would be replaced by a producer controlled marketing scheme for fatstock, preferably covering the whole of the United Kingdom. This was strongly opposed by trade interests such as the Belfast Livestock Salesmens' Association and the Northern Ireland Master Butchers' Association but was also unacceptable to the British Government because it infringed free trade, consumer choice, and an undertaking that private traders would have their businesses returned after the war (Cmd 8989, 1953, para. 12).

The Unions lowered their sights to a scheme for bacon pigs only which would also develop the voluntary marketing of other fatstock (CAB9E/57/5). When this suggestion was withdrawn in the light of the poor performance of the commercial Fatstock Marketing Corporation established by the Unions, the UFU again turned its attention to regional marketing schemes with full statutory powers established under the 1933 legislation, with the ultimate objective of all fatstock being exported 'on the hook' (Farmers' Journal, March 1955, p. 45). However Moore refused to agree to a fatstock scheme for Northern Ireland alone. The UFU attributed this reluctance to an unwillingness to act before the British Government did so, the malign influence of cattle traders, and vocal libertarian and urban elements within the Unionist Party which opposed producer controlled marketing as a restrictive practice which was contrary to the interest of consumers.

The issue of fatstock marketing came back onto the agenda when the Verdon-Smith Committee was appointed in April 1962 to report on how meat production, marketing, and distribution could be made more efficient, thereby reducing Exchequer expenditure on fatstock guarantees which had increased sharply. The remit of the Verdon-Smith Committee extended to Northern Ireland where variations in marketing strategy reflected the different characteristics of the Northern Ireland fatstock industry, particularly the substantial price differential caused by relative remoteness from main markets in Britain. Verdon-Smith was unconvinced by the Farmers' Unions arguments for a statutory producer controlled board on either a national or regional basis. Although regional conditions made a board more suited to Northern Ireland, it was not the best means of improving meat marketing and there were great dangers in departing from market forces. The

> operation of a single buyer and seller might well discourage the innovation and experiment which the Northern Ireland sector needs at least as much as the rest of the industry. In its marketing activities within Northern Ireland itself the Board would be subject to most of the criticisms levelled at the monopoly position of a United Kingdom Board (Cmnd 2282, 1964, para. 867).

The UFU was disappointed by the endorsement of free market forces which were responsible for the 'parlous state in which the industry finds itself today' and continued to press for a statutory producer controlled marketing board to strengthen the bargaining position of producers (Farmers' Journal, 3 July 1964, pp.

32-3).

The Committee also considered the advantages of the development of a viable dead meat industry in Northern Ireland. Despite the efforts of the Ministry, in 1962 exports 'on the hook' still amounted to less than nine per cent of cattle exports and about 30 per cent in the case of sheep. Verdon-Smith supported these efforts but concluded that the benefits of carcase marketing had been greatly overstated in terms of narrowing the price differential between local and British cattle because it would not solve the problem of seasonal fluctuations in supply and excess slaughtering capacity. The development of a dead meat industry might foster rural development and provide employment but the creation of a board to facilitate this goal was outside the remit of the Verdon-Smith inquiry and was a matter for the Northern Ireland Government.

Some action to improve meat marketing was necessary, however. For Britain Verdon-Smith recommended the creation of a Meat and Livestock Commission but it was considered neither advantageous nor appropriate for its responsibilities to extend to Northern Ireland where the Ministry of Agriculture should perform the same functions (Cmnd 2737, 1965, para. 25). To help formulate a new regional strategy a white paper on fatstock marketing was published (Cmd 500, 1966). On the question of a new fatstock marketing organization a balance had to be struck between the trade associations which favoured the status quo and the UFU which wanted control of a new body with substantial powers.

The Ministry's cautious approach was generally supported by MP's who were unenthusiastic about a compulsory producer controlled board, particularly in the light of the contemporary controversy about the performance of existing marketing boards. Even some producers such as Phelim O'Neill, a future Minister of Agriculture, preferred vigorous competition rather than the introduction of a monopoly buyer (NIHC Deb 63, c. 1231). Trade associations such as the Northern Ireland Livestock Auctioneers' Association (NILAA) welcomed Verdon-Smith's 'vote of confidence in fatstock sales by auction' (Farmweek, 21 April 1964). NILAA believed that a census of fatstock producers would demonstrate 'overwhelming support for the auction mart system' and that marketing boards had become 'an obsession with UFU leaders' (Farmweek, 9 February 1965). For NILAA private enterprise and free competition was absolutely imperative and all should have the 'opportunity to earn the living to which their ability entitles them and so that all can play their part in stemming systems which must eventually lead to Communism' (Farmweek, 4 May 1965).

The Minister, Harry West, was irked by the intensive lobbying of NILAA and warned that it should not 'dictate policy either to the consumer or to the producer' (NIHC Deb 64, c. 2785). Nevertheless, despite his past attachment to the principle of producer marketing when UFU President, West decided that any new body would be neither 'monopolistic nor purely advisory, since the one seems to entail powers which would be too sweeping for present circumstances, and the other would be scarcely effective enough to deal with the main difficulties' (Cmd 500, 1966, para. 39). This caution disappointed the UFU for whom the proposed body did not have 'strong enough powers to carry out the reorganisation which is vitally necessary in the interests of producers, consumers and the trade, and to enable the livestock industry to make its fullest contribution to the economy of the Province' (Farmers' Journal, August 1966, p. 19). It was gratuitous for the Ministry to

> extol the virtues of statutory marketing and yet refuse fatstock producers the rights which are enjoyed by producers of milk, pigs and all other major commodities; it was pointless to recognise the financial plight of fatstock producers and yet deny them a marketing mechanism; and it was time-wasting to go through the prolonged process of consultation and discussion and yet discard the views of everyone other than the Minister's own advisers (Farmers' Journal, December 1966, p. 22).

The proposals in the Livestock Marketing Bill introduced in April 1967 represented a further victory for caution. The new Livestock Marketing Commission established as a result had promotional and advisory functions but no trading powers. Although the Bill was generally welcomed in the House of Commons, some including Phelim O'Neill felt that the Commission was too weak and did not have sufficient powers. The UFU, of course, shared these sentiments and resented the further emasculation of the new body. In any case, however, the UFU was not interested in tinkering with the powers of the Livestock Marketing Commission because it was regarded as totally inadequate to deal with the serious problems of meat marketing.

Marketing and state-farmer relations

From the outset agricultural marketing policy was highly controversial. There was significant opposition in the agricultural community to the Ministry of Agriculture's conviction that general conditions in Northern Ireland 'necessitated a greater of degree of state intervention in and control of agriculture than in the rest of the United Kingdom' (Buckland, 1979, p. 131). Debates in the regional Parliament were littered with objections to policies which extended state inspection and bureaucracy. In a barbed reference to legislation on sheep worrying, for example, George Henderson commented that 'if we go on for a year or two as we are doing, there will be as nearly as big a demand for a Bill to prevent the worrying of the people by officials' (NIHC Deb 8, c. 100). Libertarian conservatives complained that 'socialist' marketing legislation interfered with private enterprise whereas representatives of the working class demanded strong democratic accountability to protect the interests of consumers. The most notable libertarian critic of agricultural policy was R.J. Lynn, the editor of the Northern Whig, who objected to the infringement of individual freedom by increased state power. Thus the 'great industries of Ulster had been built up by the private enterprise of its people without the help of the Government or Department of any kind...we are reaching this stage when we are getting to be the most official class in the whole of Europe outside Russia' (NIHC Deb 12, c. 1701). For the Independent Unionist, Henderson, the comparison was with Germany and the marketing legislation was 'Hitlerism run mad. The Potato Marketing Board, the pig board, the dog board and the hen board - there is no board under the sun which Northern Ireland has not secured, and they are retarding the progress of the farming community' (NIHC Deb 21, c. 1901).

Such complaints could be marginalized if the support of farmers was secured for Ministry policy. To overcome the Ulster farmers' suspicion of the state, not always successfully, the Ministry of Agriculture fostered close relations with organizations representing the farming community such as the UFU and the Ulster Agricultural Organisation Society (UAOS), often through government grants to promote cooperation amongst farmers. This reflected the conviction that agricultural progress would be 'greatly accelerated if farmers were better organised' and that 'the work of the Ministry can be done more efficiently and economically through organised bodies of farmers than through private individuals' (NIHC Deb 7, c. 605). The Ministry also pointed to the extensive consultation process which it undertook prior to the introduction of legislation. Potato marketing legislation, for example, was 'discussed with the Executive Committee of the Merchants Association and with the Ulster Farmers' Union. They are satisfied and support the measure wholeheartedly' (NIHC Deb 21, c. 1772). After the controversy over the Marketing of Fruit Act Craig insisted that outline legislative proposals be put to farmers meetings and that resolutions of approval be obtained from the UFU and other agricultural bodies (CAB9E/57/2).

Nonetheless there were significant differences between the Ministry and the farming community on marketing policy. Whilst the UFU leadership supported the general thrust of policy and was probably the staunchest advocate of marketing reform, much of the membership had serious reservations about marketing legislation which occasionally led to severe stress in the relationship with the state. Producer controlled marketing acquired totemic status although the UFU was initially equivocal about marketing boards. However, if they were the price to be paid for government assistance then it was 'necessary to take this great plunge in the dark and put up various schemes. All that farmers can now do is to see that the schemes are well thought out and try to get as free as possible from Government control' (Farmers' Journal, June 1933, p. 4103).

The attitude of the UFU to marketing legislation was framed firstly by opposition to deviations from British practice when this went against the perceived interests of farmers, and secondly by the demand for as much producer control as possible in the administration of the schemes. The breakdown in UFU-Ministry relations in the late 1930s was caused by a conflation of these considerations. Throughout the 1930s the UFU objected to the Ministry's penchant for framing special legislation to introduce marketing schemes rather than set up producer controlled boards under the 1933 Agricultural Marketing Act which was used only for the pigs, bacon, and butter/cream schemes. This was unfavourably compared with Britain where producers had more control over both the formulation and administration of schemes. Colonel Gordon of the UFU expressed grave dissatisfaction at the increasing tendency

> for more and more power to be given to the Ministry of Agriculture both as regards price determination and the administration of schemes...the producers affected should have, through their elected representatives on the marketing boards, exactly the same rights as have been given by successive British Governments to producers in Great Britain...To vest the fixing of prices, in addition to the general administration of the scheme, in the hands of a Government Department is a departure from all British democratic principles so glaring that we cannot allow it to pass without making the most vigorous protest possible. No similar attempts to set up departmental dictatorships to run schemes and fix prices for farm produce have yet been made in Great Britain or in any other of her Crown Colonies, nor are any such, in our opinion, likely to be attempted (NIHC Deb 18, c. 1323).

Ministry control of schemes was prompted by the need to coordinate regional schemes with those in Britain, by the conviction that farmers did not possess the necessary expertise to either formulate or administer schemes, and also by a more general concern for the public interest. For example, the Ministry claimed that it disliked bureaucracy as much as anyone but that the individualism of the Ulster farmer made it necessary assume a greater degree of state control than in Britain. Producers did not possess the expertise needed to administer schemes immediately and for 'months after the scheme comes into operation the Ministry will in actual fact have to run it for them, whilst they appear publicly to be doing so' (CAB9E/122/1). After the launch of the pigs scheme the Ministry had to second officials to the Board who had 'to attend practically every meeting of the Pigs Marketing Board and guide them in their policy and through their difficulties' (CAB9E/122/1).

Relations between the farming community and the Ministry reached their nadir with Brooke's sacking of the UFU dominated Pigs Marketing Board in 1939 (three of the UFU's representatives on the Board were also prominent Unionist MP's - Elliott, Gamble, and Moore). Later Brooke accepted that the Ministry had acted harshly and he 'attributed this in part to his failure to curb his own over zealous officials' (Barton, 1988, p. 112). Prime suspect was the Permanent Secretary, George Scott Robertson who provided the crusading zeal in agricultural policy. On one occasion, for example, Grant gave public vent to distrust of Ministry officials and was moved to remark that the 'time has arrived in Northern Ireland when we are not going to be dictated to by civil servants' (NIHC Deb 21, c. 418-9).

Sectional differences were buried in the national interest on the outbreak of the Second World War but the UFU tried to exploit its increased political influence to secure the Ministry's commitment to producer control of marketing schemes after the war. No part of the United Kingdom had made a greater war effort than Northern Ireland and it was 'for the ideals of democratic government that Britain and her allies are fighting this war, and when it is won this organisation and the farmers of Ulster generally are determined that their industry shall secure the same freedom of action and the same control of their own affairs as are enjoyed by their fellow farmers in Great Britain' (CAB9E/57/3/I). However, during the war Andrews refused to give any commitment which might prejudice the consideration of post war policy. Indeed it was argued that British policy had actually moved away from producer control and towards that of the Northern Ireland Government in the late 1930s. The UFU pressed the Babington Committee to accept the principle of producer controlled marketing but the Committee was worried about the conflict of interest between monopoly boards and the consumer and other trading interests. Babington effectively rejected the Union's argument by recommending the retention of the pre war mixed boards with producer representation equal to that of traders and processors combined (Cmd 249, 1947, p. 97).

The Babington recommendations and the determination of the regional Government to resist the widespread use of national marketing boards set the context for state-farmer relations in the post war period. The UFU was eager to see national marketing schemes created to underpin price parity but the regional Government wanted to continue to frame its own marketing legislation to deal with the particular problems of Ulster agriculture. In 1954, for example, Moore delayed the proposed United Kingdom fatstock marketing scheme because it entailed the complete repeal of the regional pigs marketing legislation and involved the 'almost complete surrender of our control over the marketing of the major items of our agricultural output' (CAB9E/57/5). The Ministry's cool attitude towards the scheme threatened the cordial relations with the UFU. An ex-President of the Union, Moore accused his successor of being obsessed with the alleged benefits of the scheme and of having 'surrendered the independence of our farmers and the curing industry, lock, stock and barrel, to the bigger Unions in Great Britain' (CAB9E/57/5). Moore was

> most anxious to maintain the good relationship which exists between my Ministry and the Ulster Farmers' Union, but I am not prepared to do so if it is to the detriment of any section of our livestock industry. I am particularly averse to handing over to an outside and virtually independent body the control of the major income block of our agricultural production, and to be forced into a position where in the event of the Board failing in its task or neglecting the interests of Northern Ireland producers, I would have to answer in Parliament that the responsibility rested with a United Kingdom Board not under my jurisdiction (CAB9E/57/5).

Brooke also voiced concern that the Ministry's decision would endanger its good relationship with the UFU and the Minister of Finance, Maginness, favoured inclusion in a national scheme because he feared that a regional scheme would require financial assistance from the Government. Moreover, Moore had argued for inclusion in the enabling legislation on the grounds that ample provision existed to protect the interests of Northern Ireland within United Kingdom marketing schemes. The result was a Cabinet decision that there was no satisfactory alternative to inclusion in a United Kingdom marketing scheme although modifications to protect the local curing industry were desirable.

In the event the United Kingdom fatstock scheme did not go ahead but Moore's resistance to regional marketing schemes continued to put a strain on the relationship with the UFU. Moore's approach may have reflected the desire of his senior officials to retain as much power as possible over agricultural policy once participation in the system of guaranteed prices had been secured, or even his own conversion from the time in the late 1930s when he led the UFU fight against the Ministry on the issue of producer control. Whatever the reason West's promotion to Minister in late 1960 was followed by immediate discussions with the UFU on marketing schemes for grass seed, seed potatoes and poultry. Although West remained sympathetic to the UFU position, however, the general attitude to producer controlled boards became increasingly hostile in the mid 1960s, not only amongst the public but even within the UFU itself. Officially endorsed UFU candidates were opposed and even defeated in board elections by other Union members and by non union opponents. The Union was also accused of being too closely tied to marketing board interests and of being unable to distinguish between the interests of farmers generally and the interests of the boards. In 1969, for example, two thirds of the UFU's President's Committee were also members of marketing boards. There was widespread dissatisfaction amongst farmers about the performance of marketing boards and many producers claimed that the prices paid by marketing boards were lower than those outside the schemes. Nationalist MP Patrick Gormley, for example, called on the Ministry to investigate whether marketing boards were of any advantage to producers and alleged that the farming community had turned completely against boards which had done nothing to help increase incomes (NIHC Deb 60, c. 1578).

A number of events crystallized the issue. These included the losses of £100,000 sustained by the Herbage Seeds Marketing Board which led to its demise in November 1966, the severe criticism of the prices paid by the Seed Potato Marketing Board in late 1965, and the collapse of the UFU's voluntary processing company, Northern Ireland Co-operative Canners Ltd, in the autumn of 1965. All these developments were the subject of vociferous and sustained criticism at Stormont and within the agricultural community. The operations of the PMB were particularly controversial, especially the huge losses incurred by its wholly owned subsidiary, Belfast Food Products Ltd (BFP), which went into liquidation in December 1966. West resolutely defended the PMB but after his resignation in April 1967 Chichester-Clark proposed changes to the scheme which the UFU interpreted as yet another attack on the principle of producer control and a precursor of attempts to whittle down the powers of other boards. After prolonged negotiations during which the UFU appealed directly to the Prime Minister, an agreement was reached and Chichester-Clark announced five main changes to the Pigs Marketing Scheme to make it more commercially efficient: the reduction of producer representation on the Board from eleven to eight (a compromise on the original proposal for six), the creation of a separate company to manage the Board's processing investments, Ministry approval for substantial capital investments in bacon factories or processing plants, more information for producers on the results of Board investments, and a ban on the PMB chairman acting as a director of a subsidiary company of the Board (NIHC Deb 69, c. 734 et seq).

From the back benches West, a pig producer himself, launched a vehement attack on the proposals. Given that the PMB had 'done a magnificent job' and been 'run well and efficiently' West demanded assurances that the principle of producer controlled marketing was not being abandoned (NIHC Deb 70, c. 677). Old enough to recall the exploitation of farmers and chaotic marketing before the establishment of marketing boards, West retained 'a fervent belief in the right of the agricultural producer to organise the marketing of his own product' and warned the Government that if any effort were made to 'weaken producer -controlled marketing or to replace it with any other method of marketing of the products now handled there would be a tremendous row. I would be utterly opposed unless there were very good reasons for changing the system' (NIHC Deb 70, c. 672-3). Pig producers in general had confidence in the Board and it was a mistake to equate criticism levelled by small unrepresentative groups with the feelings of most farmers whose views were reflected by the UFU. Public spirited men who had devoted most of their lives to improving the marketing of pigs had been the recipients of 'some of the most unjust, scandalous...cowardly type of criticism under the cloak of privilege' (NIHC Deb 70, c. 678). In reply Chichester-Clark stated that he had 'no designs on other marketing boards at present and I am only likely to have designs on them in the event of their running into the same sort of problem' (NIHC Deb 70, c. 709). In a long and very successful career the PMB had, with the exception of the BFP affair, done an extremely good job for producers. It was now hoped that the Board could put these difficulties behind it and go forward to further success and to better returns for pig producers.

The Report of the Ashton Committee on pigs marketing confirmed the trend away from producer control (Cmd 545, 1970). The recommendations that the PMB monopoly be replaced by a system of direct contracts between producers and processors, and that it be divested of processing functions, shocked the UFU which claimed they would destroy thirty years of work towards orderly marketing. For the Ministry of Agriculture the value of the report was not to be measured in terms of the number of recommendations accepted but by the thoughtful and useful discussion which it had provoked. With the likelihood of EC entry and domestic political instability the Ministry was unwilling to inflict further uncertainties on the agricultural industry and rejected the central proposals. For the UFU it was a 'matter of great satisfaction to us all that this dangerous attack on orderly marketing had been repulsed' but it also opposed a decision to give the investments arm more independence from the Board itself on the grounds that it was entirely wrong for the control of producers money to be taken out of their hands (Farmers' Journal, January 1971, p. 13).

These developments mirrored national trends away from monopoly producer control to a free market and voluntaristic approach. In 1968, for example, the Report of the United Kingdom Re-organisation Commission for Eggs led to the removal of the price guarantee on eggs and the abolition of the British Egg Marketing Board (Cmnd 3669, 1968). Naturally the three Farmers' Unions opposed the changes and West argued that the 'fact that the Egg Marketing Board is going to be wiped out and a free market established is...a disastrous step for the industry in Northern Ireland' (NIHC Deb 74, c. 1615). West believed that the regional Government had not done enough to prevent the 'disaster' and was particularly concerned about the effects of the removal of the system of pooled transport costs which ameliorated the disadvantage of remoteness. However, Phelim O'Neill claimed that his Ministry had continually stressed the benefits of the scheme to Northern Ireland producers in the discussions. As a result the British Government had agreed to the Sea Transport Subvention (Eggs) Scheme which in 1992-93 still amounted to £400,000.

Marketing and the European Community

Efficient marketing remained a central element in the Department of Agriculture's strategy for improving the competitiveness of the Northern Ireland agri-food industry after 1972. EC membership also had a profound impact on marketing, particularly the concept of producer controlled boards. Even before 1973, however, the trend away from producer controlled marketing towards a more voluntary and cooperative structure was evident. This was reflected in the controversies of the mid 1960s, in the Ashton Report, and in the abolition of the British Egg Marketing Board. Nevertheless during the EC negotiations and afterwards the Farmers' Unions fought to retain marketing boards which they believed were fully compatible with the Treaty of Rome. For the UFU it was 'imperative that the essential features of our marketing board system be retained and that no obstacle be placed in the way of such developments as may be required in this system to help our producers earn a better market return under the E.E.C's free competition rules' (Farmweek, 12 October 1971). In 1976, 17 producer controlled agricultural organizations in the United Kingdom agreed to form the British Agricultural Council to fight for the retention of producer controlled marketing boards with full powers.

Although the British Government agreed that marketing boards should be retained with their essential powers and functions intact there was concern about the attitude of the EC Commission and the prospect that the compulsory powers of Boards would be judged contrary to community law on competition and the free movement of goods. Discussions between the British Government and the European Commission eventually led to an agreement in 1978 to allow the Milk

Marketing Boards to continue with their powers of monopoly purchase and price equalization intact. This was subject to a vote for the retention of the Board by over 80 per cent of producers accounting for at least 50 per cent of production. The UFU with the support of the UAOS sent out 500 canvassers to lobby for a yes vote. In November 1978, 99.1 per cent of milk producers in Northern Ireland accounting for 95.9 per cent of production voted for the retention of the Milk Marketing Scheme which was amended in 1982 to put the Board on the same footing as those in Britain.

At the same time, however, producer controlled marketing was fatally undermined by the European Court of Justice in the case Pigs Marketing Board vs Redmond. The Board's powers of compulsory purchase were adjudged incompatible with the Treaty of Rome and the pig meat regime. As a result the Agricultural Marketing (Northern Ireland) Order 1982 amended the marketing legislation to make it compatible with community law. Framed under this legislation the Pigs Marketing Service Scheme 1984, agreed in consultations between the Department, the UFU, and curers, put the PMB on a voluntary basis, although by this time it was handling just 45 per cent of pig production. The UFU strongly advocated the continuation of the PMB and in fact had several amendments inserted in the draft scheme which was also supported by 11 of 13 curers (NIA 161).

Two dissident curing companies accounting for 40 per cent of total curing capacity opposed the continuation of the Board. Henry Denny & Sons (Ulster) argued that radical changes in the structure of the industry, in which just three firms accounted for over 60 per cent of pigs, made the continuance of the Board inappropriate. Indeed for Denny's the Board had 'a long history of the promotion of sectional interests which have seriously divided the industry' and its continuance would perpetuate old divisions and mitigate against the cooperation necessary between farmers and processors (NIA 161). Moreover, 'if the farming industry in Ulster is sincere in its commitment to the E.E.C. surely the Ulster Farmers' Union should be promoting agricultural co-operation rather than attempting to perpetuate local organisations, whose past benefits we do not dispute, long after their useful life' (NIA 161). Such vehement criticism of a voluntary scheme is hard to understand but perhaps explained by the fact that after the discontinuation of a "gentleman's agreement" under which most pigs continued to be sold through the Board between 1978 and 1983, producer prices fell below those received in Britain for the first time in many years (Stainer, 1985, p. 24).

Other developments contributed to the demise of the system of producer marketing. Producer controlled monopoly marketing schemes existed uneasily in the new economic order instigated by the Thatcher administrations and the EC Commission in which the free market, competition and deregulation were paramount. In 1982 the Northern Ireland Seed Potato Marketing Board was wound up but the final nail in the coffin came in December 1991 when the Milk Marketing Board declared its intention to move to a voluntary cooperative structure in line with developments in Britain. After 1978 increasing numbers of producers in Northern Ireland (over 400 by 1992-93) withheld milk from the Board and preferred to export it directly, for example through the Omagh based export concern Strathroy Milk Marketing. For the MMB the Board structure established in 1955 had brought stability but had served its purpose. It was now time to return to 'a totally free and open market; we want rid of all the old outdated practices of compulsory purchase, milk allocation and end-use milk pricing....Choice and free markets will be the buzzwords of the diary industry in the future' (Belfast Telegraph, 7 October 1992). This did not mean the end of producer cooperation which was now even more necessary to help secure the best prices for farmers in the face of new market realities, increasing international competition, and the growing influence of powerful processors and supermarkets. Northern Ireland's 6,000 milk producers, facing a handful of buyers, had

> a golden opportunity to create a strong, commercially based organisation which they own and which will retain their strength through unity...It will provide producers with a balance of power against the might of the large processors of milk and the ever increasing power of the supermarkets, whose shareholders' objectives are not the same as those of the producer (Belfast Telegraph, 17 April 1992).

These proposals were not universally welcomed. The UFU was sad to see the end of the MMB but recognized contemporary realities. The objective was to ensure that the new body represented as many milk producers as possible in order to retain their influence in the dairy sector. The retention of the Board's commercial processing arm, Dromona Quality Foods, as a wholly owned subsidiary of the new organization was criticized by processors and manufacturers as an effective retention of the monopoly. After much dispute and negotiation the MMB proposals were generally accepted and embodied in the Agriculture (Northern Ireland) Order 1993. A new voluntary cooperative, United Dairy Farmers, came into existence in 1994. The cooperative controlled about 70 per cent of milk supplies in Northern Ireland and retained Dromona Quality Foods, much to the dissatisfaction of processors.

By 1994, therefore, the edifice of statutory producer controlled marketing which had been gradually constructed from the early 1930s had largely been replaced by voluntary cooperatives. The old approach was no longer relevant in the changed economic and political circumstances of the 1990s. Nonetheless marketing was still a central element of the Department of Agriculture's strategy to promote competitiveness. To meet consumer demand the

> industry will need to develop products and marketing arrangements which bring farmers closer to the market so that they are better able to meet the changing needs of their customers. It will also require comprehensive education and training provision, the application of innovative science and technology and sound advice on all aspects of marketing and business development (Department of Agriculture, 1993, p 27).

4 Guaranteed prices and remoteness

The primary rationale for the introduction of marketing schemes was to help increase the prices which farmers obtained for their products. Many farmers, however, were sceptical about the value of this approach and preferred import control or direct financial support. Initially the demand was for reductions in land purchase annuities, rate relief, and cheap credit facilities. In Northern Ireland rate relief did little to improve the position of farmers and the Government refused to reduce land annuities or provide cheap credit. Farmers also regarded comprehensive import control as a panacea for their ills but this was beyond the pale of practical politics for any British Government because of the primacy of the cheap food policy. Direct price subsidies and production grants were the main alternative and gradually displaced import control as the central demand of farmers in the United Kingdom.

Although the state was increasingly active in the agricultural sector, direct financial assistance was eschewed for much of the inter war period. In the 1930s, however, British Governments began to make direct payments in lieu of import restriction, for example to beef and milk producers, although the Treasury insisted that these were loans to be repaid through a levy when prices recovered. Nonetheless they did represent the first steps towards a policy of guaranteed prices, reinforced by the development of the concept of price insurance for sheep, oats and barley at the end of the 1930s.

In Northern Ireland the UFU's hope that devolution would facilitate the provision of guaranteed prices for products such as flax and potatoes was ruled out by the Government. Economic policy was orthodox, increased public expenditure was strenuously opposed by sections of the Unionist Party, and in any case general production subsidies were beyond the means of the regional administration without the help of British subventions. There was occasional assistance for certain sectors of the industry but never any prospect of a comprehensive regional system of price guarantees. For policy products such as import controls and guaranteed prices, therefore, Ulster farmers had to look to the governments in London. As a result the UFU got increasingly involved in negotiations with the British Agricultural Departments as part of a United Kingdom farmers network in the inter war period. This reflected the increasing integration of Northern Ireland into a wider policy framework in which farmers received Treasury payments for milk, beef, fertilizers and ploughing up of grassland. The Treasury strenuously resisted this process and objected to funding assistance for farmers in Northern Ireland. However, the formulation of a common food policy for the United Kingdom during the Second World War, and the adoption of guaranteed prices and assured markets as the key components of post war policy, had profound consequences for regional agricultural policy.

Northern Ireland and the 1947 Agriculture Act

With the inclusion of Northern Ireland in Part I of the 1947 Agriculture Act the regional Ministry effectively relinquished its constitutional power to formulate an independent price and production policy. After the war there was little option but to participate in the British scheme for guaranteed prices even though this emasculated the powers of the Stormont Parliament and required adherence to a price and production policy for the United Kingdom which might not necessarily suit the particular conditions of Northern Ireland. Despite the fact that agriculture was a transferred power an integrative dynamic in post war policy left the regional Government impotent in many important areas and there was little that it could do except hope that its representations would be favourably considered by the British authorities. On the other hand the attenuation of formal powers was the price which the Ministry of Agriculture was prepared to pay for Treasury funded guaranteed prices. It was also integrated into the national policy and Annual Review machinery, although the Home Secretary was formally responsible for the interests of Northern Ireland at the national level.

The Ministry of Agriculture had to promote and defend the interests of regional agriculture within the context of a larger and complex policy network. However, as it was a small cog in a big wheel its ability to do so was limited in certain respects. For example, the Ministry found it difficult to defend producers of important regional commodities such as milk, pigs, and eggs when these were in surplus at the national level and the overall objective was to discourage production. In 1953, the Ministry opposed a Treasury proposal to reduce the guaranteed price for pigs because they were an integral part of the small farm economy in Northern Ireland and if support was 'removed or seriously weakened the whole fabric of such farms will collapse' (CAB9E/57/4). Constitutional convention and political necessity dictated that the Ministry of Agriculture had to defend collective national decisions in public, even if this incurred the wrath of farmers. On several occasions the Ministry had to justify decisions with which it disagreed, for example over price determinations and the calculation and distribution of the remoteness grant.

The new situation affected relations with the UFU and made it more difficult to construct a regional consensus on policy issues. In the inter war period the Ministry and the UFU had often created a domestic policy consensus before approaching the British authorities to make an allocation. After the war, however, when the Ministry was an integral part of the British state apparatus and the UFU a constituent part of the Farmers' Unions negotiating team, they could no longer work in overt cooperation. The Union was slow to adjust to the changed state-union relationship in the post war era. For example, the UFU wanted to go into the 1952 Annual Review negotiations 'fortified by an assurance of sympathy and support on the part of the Government of Northern Ireland' (Farmers' Journal, February 1952, p. 30). This demand for explicit support failed to recognize that the UFU and Ministry were now on opposite sides of the table. The Ministry had to try to defend the interests of Northern Ireland agriculture through inter-governmental negotiations and public support for the UFU, even if it agreed with its position, would have amounted to the Ministry opposing the collective policies devised for United Kingdom agriculture as a whole. Gradually the UFU developed a coherent lobbying strategy on national policy issues. The Ministry of Agriculture was assumed to fight the Northern Ireland case within government so the UFU concentrated its efforts on lobbying Westminster MP's. This, however, was largely ineffective and very much a last resort. Policy was difficult to alter once a decision had been taken and there was little that a handful of Westminster MP's could do to overturn important decisions.

The UFU was also constrained by cooperation at the national level. Prior to Annual Reviews the three Farmers' Unions formulated a joint negotiating position but it was the NFU which acted as the voice of agriculture on national issues and which took the lead on most matters. Review teams were not tied by any specific instructions from their members. Although the Scottish and Ulster Unions were disproportionately represented (in 1949 the negotiating team comprised six members from the NFU, four from the NFUS, and four from the UFU) the NFU was the dominant influence. On a number of occasions in the 1960s when the results of Annual Reviews were unsatisfactory, some UFU members mooted the possibility of a regional approach to the Review rather than a national perspective. For the leadership this was out of the question. It was convinced that 'the day the Ulster Farmers' Union decided to fight its own battles without the support of the other two Unions would be a sorry day indeed. The Union would only be so much weaker than it was should such a decision ever be taken' (Farmers' Journal, May 1960, p. 61). Generally, however, the potential for disagreement between the Farmers' Unions was small because they could request a financial sum to accommodate all demands. In disputes with the Government the Unions were invariably in harmony and the UFU position mirrored that of the NFU. A common approach was inevitably taken on developments in agricultural policy generally and to the determinations made at Annual Reviews in particular.

Immediately after the Second World War increased food production was accorded a high domestic priority. Northern Ireland farmers had an important role to play in the Agricultural Expansion Programme introduced in 1947, the success of which was linked to a high level of state support (Ministry of Agriculture, 1951, p. x). General expansion of domestic production, however, became increasingly less important as food became more plentiful. In the context of decontrol at the beginning of the 1950s the British Government moved towards selective expansion linked to improved efficiency and quality. Policy was predicated on the assumption that increased efficiency would lead to higher farm incomes and also allow the cost of agricultural support to be reduced. In fact state support increased as over production depressed prices. Production grants, including subsidies for fertilizers and beef calves, increasingly replaced general price rises and amounted to more than £100 million per year by 1960-61 (Open University, 1975, pp. 66-7).

Disagreements over price determinations became more frequent as governments grew increasingly concerned about the extent of Exchequer liability. The three Farmers' Unions opposed freer market conditions, selective expansion, and reductions in the level of price guarantees. Despite spiralling state spending the Farmers' Unions complained about Annual Review determinations. Reaction was particularly strong in Northern Ireland and in 1960, for example, the UFU Council expressed shock and disappointment that agriculture was again being

> relentlessly downgraded to the position of Cinderella amongst our great industries. Under-recoupment, since the Review of 1947, has amounted to £174 million, and we must now insist upon an injection of this money into the industry, if the downward trend in nett income is to be arrested. It is our considered opinion that there should be an all-round increase in the guarantees of our farm produce in order that farm incomes should be restored to a realistic level (Farmers' Journal, March 1960, p. 27).

The crux of the problem lay in the structure of the support system which was based on generous undiscriminating aid to farmers generally. However 'once the level of aid began to be reduced, the less successful farmers found themselves in difficulty' (Self and Storing, 1962, p. 84). Unfortunately there was a high proportion of small farmers in Northern Ireland who depended upon the production of those commodities which were discouraged by the manipulation of guaranteed prices, including eggs, pigs and milk. Disaffection steadily increased from the 1951 Review and culminated in the first repudiation of an entire price 'settlement' in 1956. This caused particular controversy in Northern Ireland because of the abolition of the fatstock guarantee on individual animals which was of great value to small farmers. For example for the nine months after decontrol in 1954-55 Northern Ireland producers received over £5 million from individual payments, more than three times the amount from the collective guarantee. The individual guarantee on fat cattle amounted to over £1 million, 38 per cent of the total United Kingdom payments, compared with only £141,000 from the collective guarantee. The Treasury wanted to abolish the individual guarantee for general financial and administrative reasons but it was also well aware that the decision would significantly reduce its expenditure on agricultural subsidies in Northern Ireland. The issue was also bound up with contemporary controversy on the general question of Exchequer support for Northern Ireland agriculture. Low prices in Northern Ireland depressed national average prices and caused a consequent rise in United Kingdom deficiency payments and Exchequer expenditure.

It was not surprising that a 'tide of indignation swept Northern Ireland...as Ulster farmers realised the full significance of the abolition of the Guaranteed Individual Price for all classes of fatstock' (Farmers' Journal, April 1956, p. 15). The UFU passed a vote of no confidence in the British Government and held emergency branch meetings from which Northern Ireland MP's at Westminster were 'bombarded with letters and telegrams asking that they should do all within their power to have the Northern Ireland case ventilated' (Farmers' Journal, April 1956, p. 15). There was sympathy but no success although Westminster MP's agreed to explore suggestions designed to offset the disadvantage caused to Ulster farmers. Nevertheless, the UFU left Westminster MP's 'in no doubt as to the feelings of Ulster farmers over the disappearance of the individual guarantee, and farmers in this country are still very angry that more positive action was not taken to have it restored' (Farmers' Journal, August 1956, p. 13). One UFU Council member actually claimed that the Westminster MP's were 'not giving any service to agriculture in Northern Ireland and in fact are grossly neglecting it' (Farmers' Journal, July 1956, p. 15).

The Minister of Agriculture simply stated that the matter was one for the British Government and expressed the hope that the removal of the individual guarantee would not turn out to be as serious as feared (NIHC Deb 40, c. 1038). However the suggestion that Northern Ireland had done as well as could have been expected in the Review was disputed by farmers. For West it would 'hardly be right to say that we came out of the February price review not too badly when those commodities, which are of such vital importance to the small farmers of Northern Ireland, got so little recoupment compared with the increase in costs during the past twelve months' (NIHC Deb 40, c. 1033).

The general complaints by the three Farmers' Unions at the level of price guarantees resulted in Long Term Assurances introduced under the 1957 Agriculture Act which limited the extent to which prices could be reduced on a year to year basis. For the Unions these were of great value, particularly for the smaller producer 'who has tended in the past to suffer from substantial price reductions concentrated on the three or four commodities of key importance to his farming pattern' (Farmers' Journal, January 1957, p. 31). This was over optimistic. At the end of the 1950s the Government opposed the further expansion of eggs, pigs and milk unless this could be done at a 'substantially lower cost of production and without prejudicing the aim of relieving the taxpayer of the increasingly heavy burden of subsidy cost' (Cmnd 390, 1958, para. 9). State support was still reduced incrementally and Long Term Assurances failed to inject much cordiality into the relations between the state and the farmers. Outright rejection of Annual Review 'settlements' became more and more common and the representatives of the farmers refused to give their endorsement to the review determinations in 1958 and again in 1960.

In the 1960s the Farmers' Unions continued to criticize the general 'restrictionist' approach of the Government and low farm incomes in particular. The Government refused to accept that increases in guaranteed prices were the best way to raise incomes and emphasized improved productivity and efficiency to absorb rising costs and help reduce Treasury liability. Moreover the Government was not even convinced that the level of farm income, either in relative or absolute terms, was as low as the Unions contended. Farmers blamed high levels of state support on the failure to control imports and turned back to import restriction as a way of improving prices without obvious additional Exchequer expenditure. The 1964 Annual Review was regarded by the Farmers' Unions as a first step towards their demand for a 25 per cent increase in income over three years and parity with other sectors of the economy. The 1965 determinations brought renewed criticism however. For the Unions the 'confidence of farmers had been shaken by the 1965 Price Review discussions, and the depth of feeling of injustice and frustration which now prevails' (Farmers' Journal, 4 June 1965, p. 12). The Government agreed to discuss some of the concerns of the Farmers' Unions including the request for an increase in the standard quantity for milk and an increased share of the bacon market but refused to reopen the Annual Review.

Partly as a response to this pressure from the Farmers' Unions for expansion, and partly as a response to economic difficulties, the Labour Government's National Plan in 1965 changed the emphasis of agricultural policy within the overall context of the 1947 Act. This stressed the contribution which agriculture could make towards import saving, an issue close to the hearts of the Farmers' Unions. A programme of selective expansion was also introduced, particularly of meat production based on home grown feed stuffs. The assumption was that improved productivity and the release of manpower for other expanding sectors of the economy would leave a larger slice of the cake for the fewer farmers left on the land. Whilst the Farmers' Unions welcomed what they saw as the first expansionist agricultural policy since 1947 they were unconvinced that it was sufficient to increase incomes to the extent necessary and the Annual Review was again rejected in 1969. The Unions formulated a policy objective of a net income of £650 million a year as a reasonable level of remuneration and a series of measures were agreed in 1970 to increase capital resources and improve farm income. The Government called this a substantial move towards the objective of higher remuneration but in the last analysis it was up to the industry to help itself. For the NFU, however, the measures taken as a whole, although significant, were insufficient to meet the Unions income objective. Again the Government refused to change the determinations but the case for exceptional measures to deal with greatly increased production costs was recognized when an interim Review increased the guaranteed prices for livestock commodities and cereals. The cash injection was welcomed by the UFU but Northern Ireland's £3 million share of the increase was little more than first aid and similar action was needed at future Reviews.

The problem of remoteness

The removal of wartime controls and the introduction of free market forces, albeit in the context of continued state protection, had a significant impact on the prices which farmers in Northern Ireland received for their produce. During the war the Treasury justified an attempt to pay lower prices for Northern Ireland produce than those for Britain because 'owing to transit costs, Northern Ireland producers were always at a disadvantage in marketing their animals in Great Britain' (Ministry of Agriculture, 1951, p. 47). This was resisted by the Ministry of Agriculture on the grounds that there was a single food production campaign and that farmers in Northern Ireland were subjected to essentially the same measures of state direction as those in Britain. Brooke's wartime policy was to see that local farmers 'get a fair deal, and that they get exactly the same advantages as the farmers in England. Secondly...to see that agriculture shall play its part in winning the war, so that when it is won the Ulster farmer can hold his head up with pride' (NIHC Deb 23, c. 194). It was also a central principle of UFU policy that Northern Ireland farmers 'be paid exactly the same price for their produce as farmers are paid in the rest of the United Kingdom' (Farmers' Journal, February 1940, p. 150). Stormont MP's such as Hugh Minford argued that it was unjust to 'compel the loyal people of Ulster to grow a crop and then not to pay the same price for it as is paid to the people in England and Scotland. Ulstermen should have the same standard of living as Englishmen' (NIHC Deb 26, c. 1476).

With the notable exceptions of prices for potatoes and milk, the British Government conceded the case made by the Northern Ireland agricultural community for price parity with their British counterparts during the war. In the potato sector, for example, the Ministry of Agriculture complained on several occasions about 'repeated attempts to regard NI so far as potatoes are concerned as not being an integral part of the UK' (AG18/11/4). In general, however, Westminster's overall responsibility for the war effort in Northern Ireland made it politically difficult to differentiate on prices and the inclusion of Northern Ireland in the pre war schemes to increase soil fertility set something of a precedent. Most important, perhaps, the contribution of Northern Ireland agriculture was vital and the less generous treatment of farmers in Northern Ireland could undermine the whole food production campaign. This did not represent a general acceptance of the principle of parity by the Treasury which used the process of decontrol after the war to limit its liability on agricultural subsidies in Northern Ireland.

The Farmers' Unions feared that decontrol would be exploited to undermine the system of guaranteed prices and assured markets. For the UFU the threat was also to the sacred principle of price parity which recognized the Ulster farmer as an integral component of United Kingdom agriculture. The bottom line was that there should be no change in 'the parity price position of Ulster farmers in relation to their brothers across the water, as a result of decontrols. The Province is part of the United Kingdom and as such must be treated fairly in all agreements directly affecting British agriculture' (Farmers' Journal, February 1953, p. 5). This position was universally shared in Northern Ireland and even Nationalists such as Cahir Healy, not usually advocates of parity with Britain, urged the Government to 'insist upon parity with the English farmers' (NIHC Deb 37, c. 702).

Lower prices caused partly by relative remoteness from British markets were the crux of the difficulties faced by Northern Ireland farmers. Uniform United Kingdom prices such as those paid during the war were to the great benefit of Northern Ireland producers as they reduced this comparative disadvantage. For the UFU price parity implied that the state had to 'provide the means by which Northern Ireland produce can arrive at the consuming centres of Britain so that our producers may not be at a price disadvantage under existing conditions where costs of wages and the social services are practically the same' (Farmers' Journal, June 1953, p. 5). Mechanisms such as deficiency payments based on average prices were opposed by the UFU because they did not ensure roughly equal prices throughout the United Kingdom. Indeed it was possible that Northern Ireland producers might receive prices below the guaranteed threshold but not qualify for deficiency payments because higher prices in Britain pushed the average above the guarantee threshold.

The remoteness grant

The Northern Ireland Government was acutely aware of the problems which decontrol would pose for local agriculture. In September 1953 Brooke made a personal approach to Dugdale in which he stressed the difficulties which Northern Ireland agriculture would encounter in a free market. Remoteness was also a problem for farmers in northern Scotland but Brooke was concerned about the

> prospect of finding ourselves no longer part of the trunk of the United Kingdom tree, as we have been, but a far-out branch exposed to every blast through no fault of our own. If deficiency payments are to be the solution to the problem of marrying guaranteed prices with free markets, I would strongly urge that Northern Ireland must receive special consideration if anything like parity is to be maintained with the rest of the United Kingdom (CAB9E/57/4; NIHC Deb 38, c. 1028).

The first preference was for an arrangement for fatstock 'whereby our marketing costs can be met so as to give our farmers returns that will maintain the parity of price they have had for the past fourteen years with the rest of the United Kingdom' (CAB9E/57/4). For the British Government, however, the 1947 Act did not 'guarantee uniform prices to producers, and any form of cushion between natural differentials could only be justified as a special measure to lessen the abruptness of the change or safeguard essential production' (CAB9E/57/4). Nonetheless clause 16 of the white paper on decontrol recognized that special arrangements were needed to deal with the 'particular conditions affecting marketing and prices of meat and bacon in Northern Ireland' (Cmd 8989, 1953).

Although the proposal for a separate fatstock deficiency payment scheme was rejected it was agreed that Northern Ireland producers should not 'carry the whole burden of a greater degree of price differentiation than that borne by other distant producers on the mainland' and that 'a financial adjustment should be made between the two Governments, a grant, the amount of which will be determined annually, being placed at the disposal of the Government of Northern Ireland to use for the purpose of assisting the agricultural industry' (NIHC Deb 38, c. 825; CAB9E/57/5; HC Deb 523, c. 229-30).

The special 'remoteness grant' was welcomed by some as a recognition of the special position of Northern Ireland agriculture within the United Kingdom but was also criticized for failing to maintain price parity. The UFU reaction was lukewarm in that Northern Ireland farmers 'instead of being placed at the foot of the class, will be destined to share that distinction with their fellow farmers of Ross, Sutherland and Caithness' (Farmers' Journal, March 1954, p. 8). In his maiden speech in May 1954, Harry West voiced disappointment that the 'parity of price structure which was chiefly responsible for the recent measure of prosperity in Ulster agriculture was...very unnecessarily allowed to slip from our grasp' (NIHC Deb 38, c. 2306). Brooke, on the other hand, exorbitantly claimed that the 'bit of sea has been removed and Northern Ireland agriculture has been placed on the mainland of the United Kingdom' (NIHC Deb 38, c. 1031). Even as late as 1956 Brooke was taken to task by the UFU for giving the mistaken impression that Ulster farmers received parity prices (Farmers' Journal, January 1956, p. 23). However this almost sycophantic enthusiasm ignored the fact that the crux of the matter was how much financial flesh was put on the bare bones of principle and whether this would be sufficient to maintain price parity.

Sceptical voices were proved correct. Not only was the Treasury eager to restrict its liabilities in Northern Ireland but it had a very different idea of the expenditure involved from that envisaged by the Northern Ireland agricultural community. Whereas farmers talked of fantastic sums for the remoteness grant of over £7 million per year the first provisional estimate made by the Treasury was £0.5 million, which was in turn revised downwards to £400,000 and one estimate was as low as £50,000. The initial assumption was that the grant was intended to provide prices for Northern Ireland producers which approximated to those of other distant producers in the United Kingdom. When the use of northern Scotland for comparison yielded a unacceptable figure, however, this was abandoned for an alternative calculation based on half of the difference between average livestock prices in Northern Ireland and those in England and Wales. This resulted in a sum of £1 million for two years which the Treasury still believed to be 'very generous but for the sake of agreement, and to meet the difficulties of transition' they were prepared to accept it (CAB9E/57/6). Eventually in May 1955 MAF and the Treasury agreed on compromise figures of £1.030 million for 1954-55 and of £1.245 million for 1955-56.

Besides the haggling over the level of the remoteness grant there was also disagreement on the administration of agricultural subsidies in Northern Ireland. Neither the Home Office, the Ministry of Food, nor MAF were willing to bear the cost on their votes for constitutional, political and administrative reasons. To help overcome this problem the Treasury proposed a separate, lower, standard price for Northern Ireland livestock to avoid the 'double subsidy' given to Ulster producers through national deficiency payments and the remoteness grant. It was also claimed that this system would ensure that the benefits of deficiency payments were received by Ulster producers and not be dissipated amongst farmers in the rest of the United Kingdom who became eligible because the low prices prevailing in Northern Ireland depressed the United Kingdom average.

This manoeuvring on both the level and administration of the remoteness grant was the primary source of friction between governments in Belfast and London in the mid 1950s. For the Ministry of Agriculture the sums offered by Whitehall were unacceptable and could not be 'satisfactorily explained to Northern Ireland producers' (CAB9E/57/6). The general assumption in Northern Ireland was that the grant would at least cover the price differential with the three northernmost counties of Scotland. Using this comparator, and assuming that local farmers should be expected to bear 12½ per cent of the full burden of remoteness, the Ministry of Agriculture claimed £1.44 million for 1954-55 and £1.76 million for 1955-56 as the very minimum which it could sell to producers. An emergency meeting of the Cabinet in April 1955 considered the outright rejection of the British proposals but there was little room for manoeuvre and the compromise figure of £2.275m for the two years 1954-56 was eventually accepted.

Although an official working group reported that separate guarantee arrangements for cattle and sheep would not be to the disadvantage of Northern Ireland, the proposal was unanimously rejected by the Ministry of Agriculture whose own figures clearly demonstrated that Northern Ireland producers would get considerably less under the new system. The Ministry withdrew its officials from the discussions in protest at the way in which they were being conducted, particularly the determination of prices on estimated and not actual prices. Moreover the proposal was a 'complete departure from the letter and spirit of the Home Secretary's announcement' of February 1954 (CAB9E/57/6). More fundamentally, the proposal was unacceptable because it treated Northern Ireland 'as an entity apart from the rest of the United Kingdom and not entitled to the same standards as Great Britain' (CAB9E/57/6). The Northern Ireland case was supported by the Home Office which found it 'a little difficult to feel confidence in assertions which have been made at the official level that the new proposals will result in the same recoupment for Northern Ireland as the existing arrangements' (CAB9E/57/6).

There was further disagreement when the Treasury fixed the remoteness grant for 1956-57 at £864,000. The Ministry of Agriculture claimed £1.491 million compared with the initial Treasury offer of £624,000. Moore complained bitterly that the calculation of the grant was devoid of principle except that of choosing comparisons which resulted in the least financial liability for the Treasury. He was

> strongly of the opinion that a refusal to disclose the basis on which the grant has been calculated would merely accentuate the controversy which seems inevitable and would undoubtedly tend to confirm the suspicion which I am sorry to say exists in our agricultural circles that Clause 16 is merely a temporary political expedient. Moreover, it will be obvious to you that I cannot adopt a line which would be likely to convey the impression that the award has been negotiated between the two Governments. It is, in fact, an imposed settlement which I would find the utmost difficulty in defending either to the Ulster Farmers' Union or in our House of Commons (CAB9E/57/7).

The British Government suggested a compromise figure of £1.133 million on condition that it was presented as an agreed settlement and that the basis of calculation was not revealed. For the Ministry of Agriculture the combination of a greatly reduced grant plus a refusal to make public the basis of the calculation would increase suspicion amongst the farming community and have serious political consequences which would prove even worse than that which would result from a full and frank disclosure of the facts. Even the revised sum still fell appreciably short of the amount which was justified and threatened political difficulties with the agricultural community. The UFU, for example, continually demanded public disclosure of the assumptions on which the remoteness grant was calculated and complained, with some justification, that the Government had misled farmers into thinking that they would get the same prices as farmers in the remote parts of Scotland. Moore accused some sections of the industry of over optimism and unrealistic expectations. Farmers should be 'satisfied with the assertion of a very important principle and the measure of implementation that we have already got out of that principle' (NIHC Deb 39, c. 1348). Nevertheless the Government was willing to accept the offer as the most that could be achieved and the conditions attached to it provided that 'a satisfactory basis for the assessment of assistance to the agricultural industry in Northern Ireland in respect of its remoteness can be agreed for future years' (CAB9E/57/7). This in turn was unacceptable to the British authorities but although the Minister of Agriculture risked substantial delay by insisting on the link the rest of the Cabinet accepted that there was no alternative but to accept the award without a settlement of the overall problem.

The reconsideration of national agricultural policy provided the way out of the three year impasse on the administration of the remoteness grant. The 1957

Agriculture Act embodied an agreement between the two Governments that annual haggling be replaced by an arrangement in which the remoteness grant was stabilized at £1 million per year for at least five years with provision for a review at the end of this period. For the Ministry of Agriculture the advantages of continuity compensated for the reduced annual amount. The agreement was tangible evidence that the British Government had 'once again demonstrated that they are not unmindful of the need for helping us to maintain and, where possible, improve the standard of Northern Ireland agriculture' (NIHC Deb 41, c. 593). The UFU agreed and even claimed that the statutory recognition of remoteness was 'one of the most outstanding achievements of the Union and its leaders in recent years' although there is no evidence that the Union had any influence at all on the matter or that they were even completely aware of all the developments (Farmers' Journal, June 1957, p. 10).

When the remoteness grant was reconsidered in 1962 and 1965 the UFU and Westminster MP's lobbied for its renewal at a higher figure. During 1961, for example, some Unionist MP's at Westminster, supported by Sir Hugh Lucas-Tooth who had been the Under-Secretary of State at the Home Office in charge of Northern Ireland affairs during the period of decontrol, called for a substantially increased grant. At a meeting with the Home Secretary, R.A. Butler, the UFU leadership stressed the great importance which they and Northern Ireland farmers attached to the remoteness grant. The huge increases demanded by Westminster MP's R.G. Grosvenor (at least £3 million pounds per year for five years) and J. Maginnis (£5 million) were completely unrealistic and the grant was increased by 25 per cent to £1.25 million for a further five year period. The UFU President was disappointed that the grant was not higher and promised to continue the campaign for a greater increase although 'the outcome of the representations which my deputies and I made to the Home Secretary cannot be regarded as unsuccessful' (Farmers' Journal, 6 April 1962, p. 25).

Although not due for renewal until 1967 a review of the grant was agreed at the 1965 Annual Review. Vociferous criticism of the review determinations was partially quelled when Home Office minister George Thomas announced an increase in the remoteness grant when he addressed a large protest meeting of farmers in Belfast in August 1965. However, the increase to £1.75 million per year until March 1971 was generally regarded as insufficient. For example Unionist MP's at Westminster such as Robin Chichester-Clark, Knox Cunningham and Orr typically hoped for an increase to something in the region of £2½-3 million. The final chapter in the remoteness grant story occurred in 1971 when it was renewed for a further three years at the existing level of £1.75 million. The grant was finally discontinued in March 1977 when it was decided 'that in the context of full EEC membership the Special Assistance Grant would not be appropriate and should not be renewed' (Department of Agriculture, 1978, p. 105).

Part of the attraction of the remoteness grant was that it gave the Ministry of Agriculture 'latitude to disburse the money in such a way that farmers can feel some direct, tangible results of the financial arrangement' (CAB9E/57/5). It was agreed that

> subject to consultation and agreement in broad principle with the Imperial Departments concerned, responsibility for the application of the annual grant will rest with the Ministry of Agriculture for Northern Ireland. It is desired, however, to emphasise that it is not the intention of the Ministry of Agriculture to interfere with the operation of the new system of marketing arrangements for the United Kingdom or to take any steps which might embarrass the Agricultural Departments in Great Britain. The primary objective will be to encourage improvement in the competitive marketing position of the industry in Northern Ireland (CAB9E/57/5).

This was just what farmers feared. Most assumed that the grant would provide direct financial aid and not be used for development schemes. West, for example, warned that if the money was used 'in any other way than by giving it as a direct payment to the agricultural producers of Northern Ireland, then the agricultural community will not stand for it' (NIHC Deb 38, c. 3293). As a compromise the grant was initially used to fund local production grants and subsidies. In 1965, however, the Ministry took up an idea floated at the Annual Review (and in the Wilson Report) and proposed an Agricultural Trust funded from the grant (Cmnd 2621, 1965, para. 64; Cmd 479, 1965). This institution was intended to bridge the gap between theoretical research and commercial practice and was charged with 'keeping all aspects of production, processing and marketing under review and of financing worthwhile developments in those fields which are not receiving sufficient support from purely private enterprise' (NIHC Deb 62, c. 18). Whilst the remoteness grant continued, the amount devoted to the Agricultural Trust was decided by the Ministry in consultation with the UFU and with the approval of the Agricultural Ministers in Britain. The Trust idea was actively supported by the UFU leadership and welcomed by those who regarded direct subsidies such as headage payments as little more than 'beer money' for farmers. Again sections of the agricultural community, including an element within the UFU, argued that the remoteness grant was 'paid to help compensate farmers for the transport costs of their produce and it should be used to do just that' (Farmers' Journal, 6 August 1965, p. 10). For the Ministry of Agriculture, however, the development of the Agricultural Trust funded from the grant was totally consistent with its aim to encourage 'developments which would help Northern Ireland farmers to compete more effectively and so overcome their remoteness' (NIHC Deb 63, c. 1854). The Trust was eventually wound up in 1979 as a result of a review of quangos and public expenditure by the Northern Ireland Office.

Agricultural assistance schemes funded by the remoteness grant were discussed with the UFU but also required the approval of the British authorities. Whitehall was generally sympathetic to Ministry proposals but there was some inevitable friction. On the Agricultural Trust, for example, the Ministry had 'a particularly difficult job in reaching a satisfactory agreement with the Whitehall authorities' (NIHC Deb 63, c. 1874). The UFU also occasionally questioned the need for Whitehall approval but the Ministry stressed that regional policy had to be compatible with that in Britain and not result in an extra burden on the British Exchequer. As George Thomas remarked in 1966, Whitehall approval was required because the grant was 'part of the total assistance given by the United Kingdom Government to the United Kingdom farmers and must be consistent with the Government's agriculture policy' (HC Deb 725, c. 1669). Subject to this proviso, disbursement was a matter for the regional Ministry in close consultation with the Home Office. According to Thomas, West was

> a master, as one would expect, of his own subject. He guides and he and his colleagues in Northern Ireland decide how the money is to be spent...The agricultural authorities in Northern Ireland, among whom I include the Ministry and the Ulster Farmers' Union, discuss what is best for the industry and I think that they themselves agree how best the money can be used...It would be very churlish of us on this side of the Irish sea to say that we knew better than the people in Ulster when they advise us how best the money can be spent over there (HC Deb 725, c. 1675).

The problem of the small farmer

The problem of low farming incomes was particularly severe for small scale producers who depended on commodities which were discouraged by successive governments because of surplus production. In 1958 the UFU condemned the price schedules because they impacted 'most heavily on that section of the industry least able to withstand economic pressure - the small farmer' (Farmers' Journal, April 1958, p. 29). In the same review, however, the Government explicitly recognized 'the special problem created by the fact that many small farmers are particularly concerned with the production of milk, pigs and eggs and that many of them have relatively low incomes and small resources despite the generally satisfactory condition of the agricultural industry' (Cmnd 390, 1958, para. 25). Part of the problem was that the Annual Review system disproportionately benefited the larger and more prosperous farmers. Very few production and capital grants were specifically designed to help the less fortunate farmers.

After discussions with the agricultural industry a comprehensive Small Farmer Scheme was introduced to help 'economic' small farm businesses improve their competitive position (Cmnd 553, 1958). To qualify for assistance farm businesses had to meet two criteria: a size of not less than 20 and not more than 100 acres of crops and grass, and be capable of reaching at least 275 standard man days

(Cmnd 390, 1958, para. 7). Such assistance was especially important for Northern Ireland which contained a large proportion of the estimated 90,000 farm businesses in the United Kingdom which qualified for help. With the different regional farm structure the UFU hoped that the 'interpretation of who exactly is a "small farmer" will take into account the fact that acreages in Northern Ireland are relatively smaller than anywhere else' (Farmers' Journal, May 1958, p. 15). In 1962, for example, nearly half of the 70,000 holdings in Northern Ireland were smaller than 20 acres. In this context the exclusion of farms below 20 acres, and of land held in conacre, caused much opposition within the UFU and in Northern Ireland generally. Nevertheless by March 1962 over 30,000 applications had been received by the Ministry of Agriculture and by 1965 over 15,000 farmers in Northern Ireland had Farm Business Plans approved under the main scheme. Under the Supplementary Scheme which operated between 1959 and 1962 some 23,146 small farmers received assistance totalling over £2 million and by 1963-64 over £9 million had been paid out to farmers in Northern Ireland under both of the schemes.

For governments in London and Belfast it was also necessary to encourage the creation of viable holdings through outgoer payments to those willing to give up uncommercial holdings for amalgamation (Cmnd 2738, 1965). The core value was that the state should not 'provide special financial assistance to help fundamentally uneconomic farm businesses to remain in being' (Cmnd 553, 1958, para. 5). With little prospect of vastly increased demand and production the basic policy objective was to increase average farm incomes through structural reform. The problem was that 16,000 farm businesses in Northern Ireland were too small to provide a full time occupation for one person. What was needed was the creation of jobs in other industries to absorb the inevitable movement out of agriculture and in this respect government policy was to accelerate a natural economic process. The only way to improve living standards when the overall size of the financial cake was not increasing was for the cake to be shared out amongst fewer farmers. Agricultural policy was linked with wider considerations of economic development. The Government was convinced that the best way to reduce the numbers engaged in agriculture was to

> make careers outside the agricultural industry more readily available and more attractive so as to encourage many of our small farmers and their families who cannot easily make a living on the land to leave the agricultural industry and take up alternative employment. This in turn will enable other farmers to purchase their farms and thus bring an amalgamation of small farms to form larger units (NIHC Deb 59, c. 853).

Far from objecting to farm amalgamation because it was unsuited to Northern Ireland conditions the Ministry of Agriculture was one of the principle advocates of the policy. For example, the Wilson Report's recommendation for a policy of farm amalgamation was accepted by West 'because in compiling this Report my Ministry co-operated closely with Professor Wilson. Most of the material in that chapter is based on existing Ministry of Agriculture policy' (NIHC Deb 59, c. 852). Both Moore and West also stressed that agriculture was neither a social service nor a way of life but a business which had to be competitive and it was difficult to 'justify the use of taxpayers money in order to keep non-viable units in production' (NIHC Deb 56, c. 20). It was not government policy to force farmers out of the industry but to point out the realities of the situation and leave the decision up to the good sense of individuals.

For the UFU the underlying philosophy of structural policy was unacceptable. The amalgamation strategy was rejected as totally unsuited to the particular conditions of Northern Ireland, such as the historical and political importance of land ownership and the lack of alternative employment. It was recognized that many farms were too small and that farm incomes were inadequate but it was 'no solution to our structural problems to drive more men into unemployment exchanges; it is no solution to our income problems to divide an already small income "cake" amongst a smaller number of producers' (Farmers' Journal, June 1965, p. 17). An adequate price and income structure for British agriculture rather than structural change was the only solution to the problems of the agricultural industry in the United Kingdom. Small farmers should be assisted through grants, subsidies and a realistic price policy to 'increase the output from their limited acreage to help meet the impending world shortage of food rather than encouraged to go out of business. Moreover...there should be no question of creating redundancies while so much of our food was imported' (Farmers' Journal, February 1966, p. 14). However when the UFU eventually realized that there was no prospect of the policy being reversed it switched its attentions to the effort to get better financial benefits for those prepared to amalgamate.

Many Unionist MP's at Stormont and Westminster also wanted the Small Farmer Schemes made more suitable to Northern Ireland, particularly to alleviate the position of those farmers whose holdings were too small to qualify for assistance. Unionist members for rural constituencies were hostile to the policy and protested at the likely effect of an extensive process of amalgamation on the whole social fabric of rural Ulster. Nationalist MP's such as O'Reilly and the Gormley brothers, who tended to represent rural areas with a high percentage of small farmers, were the most vociferous critics of structural policy which was portrayed as an attempt to crush the small farmer out of existence. Firstly, according to O'Reilly, the scheme was 'designed and framed to suit the English countryside and would require considerable changes to meet the needs of farming people in the Six Counties' (NIHC Deb 44, c. 993). Secondly agriculture was not simply a business but a way of life and policies had to take account of social as well as economic factors in order to halt rural depopulation. A policy which did not assist the small farmer with under 20 acres of land might possibly be justifiable on purely economic grounds but it was a threat to the social fabric of rural Ulster (NIHC Deb 54, c. 1424 et seq). Moreover chronic unemployment, especially in rural areas, meant that amalgamation amounted in reality to either the dole or emigration for farmers who gave up their land.

The regional Government was urged to provide financial assistance to help preserve small farms and to get the Small Farmer Scheme more attuned to the structure of Northern Ireland agriculture, for example by allowing land held in conacre to count as part of a farmer's acreage. Criticism reflected the general hostility to the parity policy. The Ministry of Agriculture was accused of being content to follow the British lead and not prepared to develop a structural policy to suit the special conditions of Northern Ireland agriculture. Policy was too closely tied to that in Britain and it was time for the Minister 'to loose those bonds that bind him to the scheme of the British Ministry of Agriculture and to introduce a scheme suitable to our own small farmers' (NIHC Deb 61, c. 1047). For Healy the

> small farmer in England is very different from the small farmer in this country. The British scheme was intended to benefit the British farmer and very little regard was paid to the special position of farmers here. We have been waiting for years while small farmers in England have been granted so many favours and have had so much money poured into their laps...while the tiny grants which had been given to farmers in Northern Ireland were actually withdrawn [the Marginal Production Schemes] (NIHC Deb 61, c. 1291).

If the British Government would not adopt a policy suitable for Northern Ireland then it was up to the regional Ministry to reassert its powers and dictate its own policy to deal with the salient problems. For Tom Gormley it was not sufficient to be told 'that we are dealing with United Kingdom grants and that the Minister has no powers. We might as well talk to thin air. While the present policy may suit Great Britain it does not suit Northern Ireland' (NIHC Deb 63, c. 1183).

The amalgamation policy proved totally ineffective in Northern Ireland, not least because of the very high incidence of owner occupation. By 1970 amalgamations had virtually dried up with just 271 schemes approved at a cost of just £115,788 for outgoers and £18,338 for annuities. This prompted a re-examination of structural policy at the national level but there was little that the regional Government could do on its own. Despite demands for a policy to suit the different structure of the agricultural industry in Northern Ireland, political and financial considerations dictated participation in an integrated national policy which was not specifically tailored to regional conditions. The Ministry of Agriculture played a key role in the development of the national amalgamation strategy. Indeed West remarked on one occasion that if the problem of speeding up the movement from the land was not dealt with on a national basis then it would have to be dealt with as a special regional problem (NIHC Deb 59, c. 853). Not only did the Ministry not accept that the small farmer policy was unsuitable for Northern Ireland but West and the British authorities actually argued that the schemes were eminently suited to regional agriculture. The extension of the Small Farmer Scheme in 1962, according to R.A. Butler, was 'deliberately done because we knew that the Small Farmer Scheme applied more particularly to Northern Ireland than to any other part of the United Kingdom' (HC Deb 656, c. 1735).

Direct action and the problem of farming incomes

The main cause of dissatisfaction amongst farmers in the United Kingdom was usually the relatively low level of farm incomes. Before Annual Reviews the Unions ritually reminded the Government that they expected action to raise incomes to help bring agriculture into line with other industries. In 1964, for example, the UFU President identified the three main policy objectives of the Union as the maximization of production, the reduction in the variability of income, and equality of treatment for agriculture with other sectors of the economy (Farmers' Journal, 1 May 1964, pp. 25-7). The Unions launched a campaign to secure a 25 per cent increase in farming income over three years, starting with the 1964 Review. It was hoped that this could be achieved through discussion, negotiation, and intensive lobbying but pressure for direct action built up inexorably as Review determinations failed to match expectations. The 1960s witnessed a marked increase in the militancy of farmers which first became evident with grass roots demands for organized demonstrations and token strikes after the 1962 Review. In 1964 one UFU Council delegate expressed the opinion that farmers would support action 'to the extent of demonstrating in the way the French and Eire farmers had' and there was some support for a suggestion that farmers should invade Belfast and block the Queen's Bridge and other main arteries if the demand for a substantial rise in income was not met (Farmers' Journal, 6 March 1964, p. 19).

Following another unsatisfactory price review in 1965 militant action was again mooted. For example the UFU's South Tyrone Group called on the leadership to take the 'most strenuous action, including militant action, if necessary' to bring the farmers' income into line with that in other sectors of the community and the Caddy and Glarryford branches even specifically demanded strike action (Farmers' Journal, 7 May 1965, p. 23). A subsequent Council resolution authorized the reopening of discussions on prices. However if this proved unsuccessful the Union was to 'give notice to the Government of its intention to withhold supplies of agricultural commodities from the market' (Farmers' Journal, 7 May 1965, p. 17). The UFU leadership was wary of direct action and adopted a four point plan: a public protest meeting addressed by George Thomas; the formation of a panel of speakers which was intended to enlist public sympathy, refute accusations of feather bedding, and present the farmers message to all sections of the community; increased political pressure through Westminster MP's; and an attempt to 'obtain the full and active support of the ancillary industries' (Farmers' Journal, 4 June 1965, p. 13).

By 1966 militancy had strengthened within the UFU, partly prompted by the threats of some farmers to form breakaway organizations to take much stronger action to improve farming incomes. Before the Review the UFU established an action committee to prepare a contingency plan in the event of an unacceptable outcome. The leadership struggled to keep grass roots militancy in check and keep the campaign for increased incomes 'responsible'. Despite increased willingness to resort to direct tactics the UFU leadership stressed that any action had to be coordinated with that taken by the other Unions because the contested policy was one for the United Kingdom as a whole. Militant tactics, moreover, were not certain of success and the UFU believed that 'more would be gained from talks with the Government leading to a long-term solution of the industry's problems' (Farmers' Journal, 7 May 1965, p. 17). The general position on tactics was stated by the UFU President in 1965:

> we have got to remember that the target in our campaign is the Government. The objective is to reverse as quickly as we can the unsatisfactory policy for British agriculture...I cannot therefore recommend the withholding of supplies of food from the public as a worthwhile course of action. You may well feel that limiting production would be in our best interests, but I cannot see that withholding it once it has been produced would be effective, even if there was complete loyalty in the operation. The general public is not hostile to British agriculture; it is perhaps unaware of the farmers' problems...we aim to create public support for our case by making the public more aware and more sympathetic of the basic facts and their implications (Farmers' Journal, 4 June 1965, p. 13).

When the Unions were again unable to accept the price review in 1969 the UFU renewed the appeal for a campaign of lobbying and negotiation rather than through militant action. The Review gave the Unions the opportunity

> to put their best case, to exert influence and argument. The alternative to the Unions settling for reasoned argument is to take direct action of some sort...In thinking of alternatives, we must bear in mind that only about 3% of the voters are in agriculture and also that the most valuable asset we can have is the goodwill of the public. It is open to serious question whether there is a more promising long term policy for the Unions than the present policy of reasoned argument and influence. I believe, however, that such a general policy does not rule out the occasional use of some sort of demonstration to emphasise to the Government the need for a better deal for our farmers (Farmers' Journal, June 1969, p. 20).

The UFU leadership refused to endorse direct tactics in advance of the 1970 review but some farmers resorted to unofficial action. One UFU member called for an official one day strike every week if the farmers demands were not met at the Review. In the interim he suggested 'immediate unofficial action with picketing of abattoirs, bacon factories and creameries to give the Government and the public a whiff of what to expect' (Farmweek, 20 January 1970). A so-called South Tyrone Farmers Action Committee held a tractor blockade and demonstration in Dungannon in February 1970. In the words of the organizer they were 'all loyal union men but the lid can no longer be kept on our feelings of disgust and frustration' (Farmweek, 10 February 1970). Similar unofficial protests were held by local action groups in Omagh (organized primarily by Tom Gormley, the shadow Minister of Agriculture) and in Enniskillen. In justification of this action it was argued that the demonstrations had been successful in making the Government conscious of the seriousness of the position and of the depth of feeling amongst farmers.

After the unsatisfactory outcome to the 1970 Review the three Farmers' Unions implemented detailed protest plans which had been formulated in advance by a specially constituted National Co-ordinating Committee. The NFU adopted a six point action programme including a one week ban on the marketing of livestock, a ban on the purchase of certain new farm machinery and a refusal to allow voluntary access to land for some new development. However, although the UFU asserted that the Unions were 'as one in their dissatisfaction with the Review and in their determination to continue the struggle to improve the prosperity of the industry' it did not ask its members to boycott markets (Farmweek, 21 April 1970). It was natural that farmers would want to give vent to their feeling of frustration, but

> in Northern Ireland conditions some of the measures proposed in England and Wales would not contribute to our objective. In particular, we feel that the boycott of stock markets in Northern Ireland, where supplies could readily flow across the border, would do little to strengthen our negotiating position. We do, however, appreciate the desire of our colleagues in England and Wales to express their dissatisfaction with the Review, and we are confident that our members would support the other measures which have been proposed (Farmers' Journal, April 1970, p. 29).

This illustrated the UFU leadership's resolute opposition to 'irresponsible' direct action. Demonstrations were useful for publicity purposes but their effectiveness was limited. Farmers had to recognize that the 'vital work is done...by the presentation of facts and figures, by argument, discussion and negotiation' (Farmers' Journal, June 1970, p. 8). Reflecting this the UFU decided that its plan of action should incorporate a demand for the submission of the Review determinations to the Prices and Incomes Board, an examination of Review procedure so that account could be taken at a Special Review of continuing inflation and costs, and a heightening of efforts to persuade Parliament and the public of the serious plight of farmers.

Price and structural policy in the EC

With United Kingdom membership of the European Community decisions on the nature and level of price support were gradually transferred from London to Brussels during a five year transitional period. At one level the influence of farmers on agricultural policy decreased because 'they could not have the direct input into the policy they had when it was made in London' (Smith, 1990, p.

161). On the other hand the EC decision making process also reduced the influence of the Treasury and other departments over agricultural policy and 'increased the autonomy of the Ministry of Agriculture' which was less constrained by the Cabinet (Smith, 1990, p. 159). Indeed the position of the British agricultural policy network was strengthened because the CAP was rooted in productionism and high price levels for farmers. Without the countervailing pressures exerted by other Whitehall departments, MAFF was able to join with its like minded counterparts in the Council of Farm Ministers to take decisions generally favourable to the agricultural community and frustrate CAP reform.

The relationship between the Farmers' Unions and the Agricultural Departments continued much as before. The Annual Review remained as a preparatory exercise for the European price negotiations but more importantly became the forum where 'the Unions set out what they expect the Ministers to go out and bat for in Brussels' (NFU official quoted in Smith, 1990, p. 161). Thus prior to negotiations the Unions and Agricultural Departments agreed a common line to pursue. Indeed Smith has argued that the relationship between MAFF and the NFU became more united as they looked for arguments to use to bolster the British case in European negotiations.

Despite these favourable structural conditions, however, European price packages often provoked outrage amongst the Farmers' Unions similar to that which increasingly had greeted Annual Reviews in the 1960s. Farmers in Northern Ireland habitually complained that price packages were either totally unacceptable or damaging to individual sectors such as milk, and insufficient to provide farmers with adequate incomes or cover increased production costs. The difficulties faced by producers during the recessions of 1973-75 and the early 1980s brought particular discontent, once more accompanied by increased militancy and calls for direct action. In 1974, for example, the UFU leadership attempted to keep the lid on grass roots discontent by sanctioning limited direct action including a series of public demonstrations in towns throughout Northern Ireland. Of course the UFU still preferred to join with its British counterparts to lobby for improved farm prices and capital grants through the usual responsible channels in London and Brussels. For example United Kingdom farmers received an immediate price boost from the devaluation of the green pound in 1979 and the Less Favoured Area scheme was introduced in 1975 and extended in 1984 to support small farmers on marginal land.

In addition to assistance provided to United Kingdom agriculture as a whole, farmers in Northern Ireland also received special aid. This was usually given 'in recognition of Northern Ireland's difficulties as a remote region of the UK and EC; because of the general economic situation in the Province; and because of the particular problems of the intensive livestock sector' (Stainer, 1985, p. 53). On the other hand, national political and economic considerations continued to exert a dominant influence on policy. For example, when the UFU lobbied the Northern Ireland Office for special aid for milk producers in 1980 the Government refused because farmers had to take their fair share of the monetarist medicine. As a result the UFU Executive passed a vote of no confidence in the Secretary of State, Humphrey Atkins, claiming that the medicine might actually kill the patient. However although direct action was actively considered the Union again opted to continue protests through normal democratic channels.

The result of intensive lobbying at the European, national and regional level was a series of schemes and payments, funded fully or in part by the EC or directly from the British Exchequer. For example the beef variable premium was introduced as a result of the crisis in the beef sector in 1974 and the Meat Industry Employment Scheme (MIES) was introduced in 1975 to offset the dislocation suffered by meat plants in Northern Ireland after the devaluation of the green pound in the Republic of Ireland (this totalled £42 million in 1978-79). Following a very large fall in farming incomes between 1978-80 an internal Departmental review of the regional agricultural industry and intensive lobbying by the farming community led to the introduction of special aid packages which provided assistance worth ten million pounds in 1981-82, £16 million in 1982-83, £12.1 million in 1984, and £10.6 million in 1985. This aid was disbursed in the form of programmes such as an EC financed doubling of the suckler cow premium, the introduction of a consumer subsidy on liquid milk in 1981 to enable the Milk Marketing Board to increase returns to producers, and aid to processing plants in the intensive sector.

After 1972, therefore, Northern Ireland agriculture continued to be subsidized to a substantial extent, both by the United Kingdom Exchequer and the EC. Although official figures for the regional share of CAP expenditure on price guarantees in the United Kingdom are unavailable, Trimble has roughly estimated this at some £42 million in 1982, based on regional agriculture's six per cent share of agricultural output in the United Kingdom (Trimble, 1984, p. 63). In respect of financial assistance for structural and improvement schemes Northern Ireland agriculture received over £106 million in 1992-93. Some £88.7 million (84 per cent) was provided through United Kingdom schemes with the remainder being regional expenditure. Over half of the global total (£55.6 million) was accounted for by four main schemes fully funded by the EC - the annual ewe premium, suckler cow premium, beef special premium, and milk outgoers scheme (Department of Agriculture, 1993, pp. 128-9).

The impact of EC membership on agriculture in Northern Ireland cannot be accurately quantified in the absence of information about how the United Kingdom's support system would have developed outside the EC. For Stainer, however, regional agriculture was, on balance, 'probably better off than if the UK had remained outside' and it was 'reasonable to conclude that the level of financial support has been greater than it would have been if the UK had remained outside the Community and had retained responsibility for its own market support measures' (Stainer, 1985, p. 60).

5 Parity and particularity: Devolution and the Belfast-London nexus

The relationship between Northern Ireland and Great Britain has been the dominant influence on the agricultural policy process. In practice an integration dynamic rooted in a combination of economic, financial, social, constitutional, political and ideological factors replaced the sweeping formal powers over agricultural matters conferred by the 1920 Act. There was irresistible pressure for an approach which gave Ulster farmers parity with those in Britain, especially where monetary benefits were involved. This necessarily required support from the British Exchequer as the regional Government was unable to finance its own agricultural subsidies and was powerless to regulate imports.

The key concepts of 'parity' and 'particularity' are central to understanding how agricultural policy developed during the period of devolution. Parity concerns the general claim that the farmers of Northern Ireland had a right, as constituents of the United Kingdom, to the same financial support as those in Britain. Throughout the inter war period, for example, the Northern Ireland Government tried to persuade a hostile Treasury to accept the principle that 'whatever Exchequer assistance is given to an agricultural product in Great Britain shall be given on an equal basis by the United Kingdom Exchequer in respect of that product produced in Northern Ireland' (CAB4/397). Particularity, on the other hand, stresses the distinctiveness of Northern Ireland as a region and on the right, embodied in the 1920 Act, to control its own development and formulate policies to suit its individual character. This claim could take both Unionist and Nationalist forms. For the Nationalist MP, Conlon, particularity was rooted in the reality that 'we in Ireland live under different conditions, our climate is different, our stock is different, our mode of living is different, our standards are different and everything else is different. There is no sense in legislating for us in the same way as for the people in England' (NIHC Deb 31, c. 579). The Unionist, Rowley Elliott summed up particularity thus:

> We are British citizens, and we are very proud of that fact. We want nothing more than citizens of Great Britain are entitled to. We are asked to contribute on the British basis as far as tax is concerned, and we do not object to do so.

We want no privileges British citizens do not get, but we do want a policy for Northern Ireland agriculture that is more suitable to Northern Ireland than the policy defined at the moment. It is not fair to say "That is the policy that suits Great Britain. That policy must suit you too." Surely it is possible, inside the folds of an agricultural policy, to have some differentiation made and to make the policy for agriculture in Northern Ireland more suitable to the requirements of the people here, more suitable to the land from which we have to produce our commodities, and more suitable to the climate we have to contend with (NIHC Deb 27, c. 922).

The overall policy objective of the Government was to ensure that farmers received similar financial benefits to those in Britain whilst retaining the scope to formulate specific regional policies to suit the particular conditions of the Northern Ireland agricultural industry. This approach was encapsulated by Brooke in 1953 when he countered 'an impression in some quarters that Northern Ireland is in danger of losing its independence in regard to agricultural policy' by asserting that the Government aimed 'to preserve our freedom to make, within the framework of the United Kingdom system, our own arrangements to meet local conditions' (NIHC Deb 38, c. 38). At the same time, however, the parity approach had resulted in the 'invaluable safeguards' of the 1947 Act and the 'integration of our economy with that of Great Britain during the last 14 years has been to the great advantage of the farming community' (NIHC Deb 38, c. 38).

In this approach the political acceptability of a policy was determined by the extent to which parity was combined with the particularity needed to adapt the general lines of British policy to regional conditions. This balance was difficult to achieve, especially where finance was involved, because emphasis on the position of Northern Ireland as part of the United Kingdom often curtailed the scope for policy innovation, adaptation and administrative flexibility. Moreover particularity was sacrificed in some areas in an attempt to obtain parity in others. The extension of the 1932 Wheat Act to Northern Ireland, for example, was on balance disadvantageous to regional interests but this was accepted by the Ministry of Agriculture as 'a small price to pay for the goodwill and indebtedness of the English ministry in other directions' and eventually helped achieve parity in other areas (Buckland, 1979, p. 141).

The complexity of agricultural policy development in the period after 1920 is best appreciated by using the concepts of parity and particularity as end points on a policy continuum on which overall trends, policy eras and individual policies can be situated. Whilst the equilibrium between parity and particularity in general terms was best approximated during the 1930s at the same time cattle policy was close to the parity extreme whereas milk policy exhibited a high degree of particularity. After 1939, however, the dominant trend towards parity in agricultural policy accelerated and helped produce a single 'national' policy for the United Kingdom on fundamental matters such as price and production. This parity dynamic in turn severely attenuated the ability of the regional Ministry of

Agriculture to frame policies suited to the particular conditions of Northern Ireland agriculture.

The state and the farmers: Belfast-London relations

The parity dynamic and the increasingly 'national' nature of policy development was reflected in the development of official and informal contacts between Belfast and London at both state and farmer level. The Ministry of Agriculture realized that decisions taken in London could have serious repercussions given Northern Ireland's dependence on the British market. However the Ministry was initially excluded from the British agricultural policy process in accordance with constitutional formalities. For Archdale it was 'extremely desirable that there should be closer co-operation between us in Northern Ireland and the British Government on the subject of agricultural policy generally' (CAB9E/69/1). The main worry was that the development of marketing schemes in Britain without regional input would have fundamental repercussions for regional policy. When a British scheme was agreed it would

> be extraordinarily difficult for us to secure any modification even if it should be definitely prejudicial to our interests. The only safeguard I can see is for us to have the opportunity of participating in this discussion in order that we may play our part in shaping what is after all a policy which affects not only Great Britain but the whole of the United Kingdom (CAB9E/69/1).

After discussion with the British authorities Scott Robertson took on the role of liaison officer with London although MAF insisted that this relationship be kept on an informal basis. As a result of this arrangement the regional Ministry claimed that it had been able to been able to 'keep in close touch with developments, ensure that our interests have been properly understood and, in particular, play a not unimportant part in securing the recognition of the fundamental importance of live stock and live stock products in United Kingdom agriculture' (NIHC Deb 14, c. 685). During the war, when consultation with Whitehall departments was essential, Scott Robertson also represented the Ministry on official sub-committees and was effectively permanently based in London (see Blake, 1956, pp. 26-33).

The Northern Ireland policy network was an integral element in the formulation of national post war policy. The Ministry of Agriculture, for example, had 'a hand in all these negotiations, all these conferences...We have represented the different points, the different facts, and the different factors in the whole situation to the Imperial Authorities, and our representations have been taken into account' (NIHC Deb 26, c. 1604). Increasingly the Ministry of Agriculture participated in preliminary discussions on policy at the official level. However although Harkness sat on the Food Policy Working Party, for example, he was not a representative of the Northern Ireland Government whose interests were formally channelled through the Home Office. This resulted in a situation where the regional Ministry participated in discussions leading to the formulation of British Government agricultural policy, for example on marketing reform, but the Minister could not raise the issue in the Northern Ireland Cabinet without the authorization of the Home Secretary. The development of close relations between the Agricultural Departments caused some concern within the regional Government, particularly that the Ministry unilaterally negotiated with MAF and entered into policy commitments without Cabinet approval (CAB4/696). There is some evidence to support this. For example, on 1 June 1948 MAF agreed with Harkness that Northern Ireland should be included in British legislation to permit participation in United Kingdom marketing schemes yet the issue was not discussed in the regional Cabinet until 16 June. The policy of the Minister of Agriculture was also portrayed by Jack Beattie as to 'make his Department subordinate to the policy of another place against the wishes and desires of the members of this House...We are the custodians of agriculture in this area in accordance with our charter, and we have no right to be made subordinate to a Department in another place' (NIHC Deb 31, c. 837).

In general the approach of the Ministry was to do the 'utmost to ensure that the outstanding problems of our farmers are clearly known when any reshaping of United Kingdom Government agricultural policy is taking place' and to assure MP's that its officials were fully were involved in discussions with British departments (NIHC Deb 54, c. 413). Relations between Belfast and London were on the whole cordial after 1939. Brooke, for example, described his Government's approach to the British authorities as treating 'the officials on the other side as colleagues and not as enemies' (NIHC Deb 38, c. 1029). Although the Government 'had many a tough battle', especially in the negotiations on the remoteness grant, the atmosphere had been one of mutual trust and the requests of Northern Ireland ministers had been met with 'sympathy and understanding' (NIHC Deb 38, c. 1029). The level and administration of the remoteness grant was the cause of the most serious disagreements. During the negotiations the British departments grew increasingly exasperated with the attitude in Belfast and the Home Office made it known that there was 'a feeling in Whitehall that the Northern Ireland attitude on this matter has hitherto consisted mainly of antagonistic criticism of proposals made from this side but nothing constructive from yours' (CAB9E/57/7).

The UFU also recognized that many important policy decisions, especially on protection and import control, were taken in London which increasingly became the focus of its lobbying activities from the 1930s. For example the Union sent resolutions to the British authorities, lobbied Westminster MP's, and often had face to face meetings with MAF and the British Minister of Agriculture. The UFU also participated in the discussions on price insurance with the British Government in the late 1930s after representations on its behalf by the Northern Ireland Government and Unionist MP's at Westminster. During the war UFU members were appointed to advisory committees in Whitehall, such as those for livestock and feed stuffs, and a channel was created through which 'direct representation can be made on both policy and prices to the Imperial departments concerned and the much greater influence that has thus been attained by the Union must be readily recognised' (Farmers' Journal, May 1940, p. 202). As the parity dynamic removed primary responsibility for fundamental policy matters from the remit of the regional Government, the UFU paid increasing attention to Westminster general elections. In 1964, for example, the UFU President issued an election message and candidates standing in rural constituencies in Northern Ireland were asked to 'support measures proposed in the future which aim at placing the industry on a sound financial basis' (Farmers' Journal, 2 October 1964, p. 15).

Joint action between the three Farmers' Unions in the United Kingdom also became institutionalized despite policy differences which made the NFU initially reluctant. The UFU and Scottish organizations (the NFUS and the Scottish Chamber of Agriculture) issued a joint policy statement in September 1931 but it was not until 1936 that the three Farmers' Unions established a Joint Coordinating Committee to discuss matters of common interest. Relations were further strengthened and institutionalized during and after the war when the Unions took a unanimous decision to 'stand together as one body on matters of agricultural policy for the transitional and post-war periods. With that end in view joint meetings are to take place at least quarterly and the closest possible liaison is to be continuously maintained' (Farmers' Journal, July 1944, pp. 255-6).

Particularity

The central criticism of the parity approach in agricultural policy was that it restricted the development of innovative policies designed to suit particular regional conditions. Demands for greater particularity in rural policy came from within the Government, wider Unionist ranks, from Nationalist and other opposition MP's, and occasionally from the UFU itself. Nationalist MP's were predictably the most vocal critics of the parity approach because it entrenched partition and further integrated the six counties into the United Kingdom. Cahir Healy remarked that 'one day we hope there will be a united Ireland, and it will be less disturbing to the national economy of the country when that day comes if we are to have an agricultural scheme for Ireland' rather than one tied to the British economy' (HC Deb 496, c. 1303). Schemes for agricultural improvement for Northern Ireland should be kept separate from those in Great Britain because Irish farmers had 'separate and distinct needs. Farmers should have more freedom to work out their own problems, and these problems are both agricultural and national. In short, we want to be free to spend our own money and our own taxes in the best way we can and the way common sense and expediency suggests' (HC Deb 496, c. 1304). Another Nationalist, Conlon, urged the Minister of Agriculture to 'consider the difficulties of his own people, and not to be continually and in a slavish way trotting after the heels of Great Britain' (NIHC Deb 31, c. 576). Parity in agricultural policy meant that Northern Ireland was entirely at the mercy of the British Government and the British electorate...we are mainly an agricultural community. The British people are mainly industrial, and we may take it for granted that they will always do what is best for the greatest number of their own people; they will not consider the people in the Six Counties (NIHC Deb 37, c. 701).

Nationalists argued that the disadvantages of increased state control outweighed any advantages of guaranteed prices and opposed inclusion in the post war system. Even though Northern Ireland farmers were spared the threat of dispossession faced by those in Britain, the extent of state direction was still deemed unjustifiable because it threatened hard won rights of ownership and meant the effective restoration of landlordism. For McSparran farmers had to resist a policy which

> restricts and interferes with the liberty that the farmers have enjoyed and fought for the past number of centuries...it is an intolerable thing that a Bill like this should be introduced into an agricultural country like this...it is the beginning of the Sovietising of the farms of the six counties if this Bill is passed and its powers are taken (NIHC Deb 32, c. 3885).

Unionists also demanded that the Government 'get off the beaten track of doing just what the Englishman wants them to do' (NIHC Deb 4, c. 385). James Brown, the Farmers and New Industries MP for South Down who took the Unionist whip, complained that 'carbon copy legislation will never bring salvation to this industry, and that what we require is some native genius and enterprise' (NIHC Deb 21, c. 1775). Like many critics of agricultural policy in the 1930s Brown blamed the 'imported officials' of the Ministry of Agriculture (code for Scott Robertson) who were 'incapable of understanding and appreciating the peculiar needs of Northern Ireland' (NIHC Deb 21, c. 1775).

In the immediate post war period criticism of parity focused on the acceptance of the 1947 Agriculture Act as the basis of policy. There was apprehension about the impact of the Labour Government in Britain and concern that the regional Parliament had become little more than a rubber stamp for a British policy. Mrs Calvert, for example, asserted that it was 'time that the policy of this Parliament and this people was a policy for the Ulster people and not necessarily a policy either for the United Kingdom as a whole or for any other country' (NIHC Deb 37, c. 75). Minford criticized the adoption of state directed efficiency simply because 'a somewhat similar Bill has been passed in England. Are we going to have to dance to the tune of the Socialist band? Surely this House of Commons and the farmers have a right to mind their own business' (NIHC Deb 32, c. 3909).

A.F. Wilson was the most vocal critic of United Kingdom marketing schemes under which the regional Parliament would 'sacrifice or give up any rights on the matter and agree to accept Government, in so far as that matter is concerned, from the Imperial Parliament' (NIHC Deb 35, c. 746). On ryegrass seed, for example, Wilson preferred a 'strong local policy for Northern Ireland alone' in which the

Ministry retained the 'ability to specialise along her own lines, while co-operating with the marketing and price structure on the other side. In that way we can pursue the individual characteristics of our own products and our own people' (NIHC Deb 33, c. 760). For Wilson acceptance of the UFU's demand for United Kingdom marketing schemes made the Union effectively responsible for policy decisions which were properly the function of the Stormont Parliament.

Powerful voices in the Northern Ireland Cabinet and administration also criticized the parity approach. Within the civil service, for example, there was opposition to inclusion in British legislation such as the 1946 Hill Farming Act. There was a strong conviction that 'only in the most exceptional circumstances should we consent to the UK Parliament's legislating for us on a transferred matter' (CAB9E/150/1). Giving effective responsibility for transferred matters back to Westminster forfeited the scope for independent action and an 'unchecked course of this interference obviously cannot fail to confine our already puny powers to an ever-narrowing channel until we end up with no more jurisdiction than a county council' (CAB9E/150/1).

The Minister of Commerce questioned the acceptance of the 1947 Agriculture Act as the basis of post war policy in Northern Ireland. In general Nugent thought that 'it might be dangerous to become too much tied to British policy or in any way permanently "integrated" with British Agriculture' (CAB9E/57/3/I). Nugent's particular concern was that increased state control to ensure efficient production, especially the power to throw inefficient farmers off their land, was an unacceptable encroachment on free market forces. Efficient farming required 'flexibility and initiative, a readiness to change methods and policy rapidly and boldly' (CAB4/697). This was promoted by the owner occupied structure of agriculture in Northern Ireland because an inefficient farmer 'destroys his own capital, not a landlord's, and in due course he will be sold up, and a better man will buy the farm, a natural and healthy economic process' (CAB4/697). The Ministry was urged to adopt an approach based on information, advice, and encouragement rather than state control which discouraged innovation. Dispossession, moreover, would create a 'general atmosphere of unrest and irritation, and destroy the good relations between the Ministry and the farmers which are essential to progress' and because farmers were 'of varying religious faiths and political opinions...great play will be made with the cry of religious and political persecution' (CAB4/697). Unless the system of guaranteed prices was adapted to suit regional conditions and divested of its socialist characteristics, Northern Ireland should develop a policy

> based on our conditions, rather than to turn to one which is based on English conditions, and is yet to be proved in practice...I hope that we can convince the English Ministers that our circumstances are so different that we can and should seek efficiency by a different road to the one which they intend to take. But if we fail, I think rather than surrender the most important of all the transferred powers, the control of our own agricultural policy, to English

direction, we should, even at the last moment, ask to be left out of the Bill altogether,and take our chance on the basis of world prices (CAB4/697).

The sacrifice of parity based on the 1947 Act for greater particularity was rejected but there was agreement that the general lines of policy needed to be adapted to regional conditions. Moore's initial preference for total inclusion in the British legislation with administrative adaptations to 'ensure that the legislation is suitable to our conditions' was overruled and the efficiency provisions were enacted in the Agriculture Act 1949 (AG16/26/1). This arrangement maintained parity in the form of guaranteed prices but also protected the constitutional position and allowed a measure of particularity. Most notably the decision not to assume the power to dispossess inefficient farmers in Northern Ireland was welcomed by MP's as a recognition of the need to adapt British legislation to regional conditions. Even this was not enough for some who also criticized the enumeration of 'rules of good husbandry' in clause 15 of the regional Agriculture Bill, which was closely modelled on the British example. For Healy the 'ten new Stormont Commandments' - Moore was the 'Moses of Government hill' - were nothing less than the first step on the road to economic slavery and loss of freedom (NIHC Deb 32, c. 3872). Opposition from MP's and the UFU eventually forced the Ministry to remove explicit reference to rules of good husbandry although it insisted on retention of a discretionary power to ensure efficiency.

Most Unionists accepted that some state control was necessary to secure the primary goal of price parity and were pleased that the British legislation had been adapted to regional specifications. Indeed Bailie wanted more such legislation which did not 'follow a rigid step-by-step policy with cross-channel legislation... this Bill provides for the consideration of a vital fact - that there are oftentimes conditions in this country that make a Bill not applicable here in the same way as it might be applicable on the other side' (NIHC Deb 32, c. 3924).

Although the UFU was the chief advocate of parity, and was worried that excessive particularity would threaten parity prices, it also stressed that policies needed to be adapted to regional conditions. On the 1949 Agriculture Act Moore was congratulated because he had 'made a quite good job of it by way of adapting the English legislation to suit our Northern Ireland conditions' (Farmers' Journal, December 1948, p. 116). Ignorant or unaware of the fact that Cabinet opposition led to the removal of the more unpleasant features of the British legislation even before it had seen the Bill, the UFU claimed that the 'outcome of the analysis and representation made by the UFU is a Bill altered almost beyond recognition with valuable safeguards added to it. In its amended form it no more resembles either the English or Scottish Act than chalk resembles cheese' (Farmers' Journal, January 1949, p. 151). Demands for parity were habitually accompanied by the caveat 'keeping in mind the particular circumstances existing in our own province' (Farmers' Journal, February 1939, p. 231). Indeed for the UFU parity often meant little more than equal treatment with Britain where it was to the benefit of Northern Ireland farmers. On issues such as agricultural wage regulation and unemployment insurance, for example, the UFU opposed parity because the cost of living in Northern Ireland was relatively lower but Craig insisted on following the British lead.

The Ministry of Agriculture was also concerned to retain the ability to adapt the general lines of British policy to regional conditions, especially in the area of marketing. Initially the Ministry was an enthusiastic advocate of national marketing schemes because it feared that opting out might prejudice inclusion in price guarantees, and because Northern Ireland farmers, as British citizens, had the right to cooperate with their fellow farmers in Great Britain. For the Ministry this policy was compatible with the constitutional position because regional interests would be fully taken into account in the formulation of schemes which were then subject to affirmative resolution at Stormont. This was questioned by a sceptical Cabinet, unconvinced that participation in national marketing schemes did not impinge on the powers of the Stormont Parliament.

The Cabinet adopted the general principle that 'any surrender of Northern Ireland's constitutional powers should be avoided wherever possible' (CAB4/836). By 1950 the Ministry of Agriculture had come round to Brooke's suggestion that 'it might be possible for Northern Ireland to participate in the system of guaranteed prices while retaining the freedom to devise and operate its own marketing schemes' (CAB9E/57/3/I). Now convinced that guaranteed prices were 'in no way dependent upon Northern Ireland participation in United Kingdom marketing schemes' the Ministry refused to agree to several proposed United Kingdom marketing schemes including those for herbage seeds and for apples and pears (CAB9E/57/4). Responsibility for agricultural marketing rested solely with the regional Parliament and 'any departure from that position would be a matter of grave concern to the Government' (CAB9E/57/4). Because the Stormont Parliament could exercise no control over a United Kingdom marketing scheme once approved it was 'essential that there should be clear and unmistakable evidence that participation in any United Kingdom Scheme will confer definite benefits upon Northern Ireland' (CAB9E/57/4).

Whilst definite advantages accrued from participation in national schemes for commodities such as wool which were produced in small quantities in Northern Ireland, the Ministry opted to retain regional schemes for the most important products. Moreover participation in national schemes would give British producers effective control of the Northern Ireland industry. The imperative for close cooperation with Britain did not mean that Northern Ireland should be 'absorbed in the British schemes. If this were so then there would be no need for a Parliament in Northern Ireland and the "closest possible co-operation with Great Britain in all things" would be secured by Government direct from Whitehall' (CAB9E/57/4). A suggestion for a national Agricultural Wages Board was rejected because it would require the repeal of existing regional legislation and make it more difficult to avoid United Kingdom marketing arrangements. This also raised the general question of whether inclusion in the 1947 Act meant that the 'whole agricultural economy must be integrated with that of Great Britain regardless of local conditions and the existence of our Parliament vested with the powers conferred on it by the Government of Ireland Act, 1920' (CAB4/836). Although there were some advantages to 'complete submersion in United Kingdom schemes' this would nevertheless 'involve sacrificing our right to pursue our own policies, adopted to suit our conditions, in respect of a large number of matters which clearly are within the competence of our Parliament' (CAB4/836). Alternatively the Government could maintain that participation in the system of guaranteed prices did not

> involve the surrender of any of the powers conferred on us by the Government of Ireland Act and that we must be free to work out our own arrangements in regard to wages, marketing and general agricultural policy. This is obviously the strict legal and constitutional position and is, of course, reinforced by the fact that, in so far as any subsidy is involved, we contribute to the cost of guaranteed farm prices through the Imperial Contribution (CAB4/836).

The parity dynamic

The scope for particularity was limited, however. Not only was parity an article of faith of the Ministry and the UFU but the British authorities were unwilling to countenance any policy variations which significantly benefitted farmers in Northern Ireland compared with those in Britain. The issue which first demonstrated the salience of the parity dynamic in rural policy was that of rate relief following the reduction of agricultural rates in Britain in 1923. There was unanimity within agricultural circles that farmers in Northern Ireland were entitled to equal treatment. For the UFU, for example, the farmers of Northern Ireland 'have still to pay Imperial taxation and to whatever extent the Imperial Government may come to the relief and assistance of British agriculture Northern farmers are entitled to exactly the same measure' (Belfast News Letter, 4 May 1923; CAB9E/8/1).

Although the case for parity was accepted by the British Government, in this instance through an adjustment of the Imperial Contribution, this was not regarded as a precedent. Moreover within the regional Government there was a fundamental dispute about what parity entailed. Craig and Andrews supported the UFU line that the intention was 'to put Northern agriculture on a parity with British agriculture through the provision of direct cash relief' (Belfast News Letter, 4 May 1923). Pollock and Archdale, on the other hand, did not extend financial parity into the realms of policy administration and wanted to use the money for agricultural improvement schemes. To Craig's satisfaction the Pirrie Report (Cmd 17, 1923) agreed with his contention that 'it would be inexpedient to depart from the principle laid down by the British Government in the distribution of the grant-in-aid' (CAB9E/8/1). This early decision set the tone for the future and when agricultural land was completely derated in Britain in 1928 Pollock had little option but to 'ensure that our farmers will not be placed in a position less favourable than those in Great Britain' despite the fact that the cost would be proportionately much greater as a result of the higher rate burden on Northern Ireland farmers (NIHC Deb 9, c. 1945).

The parity dynamic did not always work to the benefit of farmers. For example, demands for reductions in land purchase annuities were rejected because of the implications for the claim for parity. Craig told a UFU deputation in September 1938 that

> if the Government raised with the Imperial authorities the question of a concession of the land annuities it would at once jeopardise their position in securing the financial assistance which was being given to the Ulster farmers, either directly or indirectly, by the Imperial Government, and would thus endanger for the future the very important advantage which the Northern Ireland farmer possessed by enjoying the same assistance and the same concessions as farmers in other parts of the United Kingdom (Farmers' Journal, October 1938, p. 72).

From the outset agricultural policy in Northern Ireland mirrored that followed in Britain. Some of the legislation introduced in the 1920s simply copied British Acts, for example the Horticultural Produce (Sales on Commission) Act 1927. Some marketing legislation, including the 1928 Marketing of Eggs Act, was based upon the British equivalent and on other occasions Northern Ireland was specifically included in Westminster legislation such as the Fertilisers and Feeding Stuffs Act 1926. In the 1930s the parity dynamic and the inchoate unity of the fundamental aspects of agricultural policy was consolidated by the adoption of a protectionist policy for the United Kingdom as a whole. Thus a priority for the regional Government was to ensure that the Ottawa conference recognized Northern Ireland's 'status as an integral part of the United Kingdom in connection with any arrangements regarding publicity for Home and Empire produce, the control of imports by quota or other device, or the organised marketing of any agricultural commodity within the United Kingdom' (AG16/11/2).

Even the regional policy machinery had to be adapted to the parity imperative. For example Craig and Andrews objected to the establishment of an agricultural inquiry committee in the late 1930s because the Government was 'far safer in hanging on to what is done in Great Britain. I am afraid it will be embarrassing if the Committee...should bring in a report urging departures from British standards involving substantial additional benefits to the farming community here beyond what is proposed on a United Kingdom basis' (CAB9E/23/2).

The central force in the parity dynamic was financial because it was 'manifest that Northern Ireland cannot from its own resources give to its farmers the same benefits as can be given by the British Government to British farmers' (CAB4/397). Strongest opposition to the parity principle came from Treasury officials who resented the regional Government's cavalier attitude to both the constitutional provisions of the 1920 Act and to public expenditure. The Treasury opposed direct financial aid for Northern Ireland agriculture from Exchequer funds, particularly as it became impossible to offset expenditure against a dwindling Imperial Contribution. Indeed in 1931 the Treasury tried to reverse the Colwyn Committee decision that the Contribution was a residual charge on the Northern Ireland finances. However although there was some support within the Ministry of Finance for the Treasury's stance the Government pursued parity in bilateral, ad hoc negotiations with Whitehall on agricultural subsidies. The Treasury very reluctantly agreed to certain payments such as those for milk and beef but insisted that these did not concede the principle that Northern Ireland had a right to share in assistance given to British farmers. Craig tried to exploit the controversy over the 1938 Anglo-Irish Agreement to secure acceptance of parity but the Treasury steadfastly refused to concede the principle. Although Craig got an agreement that where agricultural subsidies were granted to British farmers no objections would be raised to similar expenditure in Northern Ireland being borne on United Kingdom votes, the important caveat was that equal assistance would be granted only where 'circumstances are such as to justify corresponding subsidies in Northern Ireland' (NIHC Deb 21, c. 662).

The pinnacle for the parity approach was reached during the Second World War when the regional authorities administered a national food production policy and farmers throughout the United Kingdom received the same prices for most products. Parity again entailed costs as well as benefits. The logic of Unionism underpinned the moral imperative for equity, fairness and equality of sacrifice throughout the United Kingdom. Craig warned against the attitude that

> we have far more food here than would necessitate such a rigid scheme as food rationing might impose...I want the people to take a full view of the United Kingdom as a whole - England, Wales, Scotland and ourselves all in one. Whatever produce we can send across the Channel makes it somewhat easier on the whole of the citizens rather than on a favoured few (NIHC Deb 22, c. 1906).

There was little explicit opposition in London to parity prices throughout the United Kingdom during the war and it was also taken for granted that Northern Ireland would be included in the post war system of guaranteed prices. The claim for equal financial assistance had greater force because of the contribution which Northern Ireland agriculture made to increased food production. For the regional Government it was morally and politically unacceptable that its loyal farmers be refused similar benefits to those in Great Britain after the war. The Government's case for the inclusion of Northern Ireland in the system of guaranteed prices was buttressed by the Babington Report and by UFU policy. Babington concluded that a system of guaranteed prices and assured markets should be introduced 'with the cost of subsidies borne by the Exchequer' (Cmd 249, 1947, p. 89). For the UFU inclusion represented the effective achievement of price parity with the rest of the United Kingdom. It assumed, mistakenly, that a standard national price structure would apply which would maintain the 'principle adopted throughout the war whereby the Ulster farmer may count on the same price for his output as the Essex or Kent farmer will get for his. A permanent policy that establishes that principle is not likely to be taken lightly by any Ulster farmer endowed with a grain of sound common sense' (Farmers' Journal, December 1945, p. 111).

For the Ministry of Agriculture inclusion in the 1947 Act was 'the culmination of the policy laid down by Lord Craigavon in 1937, of securing for Northern Ireland agriculture parallel assistance to that given to agriculture in Great Britain' (AG16/26/1). Moore proudly proclaimed that 'the agriculture of Northern Ireland has become more and more closely integrated with the agricultural industry in Great Britain and never was it more so than it is today' (NIHC Deb 32, c. 3857).

Despite the inclusion of Northern Ireland in the 1947 Act the Treasury exploited the Annual Review and the process of decontrol to reduce the amount of assistance given to Northern Ireland farmers, whilst accepting their general entitlement to guaranteed prices. Brooke tried to reassure farmers that the fundamental principles of the Government's agricultural policy remained to 'keep the closest integration between the two agricultural policies - that the policy of the farm prices, that is the production side, and the marketing, should be the same as in the United Kingdom' (NIHC Deb 37, c. 31). At the 1953 Review, for example, the Treasury attempted to make the regional Exchequer liable for an increased grant for marginal production schemes. The Ministry of Finance, however, rejected the Treasury's interpretation of the 1947 Act 'that only when the guarantees are implemented through prices should the cost be borne on your Votes, and that the cost of production grants is appropriate to our Exchequer even though we may have no hand in determining the amounts' (CAB9E/57/5). As a result of this protest the regional Government was assured that 'as a normal rule expenditure arising out of the farm Price Review should be regarded as Imperial expenditure, unless there are any exceptional features which would involve a wide diversity in the application of expenditure in Northern Ireland as compared with that in Great Britain' (CAB9E/57/5).

This partly safeguarded the general position under the 1947 Act but the Treasury continued its efforts to divest itself of responsibility for assistance to Northern Ireland farmers. The Treasury, for example, tried to persuade the Ministry of Finance to accept liability for agricultural subsidies in Northern Ireland by making them chargeable against the Imperial Contribution. The introduction of deficiency payments was interpreted by the Northern Ireland agricultural network as the end of price parity defined as fixed uniform prices. The claim for similar actual returns, not merely a single standard price for the United Kingdom as a whole, was extremely optimistic and unjustified. There was no uniform level of actual returns in Britain only an average level, and remote producers in Britain were also disadvantaged. Under deficiency payments producers in Northern Ireland continued to have parity because they were treated exactly as they had always demanded to be: as an integral part of the United Kingdom. Moreover although the remoteness grant did not make up the shortfall it was effective recognition by the British authorities that Northern Ireland agriculture was integral to the United Kingdom.

The parity dynamic was evident even in marketing policy where particularity was notably demonstrated and most highly prized. Increased cooperation between producers throughout the United Kingdom was illustrated by the marketing schemes prepared for wool and eggs. West expressed the UFU's belief that participation in national producer controlled marketing schemes was essential because they made price parity 'a much more permanent possibility, whereas if different boards are set up in Great Britain and Northern Ireland, we in this country would immediately suffer the unpleasantness of price differentials' (NIHC Deb 38, c. 3406-7). For Harden, the Ulster Unionist agriculture spokesman at Westminster, inclusion in British legislation was always welcome because it showed 'how closely the agricultural policy of Ulster is allied to the agricultural policy of this country. I sincerely believe that the future of the whole farming community of Ulster...is dependent upon being allied to the agricultural policy of this country' (HC Deb 482, c. 877). It was only natural for Northern Ireland farmers to want to participate in United Kingdom schemes because of the 'age old Unionist Policy of the closest possible co-operation with Great Britain in all things' (CAB9E/57/4).

However, the Ministry of Agriculture refused to agree to the widespread use of national marketing schemes because this would further attenuate its constitutional powers. Indeed the Ministry attempted to use the decontrol process to 'reconsider the constitutional position with a view to resuscitating those powers which have, to some extent, drifted into disuse' (CAB9E/57/4). As a result the Ministry drew up radical proposals to secure parity in living standards for the agricultural community whilst leaving it 'to deal with the general policy in the Northern Ireland Parliament as the Minister responsible for agricultural policy in this area' with its transferred powers intact (CAB9E/57/5). The key proposal was that a Treasury funded block grant, sufficient to maintain Northern Ireland prices at the British level, would be paid into the regional Exchequer and the Ministry would then bear the costs of all agricultural expenditure on its votes, including the remoteness grant.

This proposal was vetoed by the Ministry of Finance because it would likely result in a negative Imperial Contribution. Maintenance of a positive contribution of around ten million pounds was a fundamental policy objective of the Government but agricultural subsidies would easily swallow up this figure. For example, after 1955, in comparison with a Ministry budget of around ten million pounds, the amount received by Northern Ireland farmers was always over £20 million and reached nearly £40 million in 1961-62, some 95 per cent of which was provided from the British Exchequer (see Table 5.1).

Table 5.1
Support for Northern Ireland agriculture 1954-72 (£ million)

	Price subsidies	Production inc. remoteness	Capital grants	Total	MANI budget
1954-55	14.3	3.4	0.5	18.2	5.357
1955-56	14.4	5.2	0.5	20.3	5.383
1956-57	21.6	6.1	0.6	28.3	5.779
1957-58	24.6	7.3	0.7	32.6	6.079
1958-59	15.0	7.6	0.8	23.4	6.661
1959-60	14.7	8.7	1.5	24.9	7.797
1960-61	15.6	10.9	1.7	28.2	8.228
1961-62	25.6	11.6	2.1	39.3	7.597
1962-63	23.5	12.5	2.8	38.8	7.817
1963-64	19.0	11.8	2.6	33.3	8.846
1964-65	16.7	10.1	2.8	29.6	8.677
1965-66	15.5	9.9	2.5	27.9	9.516
1966-67	13.0	11.1	2.1	26.3	10.957
1967-68	18.3	12.9	2.6	33.8	11.757
1968-69	15.9	13.5	2.7	32.2	12.896
1969-70	15.8	13.6	3.2	32.6	13.886
1970-71	15.0	20.0	4.0	39.0	15.027
1971-72	12.0	19.2	6.3	38.4 *	17.159

* includes £0.9 million classified as 'other grants'.

The aim was 'to throw as much expenditure as possible on Imperial Votes' even if this appeared to involve a diminution of the powers of the Northern Ireland Parliament (CAB9E/57/7). For Brian Maginness the 1938 agreement under which the cost of agricultural subsidies in Northern Ireland was borne on British funds was of fundamental importance. This had not led to any change in the constitutional status of Northern Ireland and had probably 'saved the Northern Ireland Exchequer from bankruptcy' (CAB9E/57/5). It had also enabled the farmers of Northern Ireland to 'obtain benefits which it would have been impossible for them to have obtained if agriculture and the cost of agricultural subsidies had been treated strictly as a Transferred Service - the money was simply not available for the purpose' (CAB9E/57/5). The parity approach was still the overriding imperative and the Government's position had always been that agricultural subsidies are an Imperial charge designed in the interests of the United Kingdom economy and strategy as a whole, and therefore any proposals to alter the basis, whilst designed for the sake of establishing Northern Ireland's constitutional independence, may do so at the expense of divorcing Northern Ireland to some extent from its position as an integral part of the United Kingdom in this matter (CAB9E/57/5).

The policy of the Ministry of Finance was 'to extend United Kingdom liability for various services, but the implication is always present that any Imperial acceptance of financial responsibility involves some surrender of our powers to direct policy' (CAB9E/57/5). In addition the independence gained from Moore's scheme would be more illusory than real because the Government would 'be opening the door to incessant and vociferous demands from the farming community which we will have to refuse, but with the knowledge that such refusal will not increase our Government's popularity' (CAB9E/57/5). It would also be impossible for the regional Exchequer to accede to demands of farmers for more subsidies, 'accompanied by pressure and intense lobbying', unless the financial situation drastically improved or the British Government was content to see the Imperial Contribution used to increase agricultural subsidies (CAB9E/57/5). Moreover the Treasury would refuse to fund schemes which differed radically from those in Britain. As no Northern Ireland funds would be available 'what becomes of the independence so stressed by my colleague? In matters of detail and administration this Government might well differ from the British Government, but as the main principles must necessarily revolve on finance does not our independence become merely nominal?' (CAB9E/57/5).

A final fundamental objection of the Ministry of Finance was that agricultural expenditure borne on regional votes would make explicit the dependency of Northern Ireland on British subventions. This would 'give a handle to those who have argued that by ourselves we are incapable of paying our way. Such subsidies during the past fifteen years have been concealed and indefinite; they will in future be open and precise' (CAB9E/57/5). This alluded to the activities of the Friends of Ireland Group of Labour MP's at Westminster which aimed to force the Northern Ireland Government to operate within the strict financial terms of the Government of Ireland Act and thereby demonstrate that the state was subsidized by the British taxpayer (Purdie, 1983). MP's such as Geoffrey Bing publicly opposed the inclusion of Northern Ireland in British agricultural subsidies. Agriculture was the most important transferred power, and the whole point of establishing a regional parliament was allow it to deal separately with the different agricultural problems and conditions in Northern Ireland. As such it was ridiculous to make provision for Northern Ireland in schemes designed to meet British conditions. For the Ministry of Finance, however, the immeasurable advantage of the 1938 agreement was precisely that subsidies for Northern Ireland farmers were not shown separately in the United Kingdom Exchequer payments to Northern Ireland, and this has, from a Northern Ireland viewpoint, been of some advantage in the face of attempts at Westminster, in the Press and elsewhere...to prove that these payments to Northern Ireland more than counterbalance payments made by Northern Ireland in the form of the Imperial Contribution (CAB9E/57/5).

The Cabinet tentatively supported Moore's suggestion but the Ministry of Agriculture's enthusiasm for a separate block grant rapidly dissipated as it became obvious that the Treasury was primarily interested in reducing its liability on agricultural assistance in Northern Ireland. For the Treasury the transfer of some expenditure from MAF to Northern Ireland votes was desirable precisely because it would force the Stormont Government to keep the level of subsidies down. Moreover it would remedy the constitutional anomaly whereby MAF retained accounting responsibility without the corresponding power to actually supervise expenditure whilst the Ministry of Agriculture distributed the subsidies but was not formally responsible to the Northern Ireland Parliament for these activities. This interpretation was disputed by the regional Ministry which argued that MAF had a supervisory power over the administration of subsidies and that it simply acted as its agent under the specific provisions of the 1920 Act. When the Treasury proposed the separate, lower, standard price for Northern Ireland livestock the Ministry of Agriculture joined with the Ministry of Finance to reject the suggestion because it undermined the parity imperative and involved a charge on Northern Ireland funds.

From particularity to parity

According to Buckland the elusive balance between parity and particularity was attained during the inter war years when the regional Government was able to blend parity financial assistance with a distinctive agricultural policy. In marketing, for example, the Ministry of Agriculture was 'more interventionist and exploited its devolved powers to develop a policy of agricultural modernisation which differed significantly from the laissez-faire policy continued in Britain' (Buckland, 1979, p. 136). There is much to be said for this interpretation of the inter war period because regional policy did differ from that in Britain in several important respects, for example the Government refused demands for comprehensive agricultural credit facilities similar to those introduced in Britain in 1928. The regional Ministry was more activist because it needed to protect the reputation of Northern Ireland produce in Great Britain and because the almost peasant nature of farming in Northern Ireland impeded the creation of an educated, expert, and well informed agricultural elite with which the state could combine in the development of the industry.

Buckland's interpretation, however, ignores the fact that the greater part of the

Ministry's activities were not rooted in new primary legislation but in areas like education and research where much of the relevant policy was inherited from the pre partition period and based on British policy. Policy also developed within parameters set by the British Government. Harkness, for example, claimed that agricultural policy in the 1920s was 'placed upon the same basis as that adopted by the Government in Britain' which involved encouraging farmers to develop and modernize their industry through research, education, and cooperation (Harkness, 1935, p. xiv). Marketing was also central to British agricultural policy although the approach to implementation was essentially voluntary. In Northern Ireland there were compelling reasons for a compulsory strategy which nonetheless ran counter to prevailing ideological sympathies. Moreover the claim that the Northern Ireland marketing schemes of the 1930s illustrated the adaptability of the devolved institutions is unconvincing. For important sectors such as beef and cereals there was no adapted regional policy and Northern Ireland was included in British programmes. Regional marketing schemes for pigs and milk were framed in very close consultation with the British authorities and based upon the recommendations of the British reorganization commissions. The significant differences between the milk marketing schemes occurred largely because the regional Ministry was able to accept the recommendations of the Grigg Reorganisation Commission whereas British farmers were better organized than the UFU and thwarted the same approach because it was a derogation from producer control. Moreover, Ministry officials formulated the pigs and bacon schemes simply by editing and adding to copies of the British schemes. The administrative machinery may have differed in certain respects but the policy was essentially a national one.

Such differences do not demonstrate the existence of a distinctive agricultural policy in Northern Ireland in the 1930s but mark the limits of particularity which was very much secondary to the parity imperative. Finance was the key factor. Where Treasury help was at stake the Northern Ireland Government was quite prepared to follow the British example even when policies were totally unsuited to the region. Nevertheless the scope for particularity was most clearly present in the inter war period even though there was an inexorable trend towards parity.

The Second World War, however, was the zenith of parity when Northern Ireland agriculture was essentially directed from London with only restricted scope for administrative variation. Whilst the wartime integration was not intended to be permanent, the development of a national post war policy based on guaranteed prices ensured that the extent of particularity could not return to that possible before 1939. Inclusion in Part I of the 1947 Agriculture Act was dictated by the parity imperative and attenuated the scope for particularity in the efficiency provisions, not least because it was politically difficult for the British authorities to insist that its farmers be subject to stricter control. Moreover any significant derogation from the 1947 Act threatened parity and the hard won integration of Northern Ireland into the fundamental principles of national policy. Despite the claims of the UFU and others, the relevant sections of the Agriculture Act 1949 did not greatly differ in its essentials from the equivalent British provisions. The British authorities raised no serious objections to the absence of the power of dispossession and explicitly stated 'rules of good husbandry' in the Northern Ireland legislation not only because it was unsuitable and politically controversial but because they were satisfied that the regional Ministry had the necessary powers to ensure improved efficiency. The primary objective of the Ministry of Agriculture was to secure participation in the system of guaranteed prices and the adaptation of the British legislation was very much a secondary consideration to be pursued after parity was secure. In practice, moreover, the efficiency provisions of the 1947 Act fell into disuse after 1954 and sanctions such as dispossession were eventually repealed in the 1958 Agriculture Act.

By the 1950s the parity dynamic in agricultural policy was well established within the regional Government. The balance between parity and particularity which the Ministry of Agriculture attempted to strike was essentially chimerical because Treasury subsidies could not be conjoined with a distinctive regional agricultural policy. A compromise was agreed on the remoteness grant in which MAFF paid the money into the Northern Ireland Exchequer as a block grant. Specific expenditure was borne on Ministry of Agriculture votes but most assistance for Northern Ireland farmers continued to be funded directly by the British Exchequer. As a corollary to British support the Treasury insisted that it retain some control over the formulation and implementation of agricultural assistance programmes. The Ministry of Agriculture administered Treasury funded agricultural subsidies in Northern Ireland on behalf of MAF which was constitutionally responsible. In his guise as accounting officer, the Ministry's Permanent Secretary was responsible to ministers in London rather than his own in Belfast and it was the MAF auditors that had to be satisfied that money had been properly spent.

Whilst the Ministry of Agriculture retained some control over marketing its role was restricted to the administration of policies formulated at the national level in many important areas. It was not possible for the regional Ministry to vary schemes in Northern Ireland to any great extent. Broadly identical procedures for the implementation of guaranteed prices were essential and even schemes framed using the remoteness grant required Whitehall approval to ensure that they did not conflict with the main lines of national policy. Particularity in the administration of subsidies often reflected the extent to which the British authorities were prepared to permit differentiation and not the extent to which the Ministry wished to adapt schemes to local conditions. Two examples concerning land improvement schemes and potato guarantee payments illustrate the general point.

In Northern Ireland the Ministry of Agriculture administered land improvement schemes funded under the 1946 Hill Farming Act as the agent of MAF. In 1948 the Ministry of Agriculture's practice of allowing Northern Ireland farmers to claim a grant towards the cost of all labour including their own was questioned by the Treasury. MAF was sympathetic to the Northern Ireland case but pointed out that 'it would be very difficult to justify the variation in practice between the two countries if the matter were raised' (AG16/26/17). The Treasury was informed that 'strict adherence to the practice of disallowing an applicant's own services to rank for grant would cause considerable hardship to the majority of Northern Ireland hill farmers and might result in delay in the execution of schemes or failure to carry them out' (AG16/26/17). Such pleas cut no ice with the Treasury which could

> see no reason for treating Northern Ireland as a special case. Although, no doubt, there is a tendency towards small holdings in Northern Ireland it surely cannot be more marked than it is in North Wales...We are not influenced by the fact that for the purposes of their own schemes of assistance to farmers the Government of Northern Ireland allow personal labour to rank for grant. If they choose to increase the cost of these State-aided schemes by concessions of this kind, that is their affair and we cannot see any reason for departing from what we believe to be sound principles just because the Government of Northern Ireland make these unnecessary payments (AG16/26/17).

The issue of the 1960 potato deficiency payment also illustrates how inclusion in the system of guaranteed prices circumscribed the freedom of the Ministry of Agriculture to vary not only policy but also administration. A deficiency payment of £579,351 was allocated to the Ministry of Agriculture which administered the potato guarantee arrangements in Northern Ireland as the agent of MAFF. This was to be used for the benefit of growers but the British authorities insisted that it underwrite a stabilization fund for future price support operations. The UFU, supported by Stormont and Westminster MP's of all parties, argued that the money should be paid directly to growers of potatoes in 1960. One Westminster MP, for example, warned that 'the 1960 potato subsidy is one thing which will not be forgotten. We have a phrase in Northern Ireland, "Remember 1690". I am rather afraid that, if the Government do not do something, the potato farmers may say, "Remember 1960"' (HC Deb 682, c. 709). Whilst West was sympathetic with the growers position, little could be done. Although the Ministry had made the strongest possible representations MAFF had steadfastly 'refused us permission to give our potato producers any of this money in respect of the 1960 crop' (NIHC Deb 51, c. 945). The UFU continued to lobby on the matter and in 1965 a compromise was reached in which direct payments to 1960 growers were made with the greater part of the money and the remainder was allocated to a collective reserve support fund.

The argument of MAFF that potato growers in Northern Ireland were being 'treated no differently than those in the rest of the United Kingdom' shows how the parity principle limited the scope for particularity (Farmers' Journal, 4 January 1963, p. 45). Financial considerations were the motor behind the parity imperative but parity had more far reaching consequences in agricultural policy generally. After 1939 the basic priorities of a national agricultural policy were set at the Annual Reviews. If it was decided to discourage pig production, for example, this ruled out any regional policy designed to expand production because Northern Ireland was bound by the priorities laid down at Reviews. One of the most significant developments was the formulation of a small farmer policy for the United Kingdom. Despite the arguments of many in Northern Ireland that it was essential to have a scheme specially tailored to regional conditions which were completely different from those in Great Britain, the Ministry of Agriculture opted for a national programme which, it claimed, had been formulated with Northern Ireland in mind.

Even in marketing, the area of transferred jurisdiction most jealously guarded by the regional Parliament and administration, there was a clear trend towards parity with Great Britain. Despite resistance to United Kingdom schemes, national marketing boards were established for eggs and wool and an integrated policy was formulated for the United Kingdom. Although a separate Northern Ireland Milk Marketing Board was set up in the post war period it was necessary to have broadly uniform administrative arrangements because of the United Kingdom guarantee and standard quantity system.

Parity was the cardinal principle governing agricultural policy development in Northern Ireland during the Stormont period. There was pressure for a distinctive regional agricultural programme but the logic of parity was for regional policy, at least in its fundamentals, to be subsumed within a national policy for the United Kingdom as a whole. The Ministry of Agriculture was criticized by Nationalists for not taking a more independent line but it invariably stressed the link with Britain. West, for example, rejected a request for a regional agricultural enquiry committee because it could not serve any useful purpose. It was 'important to remember that the Northern Ireland agricultural industry operates within the economic framework determined by the United Kingdom Government' and that Northern Ireland received tremendous benefits from its inclusion in a national policy (NIHC Deb 65, c. 783). Future agricultural development could not

> be considered in isolation from that of the United Kingdom as a whole. Developments in Northern Ireland agriculture must depend largely on the agricultural policy planned for the entire United Kingdom. My Ministry is working closely with the other agricultural departments and the three Farmers' Unions in the formulation of this policy (NIHC Deb 56, c. 953).

A complex of reasons weakened the case for significant particularity in policy and indeed for administrative variation in many areas. Constitutionally the power to regulate imports belonged solely to the British Government; economically the influences of price, supply and demand were set outside Northern Ireland because of its dependence on the British market; politically it was impossible to resist the demands of farmers for equal treatment with their counterparts in Britain and parity was also a conscious political decision taken by the regional Government; ideologically the influence of laissez-faire limited the extent and nature of state action; culturally many farmers in Northern Ireland identified with their British counterparts and the UFU developed very close ties with the British Farmers'

Unions which strengthened the affinity with Britain and reinforced the parity imperative. In the final analysis, however, the key influence on the agricultural policy of the Northern Ireland Government was financial and the inability to subsidize farmers out of its own resources underpinned the parity approach. Other factors were important but financially the Government was 'not in a position to give subsidies over and above those available in Great Britain except insofar as they can use the remoteness grant for such purposes' (NIHC Deb 65, c. 790).

In a general sense agricultural policy between 1921 and 1972 can be described as one of parity but different pressures and circumstances at different times resulted in different combinations of parity and particularity. For example whilst particularity was at its strongest during the inter war period, the Second World War was the zenith of parity. Moreover individual coterminous policy decisions could exhibit diverse characteristics according to the particular influences at work in their formulation. The schemes for beef and milk in the 1930s, for example, occupied positions at opposite ends of the parity-particularity continuum. What actually developed in the post war period was a two tier agricultural policy sector, reflected in West's description of the role of the regional Ministry of Agriculture. On one level this was to

> ensure that the problems of Northern Ireland are known and understood by the Ministry of Agriculture, Fisheries and Food when matters of agricultural economic policy for the United Kingdom as a whole are being decided, for example, by the Annual Price Review, when negotiating trade agreements, et cetera, and, of course, to administer United Kingdom production grant schemes in Northern Ireland as agent for the Ministry of Agriculture, Fisheries and Food (NIHC Deb 65, c. 783-4).

At a secondary level, however, the Ministry's job was to 'initiate and carry out the various other aspects of the work which ...are purely a Northern Ireland responsibility' (NIHC Deb 65, c. 783-4). Whilst it was essential to keep the interests of Northern Ireland to the forefront the Ministry had always to

> be prepared to take a responsible view of the entire United Kingdom economy and be prepared to work responsibly within the framework of United Kingdom economic policy. There are times when in the interests of the United Kingdom as a whole we must be prepared to accept the rough with the smooth (NIHC Deb 65, c. 783-4).

Thus the formulation of overall policy goals on fundamental issues was done at a national level and here strict parity was the norm. Indeed there was really no regional policy at all but an integrated one for the United Kingdom as a whole. This was illustrated by West's pledge that the Ministry of Agriculture would 'continue to exercise the maximum influence possible in the formulation of United Kingdom agricultural policy' (NIHC Deb 65, c. 800). At the same time there was some scope for particularity in formulating programmes at a secondary policy level. There was a range of functions which were the sole responsibility of the

Ministry. These were financed purely from the Northern Ireland Exchequer and included 'items such as agricultural education, research and advisory work, crop and livestock improvement schemes, measures to eradicate and control animal diseases, drainage and minor watercourses and some type of agricultural development work' (NIHC Deb 65, c. 783-4). Nevertheless even in many of these areas it was often deemed desirable to follow the British example whilst adapting it to suit local conditions, in other words to seek a balance between parity and particularity. For example it was decided to extend the British agricultural safety legislation of 1956 to Northern Ireland even though regional conditions could justify a different policy. Some particularity was ensured because the objective was 'to ensure only that those regulations which are likely to be of special benefit in Northern Ireland will be applied here' (NIHC Deb 45, c. 395).

In terms of the general argument on the devolution experiment there is very little evidence from the agricultural policy sector to support Birrell and Murie's argument that 'in spite of very real constraints, Northern Ireland and its Government could and did diverge substantially from the standards and legislation operating at Great Britain and at Westminster. Independent action, different policies and substantially different legislation did emerge' (Birrell and Murie, 1980, p. 266). The quasi federal interpretation posits cooperation between effectively sovereign powers but in agriculture the Northern Ireland Government did not negotiate as an equal with the British Government. At Price Reviews the three Agricultural Departments in the United Kingdom cooperated but the lead was inevitably taken by MAFF because decisions taken affected all farmers throughout the United Kingdom. Moreover the Northern Ireland Ministry had the same status as the Scottish Department of Agriculture which did not operate in the context of legislative devolution.

Rather agricultural policy supports the contention that

> a small autonomous political unit within the United Kingdom could not afford politically to diverge substantially in respect of the services it provided from the standards set by the central Government and parliament in London... whatever freedom to legislate might exist in theory, financial constraints would compel substantial compliance with policies determined at the centre (Johnson, 1975, p. 4).

In Northern Ireland the political and financial limits imposed by the Government of Ireland Act gave very little scope for substantial variation in policy. The most that can be justified by the experience of agricultural policy is Buckland's contention that first and foremost the 'history of agricultural policy in Northern Ireland provides an overwhelming endorsement of the advantages to be derived from administrative devolution' (Buckland, 1979, p. 149). However the situation was not one of administrative devolution. The parity imperative was a deliberate political strategy on the part of the Ministry of Agriculture and the Northern Ireland Government which chimes with Birrell and Murie's contention that the adoption of British policies was the outcome of 'real political decisions and choices made at every stage' (Birrell and Murie, 1980, p. 266).

Even in the context of the parity imperative, legislative devolution had its advantages over the administrative variant enjoyed by the Scottish Department. In evidence to the Kilbrandon Commission, for example, Ministry of Agriculture officials stressed the greater freedom for particularity which Northern Ireland possessed and described the main difference in relation to Scotland as follows: 'if legislation is required to do something, we can have it passed within a matter of months whereas Scotland have often made the point that when they want to do something it may take them two or three years before time can be found for legislation at Westminster' (Cmnd 5460, 1973, para. 245). Although this was an exaggeration and the Ministry officials could not give concrete examples to back up their claim, there were certainly some occasions, albeit on relatively minor issues, when the Ministry was able to use devolved powers to introduce legislation quickly. Although Scottish or British legislation usually predated that of the Northern Ireland Parliament, the ability to delay legislation was equally important for the Ministry of Agriculture, for example on agricultural wages and safety. Perhaps the notion of 'executive devolution' is a better description because it allows for the existence of a regional assembly responsible for the specific implementation of policies whose general principles are set at a national level.

The inexorable trend throughout the devolution period was for agricultural policy to move steadily towards parity. However if specific policy programmes are plotted across time on a parity-particularity continuum, the policy pattern which emerges is extremely complex. In some programme areas, particularly price and production, the Stormont period saw a trend towards parity which eventually integrated Northern Ireland into a single 'national' agricultural policy for the United Kingdom as a whole, financed by the Treasury. In such areas Northern Ireland was often included within the scope of Westminster legislation (the post war Hill Farming Acts are an example). Although the concurrent nature of such policies gave the Northern Ireland Ministry some scope to implement them in the light of local conditions, the extent of particularity varied from programme to programme and was often closely related to the extent of Treasury liability. In other areas which were financed by the local Exchequer such as research, livestock improvement schemes, animal disease, and drainage, the Northern Ireland Ministry had greater autonomy and the policy pattern was characterized much more by particularity. An approximate calculation indicates that of all the agricultural legislation affecting Northern Ireland over the devolution period, 75 per cent was Stormont legislation and the rest came from Westminster. This, however, should not obscure the fact that variety is the key characteristic, even among policies underpinned by Stormont legislation. These ranged from the exceptional, where there was no Westminster equivalent (legislation relating to the flax sector for example), to parity measures which did little more than duplicate Westminster Acts.

Even in marketing Northern Ireland policy was much closer to parity in 1972 than at any previous time. By the 1960s many of the relatively wide powers over agricultural policy given to the Government of Northern Ireland had effectively been ceded back to Westminster in what amounted to a repudiation of the aims of the Government of Ireland Act. Throughout the period of devolution agricultural policy was essentially the product of tension between parity and particularity. By the end of the Stormont period however the Northern Ireland agricultural policy was assimilated into one for the United Kingdom as a whole to an extent which would have been unthinkable in 1920. Indeed the parity imperative was such that even some Stormont MP's, usually the last people to accept cheerily a diminution in their powers, openly admitted that despite the importance of the agricultural industry to Northern Ireland it was a policy sector where

> the major decisions lie not here but at Westminster. Here we have the Ministry doing a great job but its actual power affects only how the remoteness grant is paid out, how it educates people and what kind of drainage is carried out. These are the only things in which we have essential power. Most of the other aspects lie at the door of Westminster. It is there we must look over the next few years to see how the future of our agricultural industry is going to develop (John Taylor, NIHC Deb 63, c. 317-8).

6 State-farmer relations 1921-72

Formed in December 1917, the Ulster Farmers' Union (UFU) was the dominant farmers' association in Northern Ireland throughout the Stormont period. After partition the local Ministry became the natural focus for lobbying and was much more accessible than the Dublin department had been. Indeed Archdale and his officials proved to be so sympathetic that the UFU remarked that it was because relations were 'so friendly, the contact so immediate and continuous, that we are sincerely anxious that this constant contact, so mutually advantageous, shall not be jeopardized or broken' (Farmers' Journal, November 1922, p. 1022).

Consultation

The consultative status granted to the UFU was immediately evident when the first piece of agricultural legislation, the Livestock Breeding Bill of 1922, was submitted to the Union prior to publication. According to J.M. Mark, the Union scrutinized it and 'suggested some improvements which we thought might be put into the Bill, and the Ministry at once agreed and have done everything in their power to do what is fair and reasonable' (NIHC Deb 2, c. 678). Similarly, in January 1948 Harkness wrote to the UFU offering a meeting to discuss the Agriculture Bill and enclosing a 'secret and confidential' memorandum for the perusal of those members who would be attending. Having ascertained the views of the UFU, the Ministry of Agriculture went ahead with the preparation of the first draft of the Bill which was finally considered by the Cabinet on 21 October 1948 and approved after a number of alterations.

Close and regular contact with farmers was also in the interests of the Ministry of Agriculture. It was because Ulster farmers were sceptical about the benefits of expenditure on education, research and marketing, and reluctant to adopt new methods voluntarily, that the Ministry became convinced of the need for state direction and regulation. To ameliorate state intervention, the Ministry adopted a strategy which involved working with and through agricultural associations 'so as to provide that combination of effort which is essential if administrative measures for the development of agriculture are to attain the fullest success' (Ministry of Agriculture, 1924, p. 1). Above all, the Ministry's strategy required a close working relationship with the UFU and, paradoxically, the breakdown of Ministry-UFU relations in the late 1930s is a good indication that consultation was the norm. As farmers grew increasingly disillusioned with state control, a group of Unionist backbenchers - including the UFU President Moore, Elliott, and Gamble - voted against the Government on a series of marketing bills because of excessive state direction and insufficient consultation with farmers. The approach of the regional Ministry was contrasted with the position in Britain, where producer initiation and control of marketing schemes was normal, and was attributed to the autocratic approach of Scott Robertson and other senior officials. The UFU also opposed the Government on a number of extremely important rural issues which were not specifically within the remit of the Ministry of Agriculture, including land annuities, market tolls, rural electrification, and the 1935 Road Transport Act.

Such disquiet was an important element of the more general criticism of government incompetence and malaise within Unionist ranks. This was reflected in the Progressive Unionists' 1938 election manifesto which adopted in full the programme of the UFU. The UFU called for a reduction in land annuities, exemption from the provisions of the Transport Act of all agricultural produce and inputs, the implementation of marketing schemes only with the consent of the producers concerned as in Britain, and an investigation of the valuations of farmers houses (Harbinson, 1973, p. 220). During the election the UFU urged farmers to ascertain the views of all candidates before casting their votes. A questionnaire was issued to candidates asking whether or not they would vote for legislation to guarantee to producers a price to cover their production costs and amend the Transport Act, and whether they would support the adoption in Northern Ireland of the usual British practice of introducing white papers and undertaking extensive consultation prior to legislation being introduced (Farmers' Journal, February 1938, p. 230).

With the outbreak of war, however, consultation was not only re-established but raised to a new level. Dissemination of information was the key to the food production campaign and for Brooke it was 'obvious that more will be accomplished by persuasion and the general goodwill and anxiety of the farming community to help than by the instrument of compulsion' (AG16/18/16). In the United Kingdom as a whole the war institutionalized consultative procedures and in Northern Ireland, as elsewhere, the UFU and the network of County Agricultural Committees were vital conduits through which information on the tillage campaign was transmitted to farmers. Despite the deterioration in the relationship between the Union and the Ministry in the late 1930s the September 1939 issue of The Farmers' Journal affirmed that to preserve democratic principles, those which the Union had been fighting the Ministry for,

106

all sectional differences of opinion and purpose must, for the duration of the struggle, give way to active and intense co-operation with the Government of the day...As farmers, the duty will be to produce food in abundance for the fighting forces...Those in control must be supported and facilitated to the very limits. Obstruction, or even half-hearted co-operation, will be a form of national sabotage (Farmers' Journal, September 1939, p. 28).

For both the UFU and the Ministry, the success of the tillage campaign depended on continuous consultation. Shortly after the declaration of war the UFU informed the Ministry of its willingness to 'place the whole resources of the Union and its services at the disposal of the Government to assist, and, if need be, undertake the administration of any essential war-time agricultural legislation necessary in the national interest' (Farmers' Journal, November 1939, p. 84). To facilitate consultation the UFU followed the NFU example and created a War Committee which according to the Union was granted 'direct access to the Minister and to his Department at all times' (Farmers' Journal, February 1940, p. 151). The UFU also claimed that an understanding was reached with the Minister whereby meetings could be arranged at short notice on the initiative of either side, with such meetings to 'take place frequently for a free and frank exchange of views on all matters affecting farmers as they develop and arising from the national emergency' (Farmers' Journal, February 1940, p. 151; NIHC Deb 23, c. 1038-9). In reciprocation, Brooke expressed his indebtedness to the War Committee of the UFU which had been 'a great help' and together they were 'able to rub off many edges that might have created trouble in the country' (NIHC Deb 23, c. 1022).

Although fundamental policy differences were set aside for the duration of the emergency there were still disagreements on matters of administrative detail, particularly concerning the operation of the meat and livestock control scheme. One MP, for example, complained about the lack of information on grading decisions. According to Nixon surely no one was going to 'contend that it would be of any use to the enemy to know the weight of John Smith's dead cow...What is of advantage to the enemy is the bickering, discontent and disquiet that have been stirred up amongst the people by withholding information' (NIHC Deb 23, c. 455-6). An agreement was reached in early 1942 which according to the UFU gave it the right to appoint four qualified and responsible people to have confidential access to grading returns. A small committee of the Union would meet periodically with the Ministry to check upon the accuracy of the grading of livestock and also to give advice on the administration of the scheme (Farmers' Journal, February 1942, p. 131).

The close relationship between the UFU and the Ministry of Agriculture was also criticized by jealous MP's who accused the Ministry of ignoring Parliament. Such complaints led to the formation of a back bench Parliamentary Agricultural Committee and Brooke gave an assurance that he would consult with this committee on the various control schemes. From 1942-43 the Ministry also sent a confidential memorandum on its policy and work to MP's in recognition of the fact that the wartime requirement for secrecy limited public discussion.

A key assumption in the Ministry of Agriculture's consultation strategy was that the support of a responsible, representative, and monopolistic farmers' union could help legitimize state intervention, persuade farmers to accept policies, and facilitate policy formulation and administration. Indeed so central was a strong farmers' association to its strategy that the Ministry actively fostered the development of the UFU and it was partly because of this that the Ministry was generally successful in neutralising opposition to its programme, except for the period at the end of the 1930s.

The UFU performed an invaluable ameliorative role in helping the Ministry defuse criticism of policy. When the Ministry of Finance proposed to reduce the grant for rate relief in 1926, for example, the UFU leadership warned that any reduction would create internal problems which would make it much more difficult to carry the membership with them in the future, particularly in the light of the opposition which there had been inside the Union to the establishment of the experimental farm. At a meeting with Craig, Pollock and Archdale a UFU delegation stressed that the supplementary grant had been of great assistance to them in carrying 'the majority of farmers with them in a number of matters directly affecting the relationship between the Government and the Farmers' Union' (CAB9E/47/1). Archdale agreed with the UFU and warned that to reduce the amount of rate relief would 'bring about the most severe criticism, friction and bad feeling from the agricultural community' (CAB9E/47/1). During the war the UFU helped deliver the cooperation of farmers in return for the sympathetic administration of the schemes of physical control by the state. For the UFU the success of the tillage campaign depended largely on the approach of the Ministry and 'if the hand of fellowship is extended; if the whys and wherefores are explained to them; if their leaders whom they trust are consulted, and if miles of red tape and trimmings are left to one side "for the duration", then the very best will be secured from the Ulster farming community' (Farmers' Journal, October 1939, p. 58).

The 1949 Agriculture Act

The UFU's pivotal role in selling unpopular aspects of policy is clear from the controversy surrounding the 1949 Agriculture Act. The Act was needed to implement the efficiency measures which were the corollary of the guaranteed prices and assured markets provided for by the 1947 United Kingdom Act. The Ministry of Agriculture's initial proposals to ensure efficient farming were almost identical to those in the equivalent British legislation, including the last resort power to dispossess a farmer from the land. Although Nugent was the most vociferous opponent of these proposals within the Cabinet, Brooke's acute political antennae recognized they needed to be amended to make the Bill more palatable to the Government's supporters in Parliament and in the country, and to farmers generally. Whilst some state supervision was necessary for increased efficiency Brooke considered that the 'powers which the Ministry proposes to take are extremely wide, and that the justification for such powers has not been fully proven' (AG16/26/1).

Moore appreciated that the legislation would be controversial and create political difficulties but there was 'simply no option but to proceed with the Bill. Otherwise we endanger the whole economic position of the agricultural industry. What I want to do is to make the Bill as free as possible from the possibility of any charge of being autocratic or bureaucratic' (AG16/26/1). However initial modifications to the Bill, such as the decision to allow a right of appeal against dispossession, failed to assuage Cabinet unease and Moore was forced to agree that 'the proposal to include in the Bill the ultimate sanction of eviction and the power to compel an unsatisfactory farmer to let his land should be dropped' (CAB4/739). State control was therefore much weaker than in the equivalent British Acts. This was certainly a wise move because the UFU subsequently had difficulty in persuading farmers to accept the revised legislation and in any case would have been 'bitterly opposed to dispossession as a step back a century to the bad old days of landlordist evictions and Captain Boycott. We had too much of a struggle to reach our present position to stand by and see it sacrificed' (Farmers' Journal, December 1948, p. 118).

The Ministry's proposals were discussed with the UFU, the County Committees of Agriculture, and at a Unionist Party meeting. Moore emphasized to the UFU that the Ministry had 'done its best to shape the Bill so as to make it acceptable to the farming community and it would be helpful to him if he could claim that the reaction of the Union's representatives were favourable' (AG16/26/1). Although the UFU acknowledged the need for efficiency legislation, there was still some opposition to the draft bill within the UFU delegation, especially about the rules of good husbandry. Whilst a majority were prepared to accept the Bill in principle the delegation refused to give unqualified support to the draft legislation and decided to consult the membership. This reflected widespread rank and file hostility to increased state control. It also confirmed Moore's initial fear that the separation of the efficiency legislation from the 1947 Act would cause difficulties because it would give farmers the impression that they could have the guaranteed prices without state control. The time lag between the British Act of 1947 and the introduction of the Bill meant that for 18 months farmers in Northern Ireland had received guaranteed prices without being subject to the corresponding state direction to promote efficiency. As a result many ordinary farmers had difficulty in making the connection between the two and there was much ill informed criticism of the legislation, even deliberate misrepresentation. For the UFU's Omagh branch the 'threat to impose heavy penalties, terms of imprisonment and dispossession of lands is characteristic of Russia and not of a democratic country' (Belfast News Letter, 9 December 1948). Significantly, however, after hearing the leadership explain the effects of the legislation at a special UFU meeting, a delegate from Omagh refused to support his branch's resolution because it completely misrepresented the true position.

To assuage the concerns of rank and file farmers ignorant of the horse trading between Union and Government, the UFU leadership made great play of the fact that 'the essential difference between the British and Ulster Bills was that in the Ulster Bill there was no question in any shape or form of dispossession or eviction' (Farmers' Journal, December 1948, p. 118). Indeed the Ministry was praised for adapting the bill to the particular conditions of Northern Ireland. The political and symbolic importance of land ownership, for example, justified a different course of action because the vast majority of farmers in Northern Ireland were owner occupiers whereas tenant farming was much commoner in Britain.

The Ministry helped the UFU to sell the Bill to its membership. Harkness sent Wadsworth, the UFU President, a copy of the amendments to the Bill drafted after intensive discussions with the farmers' representatives which were to be introduced at the Committee stage. This was in the hope that they 'will help you with the difficult meetings which you are having this week. You know, of course, not to quote the actual words of the amendment but merely their substance. Having them in front of you, however, will I hope be a help' (AG16/26/1). This enabled the UFU to claim that it had wrought many valuable concessions from the Ministry. Although there was still some strident opposition to the Bill a large majority of delegates at a special meeting passed a resolution which approved of the leadership's action in its negotiations with the Government.

For the leadership of the UFU most of the criticism of the Agriculture Bill was ill informed, misleading and unfair. To remove any misapprehensions the UFU clarified its position in several editorials in The Farmers' Journal and the President, Wadsworth, issued a statement outlining the reasons why the Bill was necessary in the best interests of Northern Ireland farmers. It had been repeatedly explained since the end of the war that the British Government and the three Farmers' Unions had entered into 'an honourable and binding agreement' on agricultural policy under which the provision of guaranteed prices and assured markets was made conditional upon the achievement of a reasonable standard of efficiency (Farmers' Journal, January 1949, p. 151). The British Acts had been passed without controversy but when it came to the turn of the Northern Ireland Minister of Agriculture

> the first discordant note was heard. Nor was this discordant note related to this or that clause of the Bill, but was more directed towards a complete reversal of the declaration of policy made and agreed upon two years previously. This extraordinary and unusual procedure has been, and still is, very difficult to understand, and the only logical explanation of the whole affair appears to be downright lack of knowledge and understanding not only of procedure, but of the general agricultural policy involved (Farmers' Journal, January 1949, p. 151).

A great deal of sheer nonsense had been talked about the provisions to ensure good husbandry which 'have caused the most comment, and raised the most controversy, which has resulted in unfounded apprehension and misgivings by some farmers' (Farmers' Journal, February 1949, p. 192). Good husbandry simply meant managing the land well and did not imply compulsory tillage or production except in those rare cases where someone was farming badly. Furthermore the Bill incorporated many safeguards against the abuse of administrative powers but even where directions were not complied with there was no possibility of nationalization or eviction, simply a maximum fine of £100. Ministry direction did not impinge upon hard won property rights as the crops and the land would still belong to the farmer.

On the 1949 Agriculture Act, therefore, the UFU was able to consolidate its position by claiming credit for the absence of the more unpleasant features of the British legislation. In return the passage and implementation of the Act was smoothed for the Ministry by the support of the dominant and most representative farmers' union.

Monopoly representation

The Ministry of Agriculture fostered the UFU as a monopolistic association. This was helped by the absence of any credible alternative to the UFU as a sectoral organization in marked contrast to the position in Britain in the inter war period where the agricultural policy network was more akin to open competitive pluralism (Smith, 1990, ch. 3). After partition the Ministry of Agriculture continued the DATII's practice of assisting agricultural cooperation and grant aided the UAOS which, for example, received £1,200 on a pound for pound basis in 1923-24. In 1925, this grant was discontinued on the grounds that it had not been utilized to the extent envisaged. However the grant had to be restored in 1927, albeit at a much lower level, after MP's such as Rowley Elliott alleged that the cooperative movement was being discriminated against (NIHC Deb 9, c. 1558).

In its early years the inability to increase membership (which actually fell between 1920-24) threatened the very existence of the UFU. Indeed when faced with financial collapse at the end of 1922, primarily as a result of the post war agricultural depression and of the difficulties experienced in increasing membership, the UFU appealed to the Ministry of Agriculture for help. In response the Government sanctioned vital special assistance. A state grant of £1,000 represented some 47 per cent of the UFU's total income in 1923-24; in 1925-26 the proportion was 52 per cent and in 1928-29 the grant of £1,300 accounted for over 60 per cent of the UFU's income, the sum from its own resources being just £854 (AG/16/16/10). From 1930 the amount of the grant was gradually reduced until on the outbreak of the Second World War it amounted to just £300, representing some 17 per cent of the total revenue of the UFU. The desire of the Ministry of Finance to discontinue the grant during the war was strongly resisted by the Ministry of Agriculture and the UFU. Lord Glentoran supported the UFU's claim for an increase because of the 'value of the educational activities of the Union in the dissemination of information to the agricultural community in an unofficial manner at the present time when the help and co-operation of the farming community is so necessary' (AG16/16/10). In 1943 however, when the financial position had sufficiently improved under the stimulus of the war so that the grant of £100 represented only four per cent of its income, the UFU was at last able to stop asking the Government for help.

The state grant undoubtedly kept the UFU afloat but for political reasons it had to be portrayed as help for its educational and organizational work. Nonetheless the grant provoked considerable hostility. Urban trade unionists such as McGuffin and Grant argued that the Government should not subsidize a body which not only protected the farmers interests but which in practice acted as a ring for fixing prices and was against the interests of consumers (NIHC Deb 4, c. 865). Some agricultural interests, on the other hand, regarded the grant as an attempt by the Government to buy the acquiescence of the UFU with regard to agricultural policy. Elliott, for example, argued that it prevented the free and unfettered expression of independent opinion on agricultural policy and agreed with those who described it as 'hush money, or the price of silence' (NIHC Deb 9, c. 1554). Pressed to justify the expenditure, Archdale stressed the great support which the Union gave to the Ministry in its efforts to modernize agriculture: from day one the Ministry had the 'greatest support and help from the Ulster Farmers' Union...When our classes and our meetings are held in the various counties the Farmers' Union assist materially in attracting the right audiences to attend and listen to our instructors and lecturers' (NIHC Deb 8, c. 402). The UFU rejected the accusation that it was in the pocket of the Government and argued that its general support for Government policy was only given after detailed consideration and in the best interests of agriculture. According to Mark they had 'not hesitated, as occasion arose, both to criticize and oppose, and as a result of our representations we have, on not a few occasions, succeeded in securing amendments of policy which we felt to be essential' (NIHC Deb 9, c. 2102).

Such controversy reflected the fact that whilst the UFU may have been responsible it certainly was not representative of the agricultural industry as a whole, especially before 1939. The UFU led a very precarious existence for the whole of the inter war period and found it very difficult to get established, particularly in the western counties. Although the dominant farmers' association, the inability to organize even a bare majority of farmers could have weakened its claims for a representational monopoly. In 1937, despite rising membership, the UFU bemoaned the fact that after 20 years only a small proportion of farmers were members. If it represented 75 per cent of farmers then its 'power for good would be enormous, and we can only wonder that it has accomplished so much when only about 15 per cent are members. These are, of course, the most intelligent and far seeing of our men, and consequently carry more weight than their numbers might lead one to expect' (Farmers' Journal, May 1937, p. 1019). As in the case of the NFU, the war boosted the membership of the UFU and helped support its consultative monopoly. At the beginning of the 1960s, however, the UFU, in sharp contrast to the NFU, could claim to represent only 50 per cent of farmers although this was said to include four fifths of 'effective farmers'.

Despite this, the representatives of farmers on government agencies, advisory committees, and committees of enquiry were invariably drawn from the UFU. On the Pigs Marketing Board, for example, the influence of the UFU was evident from the beginning. Not only did its members dominate the Board (on the interim board appointed by the Ministry of Agriculture nine of the 11 producer representatives were members of the UFU) but Craig agreed to its suggestion that the Permanent Secretary of the Ministry, J.S. Gordon, become the first chair of the Board because of his wide knowledge of agriculture and of the confidence which he inspired in the farming community (CAB9E/57/2). The UFU was also recognized as the representative voice of Northern Ireland farmers by the British authorities for the purposes of the Annual Reviews. An amendment to the 1949 Agriculture Act followed the British practice and required the Minister to consult whichever organization appeared to him to represent the interests of farmers when appointing members to advisory committees. It was made abundantly clear, however, that this would be the UFU as no other body could claim to represent the farmers of Northern Ireland. This in fact contradicted the original reasons for the creation of such committees, notably that the Ministry was 'dependent for advice almost entirely upon the Ulster Farmers' Union. While in no way detracting from the value of the Union, it is considered that the Ministry should be in a position to call upon as wide a range of interests as possible' (AG16/26/1).

On the membership of the Agricultural Trust, West rejected an amendment that the Ministry should appoint 'not more than four' UFU representatives to the Trust. He accepted the UFU's contention that because the Trust was funded from the remoteness grant, which was producers money, farmers should therefore have a say in how it was spent. This left Phelim O'Neill with the distinct 'impression that the Minister himself is literally under the heel of the Ulster Farmers' Union' and he alleged that by insisting on four UFU appointees West was trying to safeguard against some future occasion when there would be a Minister who was 'less subservient to the Ulster Farmers' Union than he is' (NIHC Deb 64, c. 1854, 1863). Although the amendment was defeated West took note of the back bench revolt and accepted another amendment to the effect that 'not fewer than two nor more than four' representatives should be appointed from a panel put forward by the UFU.

The representativeness of the UFU and its connections with the Unionist establishment was questioned by Nationalist MP's such as Patrick and Tom Gormley, themselves Union members. On the Agricultural Trust dispute Patrick Gormley alleged that West's 'brain power is provided by the Ulster Farmers' Union. It comes up here and dictates terms to members' (NIHC Deb 64, c. 1863). This reflected a widespread concern that the UFU, and government policy generally, took insufficient notice of the interests of small farmers and cooperatives who were also overlooked when appointments were being made. A common complaint was that the UFU was 'no longer a body working for the good of the ordinary farmer in the field. There are too many marketing board interests; too much automatic acquiescence in everything the Ministry of Agriculture does or says whether beneficial to the farmer or not' (Farmweek, 14 December 1965).

Such criticism of the UFU had wider political overtones. The inability to organize more than half of the total number of farmers, for example, prompted the Nationalist MP Harry Diamond to ask if the UFU's consultative monopoly was 'based on the good old Unionist principle of one vote equals two?' (NIHC Deb 48, c. 2559). In the early 1960s disaffection with the UFU was reflected in agitation for an alternative union 'devoted to the interests of the small farmer be he Protestant, Catholic or dissenter, Orangeman or Hibernian' (Farmweek, 3 August 1965). Although the leadership stressed the non sectarian nature of the Union there was nonetheless a sectarian dimension to the low membership density which was also linked to the small farmer problem. By no means all small farmers were Catholic but much of the agitation for a new union was based in the western counties such as Tyrone which had a higher density of Catholics than those counties in the east which contained most of the larger Protestant farmers who dominated the UFU. Many Protestant farmers, however, also pressed for a breakaway union and the sectarian dimension is important precisely because it reinforced the economic cleavage between large and small farmers.

The UFU nevertheless managed to prevent the formation of a rival union until after the fall of the Stormont regime, bolstered by the Unionist Government's zealous protection of the consultative monopoly. The Ministry recognized the UFU as representative of the majority agricultural interest in Northern Ireland. An alternative small farmers' association - the Northern Ireland Agricultural Producers' Association (NIAPA) - did not become established until 1975. The fact that the UFU had some 27,000 members was, in West's opinion, 'ample justification for my regarding it as being the mouthpiece of the agricultural industry. I know myself, because I am a member of that Union, that the vast majority of worthwhile farmers in Northern Ireland are members of the Ulster Farmers' Union' (NIHC Deb 64, c. 229).

Ideological consensus

The relationship between the UFU and the Ministry of Agriculture was also characterized by a shared ideology, rooted in the parity imperative. Indeed an elite consensus extended beyond agricultural policy to the very existence of the state itself and the relationship with Britain. This helps to explain the faster development of the agricultural policy network in Northern Ireland compared with that in Britain, where the dominant NFU-MAFF relationship was essentially a post 1939 phenomenon. Although farmers generally were sceptical, the leadership of the UFU shared the Ministry's conviction that improvements in research, education and marketing, were essential to agricultural prosperity, illustrated by the establishment of the Agricultural Research Station at Hillsborough. The UFU leadership agreed that state direction was essential to improve marketing and pressed for legislation for the compulsory inspection and grading of produce for export and for the formulation of marketing schemes.

Nevertheless there was frequent conflict between the UFU and the Ministry on the issue of producer control of marketing schemes, especially in the 1930s, and on state direction generally. Although the UFU accepted the need for marketing reform, the bureaucratic, Ministry sponsored and controlled schemes in Northern Ireland were unfavourably compared with the democratic, producer sponsored and controlled schemes in Britain. Even after 1945 the UFU and the Ministry continued to disagree on the question of state control, for example to achieve the targets set for regional agriculture in the national expansion programme announced in 1947. When Moore resorted to increased state direction because farmers had ignored appeals voluntarily to plough more than the minimum tillage quota, the UFU voiced its 'entire and complete disagreement' with the Minister's decision to 'substitute compulsion and force for co-operation and good will' (Farmers' Journal, January 1948, p. 150). The reasons were familiar and were grounded in the parity imperative. Farmers in Northern Ireland were being treated unfairly compared with those in the rest of the United Kingdom where a voluntary approach had been agreed with the Farmers' Unions. The

> peoples of the British Empire fought side by side in two world wars against dictatorship, and under these circumstances it is small wonder that the farmers of Ulster are protesting vigorously...we would appeal to the Government to show real statesmanship and understanding by dropping this fetish of compulsion and give to the farmers of Ulster the same freedom of action to do the job well as is given to their fellow farmers in England, Scotland and Wales (Farmers' Journal, February 1948, p. 171).

Farmers had reacted with such hostility to the increased tillage quota because 'while English and Scottish farmers have been freed from the bondage of direction and compulsion, and are being treated as men of their word, Ulster farmers are still being treated by their Minister and the Government as a lot of slopers and slackers and shirkers' (Farmers' Journal, February 1948, p. 191). Minford, himself a Union member, contrasted the position with 1939 when Moore, as President of the UFU, had criticized the Ministry's penchant for state intervention. Either the Minister was 'putty in the hands of officials', or the 'conversion of Paul was nothing to the conversion of the Minister' (NIHC Deb 32, c. 142). Other Unionist back benchers, however, argued that the UFU was trying to dictate to the Government whose responsibility it was to govern 'not in accordance with sectional interests but in accordance with the interests of the whole community' (NIHC Deb 32, c. 154). MacManaway also pointed out that the UFU was arguing against compulsory tillage yet at the same time asking the Minister of Commerce to nationalize the electricity undertakings. Apparently 'the principle of compulsion was only objectionable when it applied to them, but they were perfectly prepared to its being applied to other sections' (NIHC Deb 32, c. 175).

Serious disputes also arose on the issue of participation in United Kingdom marketing schemes, which the UFU were convinced would protect price parity after decontrol. For example, whilst Moore appreciated the UFU's desire to cooperate with the other British Unions it was his responsibility 'to decide what was best for Northern Ireland agricultural interests even though this decision might conflict with the views of the Ulster Farmers' Union' (CAB9E/57/4). The UFU interpreted adverse decisions on the herbage seeds and fatstock schemes in the traditional manner. It was intolerable that British farmers had the right to control the marketing of their own produce whereas those in Northern Ireland could 'only look forward, at best, to some form of hybrid advisory committee which will have no effective control over Civil Service administration of the schemes' (CAB9E/57/4). The UFU would use all legitimate means to ensure that 'Ulster farmers will have no less a measure of control than their opposite numbers in Great Britain' (CAB9E/57/4).

There appears to be a fundamental ideological difference on the issue of state direction, therefore. However, whilst there certainly was always a section of the farming community opposed to any degree of state direction the UFU leadership was often equivocal. This may be explained in terms of an attempt to balance general support for Ministry policy with the need to retain that of its rank and file. It was the parity imperative which was the keystone of the agricultural policy of both Government and UFU, and underpinned policy consensus on issues such as marketing reform and the 1949 Act. Progress towards parity was slow in the inter war years because of strong Treasury opposition but it was the dominant productionist ideology of the post war period that strengthened the hand of the Northern Ireland Government in its attempt to ensure that its farmers received the benefits of high state support. The Ministry and the UFU shared the policy imperative that Northern Ireland be included Part I of the 1947 Act. There seems to have been little opposition to this in London where there was recognition of the contribution which Ulster farmers could make to increased food production. Nugent's argument that it would be better to opt out of the 1947 Act completely rather than accept state directed efficiency found little support in the Cabinet or in the farming community. Just as marketing reform had been the price to be paid for protection in the 1930s, so state direction to promote efficiency was the price of inclusion in the post war system of guaranteed prices. As usual the approach was firstly to ensure financial parity and then to secure as much flexibility as possible in administering the policy at the regional level. For the UFU leadership particularity in administration, although desirable, was never likely to take precedence over the parity imperative. The Union's acceptance of responsibility for efficient production on behalf of Ulster farmers had been approved by a large majority and had

> further consolidated their position of equality, as regards prices and markets, with English and Scottish farmers. It would be easy to lose that position by

refusing to accept the responsibility, for the British Government would not be justified in continuing to pay the same level of prices or to maintain the various subsidies to an industry which would do nothing to secure efficiency of production. Those irresponsible people who criticise the Union for this action either refuse or are unable to recognise this danger, and it is well that farmers should be aware that these people do not and cannot offer any alternative to the Bill (Farmers' Journal, February 1949, p. 190).

Policy networks and state-farmer relations

The notion of interest intermediation between governments and interest groups has underpinned most explanations of state-farmer relations. The classical pluralist model of interest intermediation is characterized by open group competition and bargaining. Corporatism, which in part developed as a critique of pluralist orthodoxy, involves a process of social closure, a concentration of power in a few dominant economic-corporate or producer groups who are in a cooperative relationship with the state. These groups enjoy self regulation to implement bargains negotiated with the state. In the alternative corporate pluralism and policy community approaches the stress is on the sectoral nature of policy making and the restricted nature of group competition; indeed such approaches, not classical pluralism, were the accepted wisdom for many years. The policy networks approach also emphasizes the 'need to disaggregate policy analysis and stresses that relationships between groups and Government vary between policy areas' (Rhodes and Marsh, 1992a, p. 4).

Jordan and Schubert have proposed 'a typology in which network is a generic label' embracing the different types of relationship between state and interest group (Jordan and Schubert, 1992, p. 10). A number of different subtypes of policy network are plotted against three main variables: the level of institutionalization (stability), the scope of the policy making arrangement (sectoral or transectoral), and the number of participants (degree to which the network is open or closed). Thus open issue networks and pressure pluralism are ad hoc and include a large number of groups (although the former is transectoral and the latter sectoral). By contrast meso corporatism and clientelism are stable, sectoral networks with only one participating group. State and societal corporatism are stable, transectoral networks with two conflicting groups. The other variants - including corporate pluralism, iron triangles, policy community, and negotiated economy - are stable, sectoral networks with a restricted number of groups. The alternative typology developed by Rhodes and Marsh has policy communities and issue networks as end points on a policy network continuum, differentiated according to the number of participants, type of interest involved, frequency of interaction of groups, continuity, consensus, resources, and the distribution of power. For example a policy community is characterized by a limited number of participants, frequent interaction and ideological consensus; an issue network by

117

many participants, fluctuating interaction and absence of consensus (Rhodes and Marsh, 1992b).

Such lists of network subtypes are not exhaustive. La Palombara, for example, has identified clientela and parentela patterns of interest intermediation. Clientela is characterized by a relationship of mutual dependence between an administrative agency and an interest group which is recognized by the agency as the natural representative of a given social sector; parentela by kinship or close fraternal ties between an interest group and a political party (La Palombara, 1964). Parentela relationships occur in political systems where there is a 'single dominant party or faction, and in which pressure groups must gain access and legitimacy through their attachment to that particular party rather than through their ability effectively to represent a sector of the society' (Peters, 1989, p. 167).

Theories of interest intermediation and agricultural policy in Britain

There is general agreement that an extremely close relationship developed in Britain in the post war period between MAFF and the NFU. Wilson, for example, refers to a 'community of shared beliefs and attitudes', Cox *et al.* to a 'sophisticated corporatist relationship', and Grant argues that British farmers had 'successfully developed a symbiotic political relationship with the state' (Grant, 1983, p. 141; Cox, Lowe and Winter, 1986, p. 487; Wilson, 1977, p. 45).

Initial analyses of British agricultural policy such as those by Self and Storing, and by Wilson, used pluralism. The close relationship between the NFU and MAFF was not that of agency capture or clientelism; rather the pattern of policy making was essentially one of departmental pluralism where MAFF was no more than the responsible department which administered Government policy 'under the supervision of the Cabinet and its adjunct of Treasury control' (Self and Storing, 1962, p. 232).

Corporatist theories have also been applied to British agricultural policy. For Cox *et al.* the Annual Review machinery created by the 1947 Agriculture Act was the 'major, if not the pre-eminent example, of corporatism in British industry', involving self-regulation of farmers in return for the privileges of a closed, monopolistic relationship with the state and the exclusion of other interests (Cox, Lowe and Winter, 1986, p. 480). The NFU was incorporated into the process of policy making and implementation and in return was expected to deliver the assent, or at least acquiescence, of the farming community to the annual price package.

A comprehensive critique of both pluralist and corporatist interpretations of the relationship between MAFF and the NFU has been provided by Smith. The pluralists' concentration on observable conflict results in a failure to examine the 'historical, ideological and structural factors' that led to the creation of consensus on agricultural policy between MAFF and the NFU (Smith, 1990, p. 19). According to Smith, corporatist explanations are an improvement because they focus on the exclusion of some groups from the policy process. Nevertheless, they over estimate the role of the NFU in policy implementation: 'despite having corporatist features the Annual Review was not a corporatist relationship' because it did not involve conflicting economic interests, the bureaucracy was not autonomous, the role of the farmers in the implementation of policy was limited, and the degree of bargaining was restricted (Smith, 1989, p. 95). In his anxiety to refute both pluralist and corporatist interpretations, however, Smith gives a contradictory account of the role of MAFF in the policy process. So whilst 'Whitehall pluralism' is criticized on the grounds that the influence of the Treasury and other departments was limited, his critique of the corporatist interpretation partly rests on the assertion that MAFF was 'basically implementing Government policy which was to increase production' (Smith, 1990, p. 27). Of course MAFF implemented government policy in a formal sense but this ignores the important role played by the Ministry in formulating the productionist policy in the first place. Indeed although Smith suggests that MAFF lacked autonomy with respect to other state structures, he goes on to argue that by incorporating the farmers, MAFF 'created the ability to develop and administer agricultural policy. This has increased its autonomy because it has closed the policy off to other departments and interests' (Smith, 1990, p. 55). If a corporatist arrangement requires both autonomy from state structures and from society, then it is in respect of the latter that the corporatist case is weakened. Indeed Smith recognizes this when he states that the incorporation of the farmers reduced the autonomy of MAFF by 'creating dependence on the farmers and limiting the extent to which any Government can change agricultural policy' (Smith, 1990, p. 55).

Smith's explanation links the policy community concept both to state autonomy and to the structural and ideological factors involved in the play of power. Thus a policy community may also be 'a means of mobilising bias so that the agenda is controlled...a social arrangement for preventing the discussion of issues that threatens the community' (Smith, 1990, p. 46). His account emphasizes the importance of mutually reinforcing ideological and institutional structures: a dominant set of shared beliefs protects the institutions by 'justifying the inclusion of certain interests and preventing the conceptions of alternatives'; the organizations and rules that are used for policy making 'protect the ideology by preventing the access of groups which could suggest new ideas and policies' (Smith, 1990, pp. 45-6).

This account has been the subject of a persuasive critique by Jordan *et al.* They argue that the policy community approach is 'clearly not compatible with a state autonomy view of politics as it assumes an exchange between bureaucrats and particularized interests' (Jordan, Maloney and McLaughlin, 1992b, p. 25). They also criticize Smith's distinction between a post war primary policy community in which the NFU and MAFF were continuously involved in policy discussions to the almost total exclusion of all other interests, and a secondary community of other groups consulted on an occasional basis. To talk of such a primary community 'ignores the overwhelming evidence of internally fragmented bureaucracies' (Jordan, Maloney and McLaughlin, 1992a, p. 22). As policy making is specialized and fragmented, both between and within departments, there is 'no single agricultural policy community, nor indeed is there a single policy perspective which constitutes a dominant 'structural setting' within which agricultural policy is made. MAFF is composed of 40 divisions each with their own aims and objectives and their own clienteles to satisfy' (Jordan, Maloney and McLaughlin, 1992b, p. 6). As a result, there is no NFU hegemony but a competitive agricultural milieu in which specific commodity associations, food processors, retailers, agricultural suppliers, environmental and consumer groups, can all play a significant role in a highly fragmented, segmented and specialized policy process. On a poultry processing issue, for example, it is the British Poultry Meat Federation which will be the credible source of expertise and information, not the NFU. For Jordan and his colleagues, therefore, the policy community model is not intended to provide a complete account of policy making but to help explain the milieu of routinized decisions at a micro or sub-sectoral level. Neither should the model imply a closed arrangement but rather a 'list of the most regular and relied upon contributors to the process of deciding particular families of policies. It is not however a static and formal list' (Jordan, Maloney and McLaughlin, 1992a, p. 23).

The rejection of the pluralist and corporatist paradigms in favour of an approach based on policy networks is an advance in the study of policy making in the agricultural sector. The flexibility of the policy networks approach is ideally suited to the diversity of an agricultural policy sector composed of several sub-sectoral policy communities. Part of the reason for the conflicting interpretations seems to lie in this diversity and in the fact that different aspects of agricultural policy and of group-state relations may be explained in a variety of ways. However, rather than lock the pattern of interest intermediation into one exclusive paradigm it is better to recognize that no single model can adequately explain the diverse aspects of policy making and change. Thus in an analysis of the dairy sector the insights provided by the meso corporatist and policy community models can help explain 'a stable pattern of policy outputs which is relatively resistant to change' whereas the negotiated economy framework provides some understanding of rapid and far reaching changes in the organization of the dairy sector (Grant, 1992, p. 65).

Grant applies the various types of policy network to a cross national study but it is equally important to recognize that territorial variations within a national policy area may be significant. In the United Kingdom the existence of territorial ministries for Scotland, Wales and Northern Ireland facilitates the development of territorial communities. These Rhodes defines as

> integrated, stable networks with continuity of membership and a high degree of vertical independence. However, membership of the network is informal and inclusive, distinguished by its territorial base and a high degree of horizontal interdependence rooted in shared territorial interests...Given their size and scale, the networks can encompass all the relevant territorial élite...It is simultaneously restricted and inclusive (Rhodes, 1988, p. 284).

Whilst the pre-eminence of functional politics at national level is a constraint, territorial communities possess other resources which increase autonomy and provide opportunities for independent action. Territorial communities, therefore, 'can and do inject a territorial component into UK Government which involves both distinct administrative processes and substantive policy variations' (Rhodes, 1988, p. 285).

Rose has pointed to both the existence of territorial ministries, and to the internal heterogeneity of Whitehall ministries both in their territorial scope and their functional responsibilities. Thus although the Agricultural Departments of the three territorial ministries have varying degrees of responsibility in their respective areas, MAFF also has a complex mix of responsibilities - some are exercised at a United Kingdom level, some for Great Britain, some for England and Wales, and some for England only (Rose, 1982, pp. 116-7). In agriculture, administrative devolution has been the norm. Many programmes are concurrent in that they have the same function throughout the United Kingdom but are delivered by different organizations in different parts. This can lead to significant variations in policy implementation. So whereas Part I of the 1947 Agriculture Act provided for price stability and the Annual Review, and applied to the United Kingdom as a whole, the efficiency provisions outlined in Part II applied to England and Wales only and were implemented by separate legislation for both Scotland and Northern Ireland. Territorial considerations were also reflected in the Annual Review where the interests of Scotland and Northern Ireland were represented at both the state and farmer level.

Explaining the Northern Ireland pattern

Using Smith's criteria, a good case can be made for the existence of a closed agricultural policy community in Northern Ireland during the Stormont period. There was an ideological hegemony between Ministry and UFU on parity, agricultural modernization, and increased production, protecting a monopolistic consultative relationship. In many respects, moreover, the analysis for Northern Ireland must resemble that for Britain. The internal logic of parity was the creation of a 'national' policy community with shared basic productionist objectives for the United Kingdom as a whole, particularly after 1939. This community found institutional expression in the Annual Review which reflected the territorial complexity of the United Kingdom. Though MAFF and the NFU were the lead institutions there were two sets of partners: the three Agricultural Departments on one side and the three Farmers' Unions on the other.

Although a policy community approach can help explain the relationship between the UFU and the Ministry after 1939, other aspects of the relationship can support an alternative analysis. For example, the way in which the Ministry fostered a monopolistic farmers' association in order to facilitate policy formulation and implementation suggests a meso corporatist explanation. Complaints about state control and the undue influence of Ministry officials such as Scott Robertson may indicate that the bureaucracy was relatively autonomous, especially given the unrepresentativeness of the UFU. Alternatively, in the inter war years, the interests of the UFU and the Northern Ireland Ministry could be seen as just two of many competing in the pluralist United Kingdom market place. All agricultural interests in Northern Ireland, including the Ministry, agreed on the need for protection but this was not within the competence of the Stormont Parliament and could only be obtained by working with other interests in Britain to persuade the British Government to change its policy. In such cases where the interests of Northern Ireland agriculture had to be promoted or defended in a United Kingdom context, the usual approach was firstly for the Ministry to try resolve local differences and then make a united approach to the British authorities, such as in the case of the campaign for the removal of the import duty on maize.

Internally, it was Ministry policy to consult widely in an effort to resolve potential conflict and get agreement on bills and marketing schemes prior to publication: for example the Ministry provided both the UFU and the Ulster Curers' Association with a confidential synopsis of the draft Pigs Marketing Scheme. The policy of consultation was partly the result of Craig's populism and his desire to do nothing which might threaten Unionist unity or stir up opposition to the Government. On the 1933 Agricultural Marketing Bill, for example, Craig suggested that the Ministry obtain resolutions from the UFU and other bodies in support of the legislation; to resolve the milk strike in 1931 Craig brokered a conference at Stormont between the producers and retailers, who were left in no doubt that no one was leaving until agreement was reached. Such attempts to resolve conflict between two conflicting groups might justify a societal corporatist analysis but explanations which focus on the resolution of conflict between competing economic interests are deficient because there was no attempt by the Stormont Government to reconcile the most basic conflict in society, that between Unionists and Nationalists. Northern Ireland is often viewed as a small state, which some have identified as a setting favourable to elite accommodation. Katzenstein, for example, identifies a democratic corporatism in small European states, where internal consensus between conflicting interests is generated in the face of an external economic threat (Katzenstein, 1985). In Northern Ireland, however, the Catholic minority - the 'enemy within' - was regarded as the greatest threat to the state, and patterns of interest intermediation were shaped by an internal conflict between Unionists and Nationalists which was not amenable to accommodation.

Any analysis of the relationship between the UFU and Ministry of Agriculture during the Stormont period must take account of this dominant political cleavage and of the fact that accommodation was essentially between conflicting interests within the wider Unionist family. To focus on the UFU as a client of the Ministry of Agriculture is insufficient. Ministry officials were undoubtedly influential but the local bureaucracy was highly politicized. Considerations of religion and ideology were an important factor in recruitment and promotion, indeed Archdale actually boasted that only four of his 109 officials were Catholics (quoted in Whyte, 1983, p. 13). A fuller explanation must recognize that group interaction with the bureaucracy in the Stormont years was determined by one key factor, namely the priorities and interests of the hegemonic Ulster Unionist Party.

It is in this respect that La Palombara's notion of parentela provides the key to an understanding of state-farmer relations in Northern Ireland during the Stormont period. Many of the salient characteristics of parentela which La Palombara identifies in the Italian system were also present in Northern Ireland: the hegemonic political party, the absence of a loyal opposition, and the fact that the UFU, like all other interest groups, gained access and legitimacy through its attachment to the Unionist Party rather than through its ability to represent farmers.

From the beginning the UFU adopted what it referred to as a non sectarian and non party political strategy. This was an attempt to prevent the alienation of a substantial section of the potential membership but the consistent opposition to putting up candidates for elections to Stormont can be interpreted as a desire not to challenge Unionist hegemony. In 1962, for example, there was some support within the UFU for a suggestion that the Union should 'prepare to take political action and put forward farmers candidates if satisfactory action was not taken by the existing Members' but this was totally rejected by the leadership (Farmers' Journal, 4 May 1962, p. 20). Membership was concentrated amongst the larger, generally Protestant, farmers of Antrim, Down and Londonderry and weaker west of the Bann where small, Catholic owned, farms predominated. Perhaps inevitably, the UFU became widely identified with the Unionist Party, an identification clearly apparent from the policy stances it adopted. The logic of parity with Britain was not acceptable to Nationalists even if the money was. A Unionist perspective led the UFU to act on 'patriotic considerations' during the Second World War, and it was the UFU which developed close political and social links with farmers' unions in Britain rather than with those in the Republic.

It is not surprising that instances of Nationalist MP's who were members of the UFU are rare (exceptions were George Leeke in the 1920s and the Gormley brothers in the 1960s). By contrast the list of Unionist MP's is long and the fraternal ties with the Unionist Party were so close that the UFU was often mockingly referred to as the right arm of the Government. Certainly Union leaders often spoke of the Government in glowing terms. For J.M. Mark, for example

> the farmers of Northern Ireland had just as good friends in their Cabinet as they had in the country...the Prime Minister would do anything in his power to help the farming industry; Mr Pollock had always been a farmers man...and so far as Mr Andrews...was concerned, he was a farmer and a member of the UFU, and they could count on their good friend Mr Archdale as being with them every time (Farmers' Journal, June 1928, p. 2793).

Indeed membership of the UFU was effectively a requirement for the post of Minister of Agriculture, and Brooke, Moore and West, who dominated the period, were all past presidents of the Union. Personal contacts and kinship ties with a tiny political and administrative elite were inevitably important. Craig frequently spoke of his 'good friend' David Wright, the General Secretary of the UFU; the UFU often by-passed the Ministry and sent deputations straight to Craig who also mediated disputes; the UFU committee which adopted its policy document in 1930 included four Unionist MP's - Brooke, Mark, Minford, and Colonel A.R. Gordon, plus Moore, a future Minister of Agriculture. If further proof is needed of the overlap between Union and Party, take Brooke's personal letter to Craig, prior to the official endorsement of the policy, wondering whether he would 'agree to having an informal talk with some of the members of the executive and perhaps E.M.[Archdale] and [J.S] Gordon could be asked to be present. My object in asking you to do this is that I am anxious that we should not evolve a policy, which would not be acceptable to you' (CAB9E/69/1).

In parentela relationships, the distribution of goods, services and even basic political benefits such as participation depend on having the proper political affiliations and are largely distributed amongst the faithful. The party subsidizes some groups in the market place of pressure groups, thereby depriving any competing groups of political benefits. In Northern Ireland the UFU was fostered as a means of extending the hegemonic party's control over as much of society and economy as possible. It thus played a vital intermediary role in regulating rural society. The weakening of the UFU's position after the collapse of Stormont and the end of Unionist hegemony in 1972, and the emergence of an alternative farmers' association with strong support in the Nationalist community, illustrates the essential point: access to decision makers was governed by the ideological acceptability to the ruling political party of certain organized interests.

Policies adopted by the participants in parentela relationships are to a large extent the function of the ideology and programme of the hegemonic party. With such close kinship ties in Northern Ireland it is hardly surprising that the UFU shared with the Unionist Party and Government an ideological commitment to parity. Parity with Britain was a coherent 'populist' political strategy which was designed to maintain the hegemony of the Unionist Party and to retain the support of the farmers and workers to whom any reduction in standards would have been unacceptable (Bew, Gibbon and Patterson, 1979, ch. 3). Parity was an ideological and political imperative for both the UFU and the Ministry. It fulfilled the dual purpose of keeping the farmers happy and underlining the link with Britain. In the final analysis, the keystone of the relationship between the Northern Ireland state and the UFU was the common belief in, and commitment to, the union with Britain. Parity and Unionism underpinned the relationship. It is inconceivable that a farmers' organization which did not share this ideological commitment, no matter how representative, could have attained the position of influence in the Northern Ireland agricultural policy sector which the Ulster Farmers' Union enjoyed during the Stormont period.

7 The agricultural policy network since 1972

In the early 1970s direct rule and EC entry radically altered the context of agricultural development in Northern Ireland. The prorogation of the devolved Parliament in 1972 removed formal responsibility for agricultural policy from Stormont to Westminster and Whitehall. Contemporaneously United Kingdom membership of the EC in 1973 shifted the locus of responsibility for agricultural policy from London to Brussels. Direct rule had only a marginal impact on policy development compared with the fundamental importance of the adoption of the CAP. The general parity approach was continued, indeed participation in the CAP made the formulation of a distinctive regional policy even less likely although there was still scope for particularity. The policy of the Ministry of Agriculture (renamed Department of Agriculture or DANI in 1973) was reiterated by the Northern Ireland Office (NIO) Minister Giles Shaw's response to a request for a white paper on agriculture. Since Northern Ireland agriculture was 'so closely integrated with UK government agricultural policy' there was little value in producing a separate white paper but he 'undertook to continue the policy of adopting special Northern Ireland measures to deal with particular problems which might arise' (Farmweek, 4 October 1978).

Direct rule and EC membership combined to change fundamentally the overall framework in which the regional policy network operated and had important ramifications for the nature and effectiveness of its strategies. The tension between parity and particularity was played out in fundamentally changed conditions. One significant development which coincided with these events, and was perhaps facilitated by them, was the fragmentation of the Northern Ireland policy network with the successful formation of a farmers' organization to rival the UFU in 1975.

Fragmentation of the agricultural policy network

According to Smith an increasingly weak farming lobby in Britain lost economic and ideological privilege as its political strength waned in the 1980s.

Retrenchment and CAP reform exacerbated sectoral strains between livestock and arable producers and threatened to fragment the British agricultural policy network. The NFU monopoly, for example, was challenged by breakaway organizations such as the Small Farmers' Association which were especially 'critical of the NFU for being too close to government and not having enough concern for the plight of small farmers' (Smith, 1990, p. 191). The agricultural network in Northern Ireland experienced similar pressures. From the 1960s the UFU was increasingly subject to internal tensions as grass roots farmers pressed for more direct action to improve incomes. Such tensions coalesced around the large/small farmer distinction with the UFU leadership accused of ignoring the interests of the small scale producer. Discontent over Annual Review determinations and the policy of farm amalgamation came to a head in 1965 when there were several abortive attempts to establish a new farmers' organization. James Peters of Rathfriland demanded

> a Union which will support the farmers of the country not the marketing boards and the Government. The Ulster Farmers' Union has had its chance, and it has done nothing for us...The leaders of the Union are so closely tied up with marketing boards and other commitments that they have got completely out of touch with the farmers of Ulster (Farmweek, 7 December 1965).

The establishment of a small farmers' organization was also suggested by the Gormley brothers. According to Tom Gormley there was 'acute dissatisfaction among the small farmers at the treatment they are receiving generally. The Minister of Agriculture wants them out and the Ulster Farmers' Union has no time for them either' (Farmweek, 6 April 1965). The most frequent complaint of critics of the UFU was that it was dominated by large farmers who had no time for the different interests of small farmers. Many small farmers were not members of the UFU 'because they see no benefit in such membership, but they can be attracted to their own organisation of small men' (Farmweek, 6 April 1965). The pressure for the new union was centred in counties west of the Bann where many Catholic owned small farms were located. The economic and social structure of regional agriculture meant that there would inevitably be large numbers of Catholics in a small farmers' union. The Gormley's, however, insisted that their prime motivation was not sectarian but concern for the well being of the small farmer and tried to ensure that all shades of religious and political opinion were represented.

These attempts to form a small farmers' association foundered partly on the Ministry of Agriculture's insistence that only the UFU would be recognized as representative of farmers generally. However the agricultural crisis in the mid 1970s stimulated renewed opposition to the UFU. The particular problems of the beef sector led to the formation of the Ulster Farmers Action Group (UFAG) in early 1975. UFAG adopted militant tactics including a demonstration at the headquarters of the Department of Agriculture when an effigy of the Minister was burnt, and road blocks in counties Londonderry and Tyrone. For one UFAG member negotiation was of little use in fighting for the interests of farmers. They did not 'have the direct lines of communication that are at the disposal of the Union, but we do not see this as a disadvantage' (Farmweek, 1 April 1975). As it had consistently done over the years the UFU condemned illegal actions and stuck to its responsible tactics of discussing grievances with those in power.

The Northern Ireland Agricultural Producers Association (NIAPA) emerged from this discontent in November 1975. NIAPA adopted the slogan "the voice of the small farmer" and claimed to be the 'unfettered voice of the Northern Ireland farmer' (Belfast News Letter, 29 September 1984). Certainly one of the primary motivations behind NIAPA was to establish an organization which could speak up for the interests of small farmers. UFAG, for example, pointed to similar challenges to the NFU in Britain and stressed that its 'only interest is in the financial plight of farmers with no voice in any other organisation' (Farmweek, 18 March 1975). In addition the dominance of milk producers in the UFU, who cared little for the suckler cow producer, frustrated its efforts to work through the Union. NIAPA successfully challenged the UFU in some areas. In elections to the Northern Ireland Committee of the British Wool Marketing Board in 1992, for example, NIAPA shattered the traditional UFU monopoly on marketing boards by winning three of the six seats with 62 per cent of the vote. As a small farmers' organization NIAPA developed close contacts with similar bodies such as the Farmers' Union of Wales, the Scottish Crofters' Union, and the Small Farmers' Association. In 1989 four such organizations, together representing some 30,000 farmers, agreed to work towards 'a joint policy position on all farming and rural community matters and explore jointly the possibility of closer cooperation with European Farmers Coordination which represents a number of small farming groups on the continent' (Belfast Telegraph, 26 August 1989).

NIAPA has often been described as a Catholic farmers' union. Although this characterization was rejected by its leadership which pointed out that farmers of all religions were members, NIAPA's distinct sectoral, regional and political profile lends some credence to the description. Centred on towns west of the Bann such as Draperstown, Carrickmore and Dungiven, and largely comprised of small hill farmers relying on suckler calf sales for the bulk of their income, NIAPA represented mainly Catholic small holders dissatisfied with the UFU which they also tended to regard as a Unionist organization. Significantly NIAPA developed close contacts with wider political elements traditionally hostile to the Northern Ireland state including the SDLP, Nationalist politicians, the Dublin Government and civil service, key Irish individuals in Brussels such as Ray MacSharry, and other farmers' organizations in the Irish Republic.

NIAPA's roots in UFAG and support for militant action, however, helped ensure that access to the Department of Agriculture was slow to be obtained. Of course the main problem was that processes of institutional consultation between the state and the farmers in Northern Ireland had been embedded over a fifty year period and could not be easily altered, even had NIAPA taken the consultation route.

Some of the hostility, moreover, may have reflected suspicion about NIAPA's connections with political elements traditionally hostile to the regional Government and administration.

After the prorogation of Stormont the Department continued to regard the UFU as the legitimate voice of Northern Ireland agriculture, even when its membership of 13,000 was barely twice that of NIAPA. The allocation of secondary milk quotas, for example, was done 'in accordance with priorities decided by the Secretary of State following consultation with the Ulster Farmers' Union' (Department of Agriculture, 1986, pp. 24-5). NIAPA also complained that it was not represented on the nine member Dairy Produce Quota Tribunal and that 'the Department of Agriculture in its appointments looked as if it has favoured the Ulster Farmers' Union rather than any other farming body...One would even be inclined to believe that the department was trying to suppress the aspirations of the province's small farmers' (Belfast Telegraph, 13 August 1984). Similarly the British Minister of Agriculture met the UFU but not NIAPA when he visited Northern Ireland in November 1984. One of NIAPA's leaders, however, commented that he didn't 'think it matters too much about such visits. We, the small farmers of the province, seldom get much benefit from them. In fact over the past ten years or so, we have got more help from the EC in Brussels than anywhere else' (Belfast Telegraph, 26 November 1984).

Surprisingly perhaps Ian Paisley, particularly in his influential role as chair of the Northern Ireland Assembly Agriculture Committee, was one of the main advocates of consultative status for NIAPA. Paisley was keen to stress that whereas the Department of Agriculture always consulted the UFU, NIAPA would receive a hearing at his Committee which would be independent and open to any group. The Committee voiced particular concern about the lack of recognition of NIAPA as representative of a substantial number of seed potato producers. After the demise of the Seed Potato Marketing Board, the UFU and the Northern Ireland Potato Marketing Association (NIPMA) established a joint private company, Seed Potato Promotions (NI) Ltd (SPP) to regulate marketing and help promote and develop the sector. SPP was pump primed by the Department to the tune of £383,300 over three years between 1982-85 but subsequently obtained its income from a levy on all seed potatoes which amounted, for example, to £66,300 in 1992-93 (NIA 81; NIA 162; NIA 165; Department of Agriculture, 1993, p. 48). The levy caused some disquiet amongst producers who were not members of the UFU. Indeed NIAPA, which claimed to represent 30 per cent of seed potato producers, strongly opposed the levy because it was used to support a private company on which they had no representation and demanded some say in how the money was spent. This was supported by the Agriculture Committee on the principle that any person liable for the levy should have the democratic right to participate in the selection of the organization in receipt of the money.

Although NIAPA professed a desire to work alongside the UFU in the best interests of Northern Ireland farmers, pro UFU sources argued that the fragmentation of the regional policy network was detrimental to the industry.

Farmweek, for example, commented that Northern Ireland 'is a small compact area. The agricultural industry is one indivisible whole. The industry must not become fragmented. Let us all think in terms of mounting a concerted effort to win a better deal for the Ulster farmer. Let us speak with one voice' (Farmweek, 28 November 1975). Moreover, the Department of Agriculture's attitudes were rooted in a historical preference for a single united farmers' voice. The Department insisted, for example, that SPP was broadly representative of the seed potato industry. For the Minister, Lord Lyell, producers who wished to participate in and influence SPP could join the UFU; moreover if producers did not wish to join the UFU their interests would still be looked after as the levy money would be spent for the good of the sector as a whole; thirdly, and most significantly, for the Department there was no organization other than the UFU which it could look to discharge the functions of SPP (NIA 165).

From the mid 1980s, however, the access of NIAPA to the Department of Agriculture improved markedly, evinced by the presence of the Permanent Secretary at the opening of NIAPA's new headquarters in Cookstown. NIAPA increasingly enjoyed good relations with senior Department officials and no longer felt routinely excluded from the policy process. The formation of NIAPA and its increasing acceptance as the legitimate voice of a section of the Northern Ireland agricultural industry can be partly explained by changed political circumstances after direct rule and partly by structural changes in Northern Ireland agriculture, including EC membership and considerations of CAP reform, increased concern for the environment, and the formulation of a wider rural development strategy for Northern Ireland.

Lobbying and the CAP

At the EC level the strategy of the regional agricultural network was to influence the formulation and implementation of policy, either directly through lobbying in Brussels or indirectly through national governmental channels. Because Northern Ireland was a region of the United Kingdom, however, the agricultural network experienced difficulties in advancing its case effectively in Brussels. Important issues such as the extension of Less Favoured Areas and milk quotas were negotiated by British Ministers at European Council level and there was only limited scope for regional interests to influence the outcome. The task of the agricultural network, difficult enough in the context of the United Kingdom, was made much more onerous within the EC where Northern Ireland was a peripheral region of a peripheral state.

The Farmers' Unions worked at two levels: direct lobbying of community institutions and pressure on the British Government, either through the Department of Agriculture and the NIO or via MAFF. Under the leadership of the NFU the Farmers' Unions developed a network of formal and informal contacts with advisory committees and institutions such as the Commission and the Directorate-

General for Agriculture (DG VI). Direct lobbying, for example, was facilitated by the Farmers' Unions shared Brussels office and participation in Comité des Organisations Professionelles Agricoles (COPA). The umbrella group for European farmers' associations, COPA has been dominated by large farmers and is widely regarded as the most influential lobby group in the Community. The UFU President attends the COPA Praesidium. The Union also saw the EC Commission office in Belfast as another valuable line of communication with Brussels. Although not able to draw on the insider institutional structures available to the UFU as a member of COPA, NIAPA developed significant contacts at the EC level through influential figures such as John Hume and Ray MacSharry, and through cooperation with other small farmers' associations. Indeed NIAPA's European profile developed much more quickly than its contacts with the Department of Agriculture. Moreover the claims of the network were also pressed in Brussels, often in concerted action, by Northern Ireland's three Members of the European Parliament (MEP's), notably Hume, Paisley, and Jim Nicholson.

Formal institutional structures impeded the extent to which the case of a small region such as Northern Ireland could be successfully pursued in Europe, independently of that for the United Kingdom as a whole. It was fundamentally important, therefore, for the regional agricultural network to influence national policy. The UFU continued to lobby government departments through direct contacts and intermediaries such as MP's. Indeed for the UFU it was 'pointless to make a case to the Commission on behalf of Northern Ireland which did not have the support of the United Kingdom Government. The first essential is to persuade the United Kingdom Government of the need for action' (Farmweek, 2 May 1981). The three Farmers' Unions agreed policy in advance of EC negotiations and the general objective of the UFU was 'to see that the Northern Ireland situation is taken into account properly in arriving at an agreed U.K. policy. Naturally the Ulster Farmers' Union view on U.K. policy does not always prevail' (Farmweek, 2 May 1981).

Building a regional consensus was one general prerequisite for effective lobbying in Whitehall but this did not guarantee that the Northern Ireland case would be accepted. The main problem was that in the national context there were three other Agricultural Departments who were also expected to fight for the interests of their clienteles. Moreover MAFF was the lead department for the United Kingdom and negotiated on behalf of all farmers at the EC level. The task of the Department of Agriculture, as an integral part of the national policy machinery, was to try to make British policy on CAP issues amenable to regional interests. At both official and ministerial level the Department ensured that 'matters of special interest to Northern Ireland are fully considered when UK policy is being decided and is normally represented in the UK teams which take part in the decision making and discussions in the agricultural affairs of the community' (Department of Agriculture, 1975, p. 10). A Department official was included in United Kingdom delegations at meetings of EC Management Committees and Working Groups when subjects under discussion had particular regional relevance. Furthermore a senior official normally attended Council meetings as an adviser to the British Minister. In 1981, responding to criticism that the problems of regional agriculture were not understood in Brussels, the Department of Agriculture divulged that on average its officials attended about 100 meetings per year in Brussels and a similar number in London in preparation for EC meetings (Farmweek, 2 May 1981).

That regional interests on CAP issues had to be defended by a Minister in charge of a Department which had no formal responsibility for the industry was often a source of controversy, although John Gummer, when Minister of State in MAFF, stated that the 'Northern Ireland Agricultural Office is extremely good at making sure we know all the problems facing farmers there' (Belfast Telegraph, 21 September 1985). On the milk quotas issue in 1984-85, for example, there was much hostile criticism of Michael Jopling's failure to defend Northern Ireland's interests. Jopling's forthright if exasperated assertion that he had no remit for Northern Ireland agriculture was greeted with incredulity by Ian Paisley who thundered: 'Well, who is responsible? None other than the man who made the decision. Anybody who knows anything about the Department of Agriculture in Northern Ireland knows all about those mad folk and how that Department is more tied to the Westminster administration than any other of the Northern Ireland Departments' (NIA Deb, 3 October 1984, p. 89). Jopling's subsequent visit to soothe hurt feelings was welcomed by John Taylor as a recognition that Northern Ireland was a part of the United Kingdom and that as the Minister representing the United Kingdom at the Council of Ministers Jopling was 'responsible for representing the best interests of the farmers and the agriculture industry in Northern Ireland' (NIA Deb, 27 November 1984, p. 289).

Whilst Nationalists such as John Hume utilized all possible channels of influence they instinctively distrusted the British authorities and preferred to work directly through Brussels. The 'malevolent indifference' of the British Government to Northern Ireland agriculture necessitated direct representations at the EC level and it was 'vital that we make the Northern Ireland case directly where we can and not just direct all our efforts at the British Government' (Belfast News Letter, 17 April 1984). For SDLP agriculture spokesman Denis Haughey the interests of farmers in Northern Ireland were not 'properly represented at Brussels by the Westminster Government. Our producers have special problems and require special representation' (Belfast Telegraph, 19 February 1987). During the bad weather crisis in late summer 1985 Sinn Féin's Jim McAllister also claimed that the 'lax and somewhat disinterested attitude of British ministers on the present crisis situation in the farming community highlights just how far the well-being of the six counties is on the Government's agenda; this in spite of the fact that the majority of large farmers here are Unionists' (Belfast Telegraph, 23 September 1985).

The 'second hand' representation of regional interests in Europe prompted demands for a permanent political presence on British negotiating teams. For Hume the British Government's treatment of Northern Ireland on the milk quotas issue demonstrated the 'inadequacy of our being represented in Brussels by British Ministers' (Belfast Telegraph, 13 April 1984). Unionists increasingly shared this view. Jim Nicholson expressed a widely held view when he called for an Ulster voice in Brussels and implored the Minister of Agriculture

> to pay special attention to Northern Ireland needs in his future negotiations. It has been a bone of contention for some time in Northern Ireland that when the Minister negotiates on behalf of the United Kingdom he is also negotiating for Northern Ireland without the presence of a Northern Ireland Office Minister in his team. Is it not time that a Minister from the Northern Ireland Office was present to represent the interests of the Province? (HC Deb 56, c. 1292).

Among Unionists this complaint was also linked to the absence of regional political institutions. Thus the lack of response in Whitehall to the milk quotas campaign prompted the Reverend William Beattie to bemoan that the British Government did

> precious little for the dairy farmers in Northern Ireland. If we had our own government in Northern Ireland a great deal would have been done and this mistake would never had been made; the bungling by Mr Jopling would never have taken place. If ever there was an argument for a Northern Ireland Government, this is one (NIA Deb, 5 July 1984, p. 898).

The development of a strong and united regional voice in the non governmental sector, allied to a permanent Northern Ireland office in Brussels, was also advocated by the EC Commission representatives in Belfast. Geoffrey Martin, for example, was concerned that the particular problems of Northern Ireland agriculture could be overlooked in the context of the United Kingdom as a whole. Martin frequently urged the development of a regional case on EC matters, perhaps allied with areas with similar interests in countries such as Greece, Italy and Ireland. Of particular concern was the frequent lack of consensus amongst regional voices when lobbying in Brussels and the tortuous route which Northern Ireland views took through the British administrative machine before reaching Brussels. Martin also pointed to the absence of any Brussels based Ulster natives on United Kingdom delegations and complained that 'one seldom hears or sees anyone from Northern Ireland in Community offices around Brussels. The Northern Ireland farmer has no image at all, therefore no voice, no political muscle' (Farmweek, 18 April 1981).

There were also suggestions for an all party farm policy. Hume, for example, condemned the 'complete disregard for Northern Ireland farming interests at Westminster' and appealed to farming organizations and public representatives 'to come together to devise a common strategy to fight for and defend our agricultural industry and to ward off the repeated assaults on farmers' interests...I still believe that is the best way forward for we are in a stronger position when we speak with one voice' (Belfast Telegraph, 17 December 1984). However whilst Unionists were prepared to cooperate in the interests of regional agriculture, the development of an agreed policy was treated with suspicion. John Taylor made it clear that whilst close cooperation between MEP's was possible, a joint policy was difficult because farming and rural issues could not be isolated from constitutional politics.

The Department of Agriculture and the UFU rejected accusations that the interests of regional agriculture were poorly promoted in Brussels. The UFU stressed its cooperation with the NFU and its work through the Brussels office and COPA. The Department highlighted its actions in pressing the Northern Ireland case at the national level and argued this had resulted in EC recognition of special regional problems, for example through feed price allowances and aid to milk producers. In addition it pointed out that between 1973-81, in respect of EC money devoted to individual projects, Northern Ireland had been allocated approximately 20 per cent of the total funds earmarked for the United Kingdom. This hardly suggested 'that the problems of Northern Agriculture are not understood in Brussels' (Farmweek, 2 May 1981).

The impact of direct rule

Although less significant than EC entry the imposition of direct rule changed the institutional framework within which the regional agricultural policy network operated. Besides EC entry the impact of direct rule was mitigated by two other factors. Firstly the parity dynamic in agricultural policy integrated Northern Ireland into a United Kingdom policy framework after 1939. Secondly, direct rule removed the political head but left the administrative body to continue largely as before with the same officials pursuing the same policy direction.

Initially the Northern Ireland agricultural policy network was unaffected by direct rule and consensus persisted on the fundamentals of policy and processes of consultation. The UFU's desire for the 'continuance of the close cooperation between the Ministry and the various bodies in the industry such as the Ulster Farmers' Union' was not likely to be refused (Farmweek, 25 April 1972). Immediately on taking office, the first Secretary of State, William Whitelaw, gave a public assurance that the work of the Ministry of Agriculture would continue along established lines and NIO ministers quickly established contact with the agricultural policy network. Whitelaw, for example, met the representatives of the industry at an informal buffet in April 1972, the British Minister of Agriculture (Prior) visited Northern Ireland and met the UFU in August, and the regional Agriculture Minister, Mills, addressed the UFU Executive Committee in December of the same year.

On the other hand direct rule and political conflict contributed to a 'rebureaucratization' of the civil service, increased the autonomy of the Department vis-a-vis the rest of the agricultural network, and helped weaken the influence of the agricultural lobby. The UFU had always exploited to the full its formal and informal contacts with Unionist circles and the Stormont Government.

Direct rule removed this vital channel of access and influence for the UFU. Although the consultative relationship between the state and the UFU was maintained the fact that those politicians in charge of agricultural policy were no longer responsible to a local electorate, still less had personal and political ties with the UFU, made the Department and the NIO less responsive to regional pressures. On a number of occasions after 1972, for example, the UFU's dissatisfaction with agricultural policy was reflected in a vote of no confidence in the Secretary of State. In October 1980 the UFU President made a public appeal to the Department's Permanent Secretary to 'convey yet again to his political masters the feeling of despair and despondency within the agricultural industry' (Farmweek, 25 October 1980).

The UFU also complained about lack of consultation on several key issues including the abolition of the Agricultural Trust in December 1979 and the extension of Less Favoured Areas. However, this may not be explained solely by the absence of a regional parliament. Economic, social and political trends increasingly operated to the disadvantage of the farming lobby with greater focus on consumer, urban and environmental interests. The weakness of the Farmers' Unions throughout the United Kingdom was implicit in increasing militancy and grass roots pressure for more public criticism of government by the leadership. In 1987, for example, the NFU took the unprecedented step of passing vote of no confidence in the Minister of Agriculture.

All ministers in charge of agriculture after 1972, apart from the brief tenure of the Unionist Leslie Morrell during the power sharing Executive in early 1974, had their political base outside Northern Ireland. Indeed many were members of the House of Lords and even less responsive to public pressure. A central point of concern for the regional agricultural network was the remoteness from and ignorance of the particular conditions of agriculture in Northern Ireland on the part of most of the British politicians given responsibility for the industry. In 1965 Farmweek had eulogized Harry West as

> a practical farmer - he has been described as "the Minister with mud on his boots" - and in his home constituency of Fermanagh and elsewhere throughout Northern Ireland he is on christian name terms with hundreds of other practical farmers, is in constant touch with them, and from his conversation with other working farmers has...his finger on the pulse of the opinions and viewpoints of agriculturalists generally (Farmweek, 1 June 1965).

In this context the UFU greeted Peter Bottomley's departure with some sadness because he had been able to voice their interests on the floor of the House of Commons and had 'made considerable efforts to get to know Northern Ireland agriculture's problems and saw farming practice on the ground...We have lost a man who was shaping up to serve our industry well and we will seek to become as well acquainted with his successor' (Belfast Telegraph, 26 July 1990). The fact that NIO ministers invariably had more than one portfolio also led to criticism.

laden, as he was, with responsibility for not only farming but the environment and transport...never really had opportunity of standing out as a signal figure for agriculture. For in truth, no sooner had he made an early morning call on some farm or other but he was almost immediately booked in to speak on road safety, drink and driving or some other subject, totally unrelated to matters on the land. It was not fair to farming. It was not fair either to farmers that a man of the calibre of Peter Bottomley should have had to split his time with so many other activities (Belfast Telegraph, 2 July 1990).

Whilst the UFU and NIAPA gave a cautious welcome to Bottomley's successor, Lord Skelmersdale, they expressed concern that agriculture continued to be a 'part time' portfolio. The UFU was

> disappointed it has not been seen fit to give us a full time minister for agriculture. Ours is the largest industry in the country and we want someone who has the time to get to know it and the problems associated with it. We need someone who can get to grips with those problems and fight a strong case on behalf of Northern Ireland farmers (Belfast Telegraph, 27 July 1990)

Although boycotted by Nationalists, the Northern Ireland Assembly provided a focal point for the agricultural community between 1982-86 (O'Leary, Elliott and Wilford, 1988, pp. 96-108). The Agriculture Committee possessed a high level of expertise because all its members represented predominantly rural constituencies and most were farmers. The Chair and Deputy Chair, Ian Paisley and John Taylor, were both MEP's and at one point members of the European Parliament Agriculture Policy Committee; Paisley and Jim Nicholson were on the House of Commons equivalent. Through the proceedings and reports of the Agriculture Committee the Department was made more amenable to scrutiny by locally elected politicians. Evidence gathered from the whole range of the regional agricultural network, including the UFU, NIAPA, and marketing boards, formed the basis of some 23 reports and a similar number of minutes of proceedings on a diverse range of subjects such as Less Favoured Areas, the future of Northern Ireland agriculture in the EC, special aid for agriculture, and the effects of sustained bad weather. Paisley claimed that the Assembly was

> a rallying place...a forum in which the Agriculture Committee and the representatives of the agriculture industry have had an opportunity to come together and to have their public representatives put their case in a proper manner to the Minister responsible. If we had not had this Assembly there would have been no effective voice, and it has proved to be an effective voice (NIA Deb, 1 May 1984, p. 44).

The Committee had mixed success, however, partly because it 'devoted much of its time and effort in seeking to influence the European dimension of relevant policy, something that not only lay beyond the formal control of DANI but which, strictly speaking, lay beyond the Committee's remit' ((O'Leary, Elliott and Wilford, 1988, p. 174).

The Agriculture Committee quickly established good relations with the policy network and was generally welcomed by the farming community as offering a high profile forum for airing the views and complaints of the industry. After the appearance before the Committee of the Permanent Secretary of the Department of Agriculture (Bill Jack), Farmweek commented that 'not for a decade, perhaps never before has Ulster agriculture seen a senior member of the Department responsible for the industry publicly asked to explain policy and resultant actions' (Farmweek, 8 January 1983). NIAPA welcomed the opportunity to raise its public profile, put forward its views, and had 'every confidence that Mr. Paisley and his colleagues will put a strong case to the Minister for further help to farming' (Farmweek, 8 January 1983). For the UFU, with its well developed contacts with government, the Committee was less vital. On several occasions it replied to requests for its views on draft legislation with the simple message that it agreed with the proposals and had amendments included in the draft but nonetheless the Committee was a welcome addition to the agricultural lobby. Even the Department appreciated the assistance given by the Committee in helping to set priorities for public spending on agriculture.

Parity and particularity revisited: the case of milk quotas

In the mid 1980s the issue which dominated rural politics in Northern Ireland was the EC decision to impose quotas on milk production. At the crux of the dispute about milk quotas was the perennial tension between parity and particularity. All the familiar contradictions and confusions riddled the campaign of the regional agricultural policy network on the quota issue. The reaction to the implementation of the quota system reflected the traditional concerns of parity and particularity but also demonstrated how direct rule and EC entry changed the lobbying strategy and effectiveness of the agricultural policy network.

Dairying traditionally dominated the Northern Ireland agricultural industry with milk production the largest single enterprise in value added terms. Problems of overproduction were endemic, however. In the 1960s, for example, some producers in Northern Ireland advocated a quota system to give a better price to small farmers who suffered because of surpluses generated by larger producers. Market imbalance also characterized the CAP milk regime from its early days. Despite measures such as beef conversion schemes and the co-responsibility levy, surpluses continued to increase with adverse political, economic and financial consequences. In 1980 the proposal for a super levy applicable to milk in excess of defined base quantities marked the realization that it was no longer sensible or possible to guarantee the price of unlimited quantities of products in a structural surplus. The initial approach was to restrict price increases but this too failed to control production. At the Brussels summit on 31 March 1984, unwilling to reduce prices by the 12 per cent necessary fully to offset the additional expenditure arising from overproduction, the Council of Ministers accepted Commission proposals for the introduction of a quota system based on deliveries in 1981 plus one per cent, with all excess production subject to a supplementary levy.

The claim for particularity

Any action to tackle seriously overproduction was certain to have a significant detrimental impact on milk producers in Northern Ireland. Despite surpluses the attitude taken in the 1970s was that Northern Ireland should be allowed to increase milk production as the United Kingdom itself was not self sufficient. Surpluses were attributed to inefficient European farmers not to those in the United Kingdom where dairy production was the area of greatest natural advantage. In this context the EC proposals to tackle surpluses were given a hostile reception by producers in Northern Ireland and were also regarded as a penalty for efficiency. The quota proposals were vigorously opposed by the Farmers' Unions as an infringement of the 'right to produce' and the UFU pledged to fight tooth and nail to ensure that eventual decisions would have the least possible disadvantage to Northern Ireland. In November 1983 the three Farmers' Unions reiterated their total opposition to milk quotas at a meeting with the Agriculture Ministers. The UFU also pressed for a meeting with the Secretary of State, Prior, to ensure that at least two Cabinet members were fully briefed on the problems facing agriculture prior to the European summit.

Given the warning which farmers had received it is surprising that the Council of Ministers' acceptance of quotas came as a severe jolt to the agricultural network in Northern Ireland. The Department of Agriculture remarked with considerable understatement that the quota system caused 'substantial unrest and uncertainty' in Northern Ireland (Department of Agriculture, 1985, p. 11). The starting point was particularity. Northern Ireland milk producers believed that they deserved special treatment because of the particular conditions of the regional industry including remoteness, farm structure, and the lack of alternatives to grassland production. Significantly the claim for parity was now with farmers in the Republic of Ireland, which was said to share the same problems as the north, and not with those in Britain. Attempts were made before the Council meeting to persuade the British Government to follow the Irish example and seek a special derogation for Northern Ireland. For example, Unionist MEP John Taylor sent a telegram to Mrs Thatcher asking for a special exemption for Northern Ireland if concessions were granted to the Republic (Belfast Telegraph, 16 March 1984).

The British Government, however, was more interested in cutting agricultural support in the EC generally than securing special treatment for farmers in any part of the United Kingdom, and also opposed special treatment for the Irish Republic. Nevertheless a pledge was given that the 'claims of Northern Ireland must be given equal consideration with those of the Republic' (HC Deb 56, c. 1274). Unionists were uncomfortable with the general political implications of this argument and justified special treatment for Northern Ireland within the context of the United Kingdom as a whole. Thus George Graham of the Democratic Unionist Party (DUP) later remarked that because it was a peripheral region of the EC 'it would not be difficult to make a special case for Northern Ireland without even straining the Union - the Farmers' Union or the Union with the United Kingdom' (NIA 136, pp. 8-9)

The agreement reached did not begin to meet this pledge. Whereas the Republic of Ireland was allowed to increase production by nearly five per cent on 1983 levels, the United Kingdom was required to cut deliveries by over six per cent. With an additional cut of 2½ per cent imposed by MAFF to provide additional quota for special cases the total reduction was some nine per cent on 1983 levels. In recognition of the importance of the dairy sector, however, the Council of Ministers granted an additional quota of 65,000 tonnes (63.1 million litres) to Northern Ireland. Farmers in the United Kingdom bitterly opposed quotas and were particularly incensed at the special treatment given to producers in the Irish Republic. For Northern Ireland, where production had increased even faster between 1981 and 1983, the situation was even more serious. The decision was described by the UFU as 'a real disaster day for the agricultural industry in the province' which would mean a substantial drop in farm incomes (Belfast Telegraph, 31 March 1984).

Politicians of all parties also criticized the agreement but particular venom was reserved for the British Government because it had not sufficiently pressed the claims of Northern Ireland for a derogation. Paisley complained that Northern Ireland had not received the same concessions as the Republic, and John Hume alleged that the British Government had not honoured their public undertaking nor pressed the case for the Ulster farmer in the negotiations. The Belfast press was equally outraged. For the News Letter, Ulster farmers had 'good reason to feel that their interests have been ignored when the crucial decisions were taken in London' (Belfast News Letter, 16 April 1984). A Belfast Telegraph editorial exemplified the traditional tensions between parity and particularity. The British Government

> might argue that Northern Ireland is attempting to have the best of both worlds - parity with Britain when it suits us and special treatment, on a par with the Republic, when it does not. But the argument is that the province is too dependent on agriculture, and too much affected by prices in the Republic, to be regarded as just another region of Britain (Belfast Telegraph, 21 September 1984).

Even worse was to come with the allocation of quotas amongst producers in the United Kingdom and particular controversy arose over the additional 65,000 tonnes. The widespread belief that Northern Ireland had won limited special concessions was shattered when the regional quota was revealed. Suspicion was reinforced by a lack of clarity, deliberate or otherwise, over whether 1981 or 1983 had been used as the base year for calculation. The initial Government line was that the regional allocation was made up of 1981 deliveries plus 65,000 tonnes and a similar amount from the United Kingdom pool to ensure its reduction on 1983 was no greater than other regions (HC Deb 58, c. 876; 59, c. 245). This gave a quota which was 2½ per cent greater than 1982 production. The regional Milk Marketing Board questioned this methodology and claimed that the special allowance was absorbed into the overall United Kingdom quota which was then distributed on the basis of 1983 production. This was given some credence when the Government changed to portraying the figure in terms of 1983 production. The Government explained the methodology in a response to the House of Commons Agriculture Select Committee. It was decided when allocating quota to apply differential reductions to reflect trends between 1981 and 1983 when production in Northern Ireland increased by almost 20 per cent compared with under eight per cent in England and Wales. The reduction applied to England and Wales was 6.25 per cent compared to 10.35 per cent in Northern Ireland, considerably less than the rate of expansion. With the addition of the extra 65,000 tonnes the reduction in Northern Ireland was further reduced to 5.83 per cent on 1983 deliveries (HC 274, 1984-85).

This decision caused considerable 'feelings of anger, resentment and deep frustration' throughout the agricultural network in Northern Ireland where it had been expected that its quota would be calculated by adding on the extra 65,000 tonnes after receiving the same cut on 1983 production as the rest of the United Kingdom (HC Deb 63, c. 211). Ulster Unionist agriculture spokesman Jim Nicholson calculated on this basis that an additional 57.7 million litres had been 'hijacked from us and that we have not received the full benefit of it' (HC Deb 63, c. 213). The extra quota had been precisely intended to treat Northern Ireland producers differently because of the special conditions of the regional dairy sector, not to equalize the pain amongst all farmers in the United Kingdom. John Hume spoke of the 'ignorance, inconsistency and insensitivity' of the British Government and called for a complete reconsideration of the implementation of the quota system in Northern Ireland (Belfast News Letter, 17 April 1984). Alliance Assembly member Addie Morrow, who had been involved for many years in negotiations with governments on agricultural matters, had

> never seen such a breakdown in confidence among the leaders of the industry...Disagreements have always been part and parcel of these sort of discussions, and bitter pills have had to be swallowed over the years, but this issue has undermined the whole relationship between Government officials and the Ulster Farmers' Union and the Milk Marketing Board. The leaders of the farming community believe, the Agriculture Committee believes, and I believe, that we are being told a pack of lies - nothing less - in order to swindle us out of that extra amount of quota that should have come to us from Brussels (NIA Deb, 5 July 1984, p. 894).

The UFU was equally hostile. The quota division had been 'designed to ensure that Northern Ireland receives no better treatment than producers in the rest of the

United Kingdom. The Northern Ireland special allocation has, therefore, been redistributed to producers in areas for which it was never intended' (Belfast News Letter, 16 April 1984). The Government's treatment of Ulster producers was 'appalling and the lack of response to pressure from the Ulster Farmers' Union for measures to alleviate this most serious problem is simply both inhuman and unbelievable...Until we receive a just quota for this Province the Union will never accept the quota arrangements' (Belfast News Letter 16 May 1984).

Questions of parity and particularity were again central, especially for Unionists. For Nicholson it was

> all very well of the Minister to speak of equalising the burden, but the Government must learn that they cannot say when it suits them that we shall be treated in the same way as any other part of the United Kingdom, but when it suits them, say, "Ah, but you are different." We are not different when it comes to this and suits the Government to equalise the burden throughout the whole of the United Kingdom. Then we had to have equal rights. On every other occasion, we are told that we are different' (HC Deb 61, c. 540).

Paisley also complained that Northern Ireland producers were 'simply to be treated the same as producers everywhere else in the United Kingdom' when the special allocation was intended to put them 'on a par with those in the Republic and instead it has been used by the Government to ensure that all United Kingdom producers will be cut by the same amount' (NIA Deb, 1 May 1984, p. 34). Jopling had 'betrayed Northern Ireland farmers. He has kicked the jewel of Ulster agriculture into the mire. He is no friend of Ulster. No wonder a Dublin Minister congratulated him on his performance' (Belfast Telegraph, 27 November 1984). The only way to prove that Northern Ireland had not been unfairly treated was 'to open the books and make the calculations available both here and in Brussels. The Community at large can then judge whether or not the justifiable claims of Northern Ireland have been met and whether or not the special addition for Northern Ireland has been correctly used' (NIA Deb, 5 July 1984, p. 892).

The Northern Ireland agricultural network lobbied intensively to have the 'missing' 65,000 tonnes restored and the regional quota increased. For the UFU this would 'provide the only permanent and satisfactory solution to the problem...Any other measures are treating the symptoms rather than the problem' (Belfast News Letter, 16 May 1984). The campaign was influenced by the fact that the responsible authorities were those in London and Brussels, not in Belfast. At the regional level the UFU, Milk Marketing Board and local politicians joined together to lobby the NIO but Northern Ireland ministers were sympathetic to their case and this strategy was primarily designed to bolster the Secretary of State's position in negotiations within the British Government and Cabinet. The quota issue was one of the most significant dealt with by the Northern Ireland Assembly which was heavily involved in the campaign. In particular the Agriculture Committee played a vital coordinating role, drawing on Paisley's contacts in

Brussels and Strasbourg to raise the matter at the EC level. The Assembly adopted a motion which condemned the British Government's handling of the negotiations on milk quotas and called for compensatory measures; the issue was raised in Committee and on the floor of the Assembly on at least 20 occasions; and delegations from the Agriculture Committee had frequent discussions with the NIO ministers. Paisley saw the Assembly as a catalyst for a united front which would bolster the NIO in its battle in Whitehall. The Agriculture Committee 'must do all in our power to strengthen the Secretary of State's arm in these negotiations. He needs our help. He needs the united help of the entire Ulster community. And I trust that he will realise that he has our backing as he demands a solution to this matter' (NIA Deb, 1 May 1984, p. 36).

To focus the campaign on the quota issue a new broadly based single issue pressure group - the Super Levy Abolition Group (SLAG) - was formed in June 1984 to bring together politicians, the UFU, NIAPA, trade unions, and related industries. One SLAG meeting unanimously adopted a resolution which called for a suspension of the super levy 'until the Northern Ireland Special Allocation of 65,000 tonnes is restored and a fair and reasonable system of implementation is devised with a commitment to an increased quota for the year 1985/86 bearing in mind the special circumstances in Northern Ireland' (Belfast News Letter, 7 July 1984). There was pressure for militant action, including refusal to pay any supplementary levy. It was generally realized, however, that the Thatcher administration would not be blackmailed and that 'sustained negotiation and lobbying would be more effective' so a SLAG delegation, accompanied by Paisley, Nicholson and Denis Haughey, met the Secretary of State and Lord Lyell to explain the milk producers' case (Belfast News Letter, 4 August 1984).

At the national level the issue was raised at Westminster through parliamentary questions and during the House of Commons Agriculture Select Committee's investigation of quotas. Influenced by the input of Nicholson, the Committee regarded the question of the 65,000 tonnes 'as a serious matter and expect the Government to clear it up immediately' (HC 14, 1984-85, para. 11). Although this report was helpful, advocacy of the regional case within the British Government machinery was hampered by the structural format of negotiations in which the NIO was outnumbered three to one by the other Agricultural Departments. The NIO made it clear that, whilst sympathetic, ministers had fought hard to get a better deal for Northern Ireland and that there would be no addition to the overall quota. Indeed the position could have been much worse but for the strong case put forward by the NIO against an allocation on the basis of 1981 production. This was strongly favoured by the 80 per cent of the United Kingdom's dairy producers in England and Wales and would have resulted in a cut of ten per cent in Northern Ireland, even after the inclusion of the extra quota.

MEP's Paisley, Hume and Taylor displayed a rare degree of unanimity and cooperation in pushing the Northern Ireland case at the EC level. In July 1984, for example, they accompanied a delegation drawn from the UFU, NIAPA, the Milk Marketing Board and the Northern Ireland Economic Council in a meeting with

141

Commissioner Dalsager in Strasbourg which demanded a full scale enquiry into the fairness and legality of the quota allocation. The UFU also utilized its Brussels contacts to brief the Agriculture Commissioner on the problems faced by dairy farmers and in December 1984 Paisley tabled a resolution concerning the 'missing' quota in the European Parliament.

Despite some disquiet in Brussels over the fate of the 65,000 tonnes, and talk of legal action against the United Kingdom, there were no concessions by the British Government. Jopling maintained that 'producers generally are being treated equitably throughout the United Kingdom' and there was

> no question in my mind that Northern Ireland has had the benefit of the 65,000 tonnes. If you look at the quota which Northern Ireland has got, whether it is put against 1981 or 1983 Northern Ireland is better treated and has got an advantage under either way of working it out, compared with England and Wales or Scotland (HC 14, 1984-85, pp. 35-6).

Parity and the administration of quotas

Although the controversy over the missing quota rumbled on without solution, the focus of the regional campaign turned to the implementation of the quota arrangements for special and hardship cases. To obtain extra quota for distribution to seriously affected producers in the United Kingdom £50 million was made available over five years to compensate those wishing to discontinue milk production. The intention was to buy up about 2.25 per cent of total quota in Britain and five per cent (66.06 million litres at a cost of £8.59 million) in Northern Ireland for reallocation to priority cases. Lord Lyell stressed the element of particularity which had been obtained and was 'pleased that the efforts of Northern Ireland's Ministers to obtain a special deal for Northern Ireland had been rewarded' because proportionately more money was made available to buy up quota in Northern Ireland (Belfast News Letter, 2 June 1984).

Whilst the outgoers scheme was welcomed as a recognition of the special difficulties facing producers in Northern Ireland it was regarded by the Milk Marketing Board as insufficient to meet the quota shortfall and would 'in no way compensate for the blow that the unfair imposition of the quota scheme has dealt to the fulfilment of Northern Ireland's milk production potential' (Belfast News Letter, 2 June 1984). The problem in Northern Ireland, exacerbated by the fact that there was no viable alternative to dairying on many small farms, was that over 60 per cent of producers applied for additional quota as special and hardship cases whereas the poor response to the outgoers scheme meant that there was insufficient spare quota available for redistribution. Consequently many producers in Northern Ireland were liable for the supplementary levy because they received much lower secondary allocations than those in Britain where outgoer targets were achieved. This prompted complaints that Northern Ireland producers were being denied equality of treatment with Britain in the allocation of secondary quotas. According to the UFU even if all the outgoer funds were taken up 'the quota released would still fall short of what is necessary to achieve equality with producers in Great Britain' (Belfast News Letter, 25 May 1984). Jopling, however, argued that the central problem was the reluctance of producers to avail of the outgoers scheme, a stance which 'disgusted and disappointed' the UFU in the light of frequent assertions that the Government was trying to preserve equality of quota pain (Belfast News Letter, 25 May 1984).

This issue was of paramount importance for the UFU because it impinged directly on the parity imperative. As United Kingdom milk producers 'we do not want to be treated as second-class citizens. We do not want special treatment; we want to be put on a par with producers in Great Britain' (Belfast News Letter, 6 April 1985). The parity claim also extended to liability for the super levy which threatened 5,000 producers with a collective payment of some £5.2 million. Administration arrangements made it possible for Northern Ireland producers to be liable for supplementary levy even when total United Kingdom milk production had not exceeded the national quota. For Unionists this was unacceptable and there was no justification for the collection of supplementary levy from producers in any part of the United Kingdom until the national quota was exceeded.

A campaign for the deferment of the levy collection until secondary quotas had been allocated was mounted in Brussels by the policy network. Moreover the UFU wanted 'firm and positive support to the principle that no levies will be collected in Northern Ireland until the milk quota system has been effectively implemented in all other member states' (Belfast News Letter, 24 November 1984). On this issue Jopling was more responsive and agreed that there should be no collection of levy in the United Kingdom if the system was not effectively applied throughout the EC. After repeated postponements the Council of Ministers eventually decided not to impose a levy for 1984-85 production. This was greeted as 'not only a tremendous victory for the UFU but a great relief to many Northern Ireland milk producers...the decision is a just and fair outcome to the representations we have made' (Belfast News Letter, 2 March 1985). Also welcomed was the accompanying decision to introduce more administrative flexibility into the scheme by permitting transfer of quota between regions, an approach advocated by the UFU because it would allow spare British quota to be acquired for distribution to producers in Northern Ireland.

The parity principle had never been accepted fully by the British agricultural policy network, however. Divisions between different regional and sectoral interests in the United Kingdom, although relatively uncontentious for most of the post war period when production was generally expanding, were exacerbated by retrenchment. British milk producers were unwilling to cut back production to allow those in Northern Ireland to continue to expand. The suggestion that quota be transferred from Britain to Northern Ireland was met with hostility by British producers. There was intense political pressure on MAFF to ensure that those who contributed most to overproduction, namely milk producers in Northern Ireland, assumed a greater share of responsibility for the reduction of surpluses. For example the Scottish Milk Marketing Board opposed purchase of quota in

Scotland for Northern Ireland and Welsh farmers insisted that any surplus quota in Britain be shared out amongst British producers. For Nicholson, however, it was 'totally wrong for us or anyone else in Northern Ireland to start talking about getting quota from Scotland, England, Wales or anywhere else. We have got to make it quite clear that we are part of the United Kingdom, and being part of the United Kingdom, we are entitled to equality of treatment' (NIA 195, p. 10).

Relations between the three Farmers' Unions were strained. The UFU was disappointed that British farmers had been

> so vigorous in their opposition to any transfer of quota to Northern Ireland. There is a very shallow ring to their objection as producers in Great Britain have already received substantially better treatment than producers in Northern Ireland and part of this has been achieved using quota that was destined by the EC Commission for use in Northern Ireland (Belfast News Letter, 3 August 1985).

British agricultural interests had to look after their own producers but had 'no right to object to Government introducing measures aimed at bringing a little more equality into the treatment of all United Kingdom producers' (Belfast News Letter, 3 August 1985). According to Nicholson the NFU had 'acted in a very niggardly fashion on this issue, and the close ties that there have been between the Ulster Farmers' Union and the NFU are going to have to be strengthened, as the NFU has certainly been less than helpful - in fact, it has been totally unhelpful - on this issue' (NIA Deb, 11 June 1985, p. 121). Paisley also attributed the lack of fair treatment for Northern Ireland to the

> intransigent attitudes of farmers across the water, and the unwillingness of the Government to act against vested interests - I am referring, without apology, to the National Farmers' Union and to the right hon Gentleman who has now become the Minister of Agriculture for England and Wales only and who is not prepared to ensure fair play in the other parts of the United Kingdom (NIA Deb, 11 June 1985, pp. 117-8).

In an attempt to resolve the quota dispute between the Agriculture Departments the Government set up a Cabinet Committee chaired by the Foreign Secretary, Geoffrey Howe. For the UFU this was a significant development and if the Committee considered the case for equality of treatment in an impartial manner it would have no option but to 'accept that Northern Ireland producers have been treated most unfairly and that corrective action is urgently needed' (Belfast News Letter, 22 June 1985). On the other hand if the Government continued to treat Northern Ireland producers as second class citizens then 'the full force of the EEC must be brought to bear on the Government to force a change in attitude' (Belfast News Letter, 22 June 1985). A delegation of the UFU and politicians including the leaders of the three main parties - Molyneaux, Paisley and Hume - met Howe to present the case for equal treatment. The UFU saw the regional consensus on the issue as 'an indication of the depth of resentment among Northern Ireland milk producers as to the way they have been treated to date by the UK Government' (Belfast News Letter, 6 July 1985).

The deliberations of the Howe Committee resulted in an agreed three point plan to increase the quota available for Northern Ireland. This included the transfer of 2½ million litres of unallocated direct sales quota, the reopening of the outgoers scheme in Northern Ireland, and the use of the Department of Agriculture's outgoers funds to purchase up to 20 million litres of quota from Britain after the outgoer targets there had been reached. For the UFU these measures were 'totally inadequate and fall significantly short of that required to treat individual producers in Northern Ireland on the same basis as individual producers in the rest of the United Kingdom. As UK milk producers we have every right to expect equal treatment and the UFU will not be satisfied until this is obtained' (Farmweek, 9 August 1985). At least 80 million litres was needed to restore parity but the measures agreed would amount to only 50 million litres at best. Nicholson regarded the plan as 'most disappointing and did not in any way attempt to redress the serious problem of equality with the rest of UK dairy farmers. This decision now means that N.I. dairy farmers are being placed in a position of permanent disadvantage not only with their U.K. counterparts but also with every other farmer in Europe' (Farmweek, 2 August 1985).

After the disappointment of the Howe recommendations the campaign switched back to Brussels. The Milk Marketing Board, for example, believed that Northern Ireland producers had 'no alternative but to intensify the pursuit of their case in Brussels, where there is clearly a better understanding of our situation and a greater sympathy towards it than seems to exist in Whitehall or in the shires and the glens' (Farmweek, 23 August 1985). An emergency meeting of the Assembly Agriculture Committee decided that the regional network would make a joint direct approach to the Commission. The UFU lodged an objection with the Commission concerning the harsh treatment of Northern Ireland producers compared with those in Britain. Accompanied by the three MEP's, a UFU delegation met the Agriculture Commissioner, Frans Andriessen, in Brussels in April 1986 to press for the 65,000 tonnes and identical treatment for small producers throughout the United Kingdom.

In the short term the measures recommended by the Howe Committee had little impact as only small amounts of quota were transferred from Britain to Northern Ireland. The regional agricultural network continued to complain about the 65,000 tonnes of 'missing' quota and about the lack of equality of treatment with British producers. Eventually, however, the issue lost salience as more quota was gradually found to complete the 50 million litre target set in 1985. By 1987-88 the transfer of a further 30,000 tonnes was sufficient according to the Department of Agriculture to bring the treatment of special and hardship cases in Northern Ireland 'into line with that of producers elsewhere in the United Kingdom' (Department of Agriculture, 1987, p. 11). Some sort of parity was therefore eventually attained. The struggle to do so, however, indicated that changing economic and political conditions had again brought the whole parity issue back to the top of the agricultural policy agenda.

CAP reform, the environment and rural development

The milk quota controversy was symptomatic of the threat posed to farmers by CAP reform which itself must be seen in the wider context of structural and political change, including increased concern for the environment and rural development. In the late 1980s the Department of Agriculture shifted the emphasis of its strategy away from traditional concern with farming to a focus on the whole rural economy, the interests of the consumer, and the enhancement of the environment. Increasingly, therefore, agricultural policy was subsumed within a general strategy for rural development. Whilst Northern Ireland was not included in the legislation, the Department of Agriculture followed the example of the 1986 Agriculture Act which required the British Agriculture Ministers to balance the promotion and maintenance of a stable and efficient agriculture with the interests of conservation and enhancement of the countryside. This duty to balance economic and conservation interests was eventually given statutory form in the Agriculture (Miscellaneous Provisions) (NI) Order 1994. The Department was also involved in the development of a new policy approach on agriculture and rural enterprise which was partly a response to pressure for CAP reform. Specific schemes included grants for environmentally beneficial projects, the Farm Woodland Scheme, and Environmentally Sensitive Areas were established in the Mournes, the Glens of Antrim, and West Fermanagh and Erne Lakeland.

In 1988 the Department established a 'Conservation, Land Use and Diversification' division which reflected the conviction that 'growing concern for the environment has led to an awareness of the need to reassess agricultural policy and develop a policy for sensitive countryside management' (Department of Agriculture, 1990, p. 33). Its strategy published in 1990 aimed to incorporate countryside management as an integral element in all planning and execution of farming activity, and a Farming and Wildlife Advisory Group was established to promote consensus between farming and conservation interests. All these developments were encapsulated in the corporate aim of the Department which was

> to promote economic growth and the development of the countryside in Northern Ireland. It will assist the competitive development of the agriculture, horticulture, forestry, fisheries and food sectors, being responsive to the needs of the whole community for safe and wholesome food, the welfare of animals and the conservation and enhancement of the environment (Department of Agriculture, 1993, p. 8).

From the 1980s there was increased recognition that rural economic development involved the encouragement of off farm and non traditional activities, not least because there was little scope for agricultural expansion. This was accompanied

146

by the emergence of the notion of 'integrated rural development' which stressed a multi sectoral approach in which agriculture was just one component. Thus 'agricultural development is to be integrated with other sectors to increase incomes and create employment opportunities. Social development is to be integrated with economic development to increase the attraction of rural areas and to lessen out-migration' (Greer and Murray, 1993, p. 11). Integrated rural development was taken up by the EC in the late 1970s to improve coordination of agricultural and regional expenditure and to focus attention on lesser developed areas. It became a priority area for the Commission which in 1988 agreed to reform structural funds to allow greater financing of rural development through the diversification of agriculture and was embodied in programmes such as INTERREG (transfrontier cooperation) and LEADER (community based economic development).

Suggestions for an integrated rural development programme for Northern Ireland to help small farmers and stem rural depopulation emerged in the mid 1980s from essentially Nationalist sources, particularly the SDLP. John Hume raised the issue in the European Parliament and aimed to persuade the Commission to prepare an integrated plan for regional development for Less Favoured Areas in Northern Ireland, covering not just farming but also housing, small industry and forestry. The SDLP proposed the creation of a new unitary rural development agency which would 'represent the EEC, government, agricultural interests and community groups with a brief to investigate the opportunities for off-farm employment in rural areas and to encourage local community groups to initiate new policies and analyze, advise and monitor new projects for submission to the EEC for grant aid' (Farmweek, 15 November 1985). This was accompanied by a number of other proposals such as the creation of a rural investment bank, a differential support structure to take account of the relative disadvantages of small farmers, and the reversal of the growth centre strategy to economic development. The key element of a rural development programme was the integration between agriculture and other sectors which required 'the integration of agricultural, regional and social policies of both the EEC and national governments' (Belfast Telegraph, 7 November 1985). NIAPA also complained that the Department of Agriculture took a segmented approach to rural areas and was 'primarily concerned with the efficient on-farm management of resources. Today, the trend is to view the rural area as a totality and to examine housing, welfare services, off-farm employment, recreation, education, transport and farm structure together' (Belfast News Letter, 9 February 1985).

John Hume's efforts were primarily responsible for the appointment by the European Parliament of T.J. Maher, the Irish MEP and ex-president of the Irish Farmers' Association, to report on an integrated regional development programme for Northern Ireland. Maher paid a series of visits to Northern Ireland during 1985-86 and his draft report was issued in June 1986. Welcomed by John Hume for its adoption of many of the proposals made by the SDLP, the Maher Report's central conclusion was that the EC should draw up an integrated development programme for the whole of Northern Ireland outside the Belfast travel-to-work area. There was also a need to encourage diversification in agricultural production away from grassland based enterprises such as beef and dairy, provide direct income support for small farmers (linked to the attainment of agricultural, social and environmental objectives), encourage tourism and craft industries, expand local training facilities, assist local community and voluntary groups, establish a rural invest bank, encourage cooperatives, and relax planning controls to permit more rural housing and small businesses (Farmweek, 6 June 1986).

The realization of such plans, however, required a financial contribution from the British Government at precisely the time when public expenditure control was paramount. Whilst the comprehensive programme was not introduced, policy in Northern Ireland developed in the general direction suggested by Maher. A series of initiatives were taken as a result of the deliberations of an inter-departmental committee established in 1989, chaired by the Permanent Secretary of the Department of Agriculture, to suggest ways to tackle the problems of rural areas. In 1991 the Department of Agriculture was given responsibility for rural development and established a Rural Development Division. A Rural Development Council (RDC), funded by the Department and the EC but managed by a broad range of private rural interests, was also set up to provide a source of expert advice to local communities on the general process of rural regeneration. The strategy was essentially to encourage rural communities to adopt a self help approach to regeneration. The function of the RDC was to give advice and assistance in the development of ideas and to support and facilitate rural community organizations. It also assumed responsibility for the administration of the International Fund for Ireland's (IFI) farm diversification programme. This was intended to assist innovative projects outside existing government and EC support schemes, provide non traditional on farm alternatives such as mushroom production, and stimulate economic and social regeneration in disadvantaged rural areas. The Department of Agriculture's Annual Report for 1990-91 included a section on rural development for the first time. It was recognized that the contribution of the agri-food industry in Northern Ireland

> by virtue of its distribution, structure and activity at local level, plays a principal role in sustaining the Province's rural communities, contributing social as well as economic benefits and keeping the countryside inhabited, active and cared for. Additionally the industry provided the regional base for a diverse range of service and support activities, which in turn provides a source of income and employment for the rural population and further helps to support the rural infrastructure (Department of Agriculture, 1991, p. 49).

One of the first tasks of the RDC was to help prepare the Northern Ireland Programme under the EC LEADER scheme to promote rural community regeneration. Some £2.66 million was secured from the LEADER Programme in November 1991 which with government co-financing provided the RDC with a budget of around £4 million to spend on projects designed to encourage job creation, tourism and other activities (Department of Agriculture, 1992, p. 61).

Rural development funding was boosted by the partnership arrangement between the Department of Agriculture and IFI which provided a grant of £572,000 to the RDC in October 1991. IFI's Rural Development Programme announced in March 1992 also helped to optimize funding available under EC programmes. The joint INTERREG programme, for example, was designed to assist border areas in Ireland overcome the problems associated with underdevelopment and peripherality and 'to promote networks of cross-border cooperation' (Department of Agriculture, 1992, p. 93). Under INTERREG £3.29 million was allocated to help community organizations in border areas to consider their development needs and to put forward plans in areas including agriculture, fisheries, forestry, and rural community development.

Productionism or stewardship?

The fragmentation of the agricultural policy network in Northern Ireland embodied fundamental disagreements about the nature of agriculture, environmental protection and rural development in the context of CAP reform and reduced state support. Farmers increasingly have been faced with a choice 'between strategies which emphasise agricultural production and those which stress environmental protection or enhancement of the land' (Collins and Mack, 1995, p. 10). These reinforce and overlap attitudes to viability and non viability. Adherents of the productionist strategy emphasize that farming is a business which needs to be economically viable, efficient, competitive and technically advanced to survive in a world market. The problems of low income farmers need to be addressed through social policy and structural reform not primarily through agricultural policy. Proponents of the stewardship approach, on the other hand, emphasize the farmer's role as custodian of the land, environment and rural economy and argue that agricultural policy should support the maintenance of farmers on the land. The essential choice is between protecting agriculture as a form of social policy for rural areas in a pluriactive context, or working towards greater rationalization with fewer farmers obtaining a bigger slice of the cake. The latter approach has usually been advocated by economists such as John Simpson who posed the important question as 'whether there is a need for a change of official policy towards farming and farm incomes. If there were 28,000 small manufacturers, many producing on such a small scale as to be non-viable, the logic of any policy debate would be about rationalisation, creation of viable units, and redeployment or early retirement' (Belfast Telegraph, 9 May 1995).

In the Northern Ireland context the UFU is generally aligned with productionist ideology and NIAPA with stewardship. So the central disagreement between the UFU and NIAPA 'is expressed ideologically in terms of dichotomy between a production or end price orientation to agriculture and a commitment to maintaining family farms as the bulwark of the social fabric of rural areas' (Collins, 1993, p. 33). The UFU, however, has always claimed that it 'has a responsibility for the whole agricultural industry and represents the needs of all Northern Ireland farmers, be they large or small farmers, or wherever they farm' (Farmweek, 19 October 1984). In Northern Ireland, moreover, there were 'important social reasons for keeping as many people directly working on the land as possible' (Farmweek, 5 October 1984). Nonetheless such sentiments were often coupled with the viability imperative. Thus it was necessary to examine whether farm output could 'be geared profitably towards more labour intensive products, without necessarily stepping back in technological time unless it is economic to do so' (Farmweek, 5 October 1984). At core, therefore, UFU ideology focused on the commercial viability of the whole agricultural industry and regarded farmers as producers not as individual guardians of a rural way of life. The UFU's first policy objective outlined in 1984, for example, was to secure 'conditions in which our members can survive in the context of an efficient and viable industry... maintenance of viability and income levels is obviously paramount' (Farmweek, 5 October 1984). Pressures for more environmentally sensitive farming were also greeted with scepticism. For the UFU farmers were 'in business as producers of food, not park-keepers' although no one was 'more conscious of the need to preserve a sensible rural environment than those who live and work within that environment' (Farmweek, 19 October 1984).

Whereas the dominant UFU discourse 'stresses the realities of commercial discipline as opposed to the ethical notions of rural life', the NIAPA line emphasizes 'community values and the sustainability of traditional family farms' and is 'frequently defended with rhetoric drawing on Irish history and conspiratorial theories' (Collins, 1993, p. 30). NIAPA argued for an integrated rural development programme and habitually complained about the bias against small farmers in the EC price and structural support system. Productionist policies resulted in a situation in which 80 per cent of resources went to just 20 per cent of farmers and helped force small farmers off the land. Thus the large farming lobby, in which NIAPA included the UFU, the Department of Agriculture, and most Department sponsored academics, had dominated the United Kingdom agricultural industry for years and had 'a vested interest in blatantly depriving small farmers of their right to exist or from gaining access to the grants they so desperately need' (Belfast News Letter, 2 March 1985). NIAPA hoped that the days were over 'when the powerful established minority who have manipulated the industry for years with the connivance of the bureaucracy, can dictate terms which suit themselves, but are a disadvantage to the vast majority of farmers and the economy of Northern Ireland in general' (Belfast News Letter, 2 March 1985).

NIAPA's stewardship approach focused on stemming the drift from the land which has 'gone much further than anyone has imagined. Those who have permitted this vast exodus have, at this late stage, realised there is more to farming than just the price of milk or beef' (Belfast News Letter, 9 February 1985). With other small farmers' unions in the British Isles NIAPA proclaimed a 'high level of agreement on the need for agricultural support policies to give priority to sustaining farming families in the countryside rather than making rich farmers richer' (Belfast Telegraph, 26 August 1989). Viability was important for NIAPA but this was conceived in a more organic terms as the viability of rural areas and communities as a whole.

The divisions between the UFU and NIAPA became focused on proposals for CAP reform. The original MacSharry proposals, for example, were welcomed by NIAPA because they shifted emphasis away from price support for increasing production towards direct income supports. The UFU on the other hand, stressed the importance of ensuring the survival of the full time family farm and criticized the MacSharry proposals because they would 'remove the incentive for farmers to be progressive, innovative and competitive' (Belfast Telegraph, 21 May 1992). It appears, therefore, that the EC agenda swung decisively towards the NIAPA position in the late 1980s, reinforced in turn by the Department's increased concern with integrated rural development. However NIAPA subsequently complained that the original MacSharry proposals were watered down under pressure from the big farm business lobby of COPA which accepted that a reduction in the number of farm businesses was essential to help maintain farm incomes.

The MacSharry proposals may be interpreted as an attempt to defend the power of agricultural interests in the EC and to safeguard the essential principles of the CAP. For example, the United Kingdom Farmers' Unions acceptance of price restraint and acknowledgement of environmental concerns has been viewed as largely a tactical move to limit the damage to agricultural interests. Some change was necessary to prevent more radical change. So whilst the NFU acknowledged that prices and production had to be reduced its goal was 'to achieve these reductions in a way that is least harmful to the farmers' (Smith, 1990, p. 193). Smith has questioned the notion of a radically new agricultural agenda and pointed to the continued strength of the European and British agricultural policy communities. Although the influence of environmental and consumer groups has increased in the United Kingdom the general structural conditions of agricultural policy making remains intact and continues to protect the farming interest. Despite the weakening of the productionist paradigm, therefore, there is no real prospect in the medium term of a wholesale shift in EC policy towards a stewardship approach.

8 North-south cooperation

> As might be expected from two contiguous regions on a small island, the agricultural economies of both are very similar and have important linkages. In many respects the island of Ireland still functions like a single economy to-day despite partition (Sheehy, O'Brien and McClelland, 1981, p. 68).

The notion of a common Irish farm economy has always informed the debate about the proper political and institutional framework for agriculture in Ireland. It has been widely accepted that Irish agriculture, north and south, had common characteristics and differed in several important respects from that in Great Britain. For example in both areas the agricultural sector made an important contribution to gross domestic product and employment, possessed a similar farm structure, was export oriented, and climatic and geographical conditions dictated predominantly grassland enterprises. Historically this was reflected in the development of a separate institutional and administrative structure in the form of the Department of Agriculture and Technical Instruction for Ireland. Partition was seen by many as undesirable for agriculture in Ireland and the industry was widely regarded, not least in Britain, as an integrated whole for which it would be inadvisable to divide responsibility between two parliaments. 'Irish control of Irish agriculture' was a key element of the Nationalist political case. Moreover, there is little doubt that the British Government would have much preferred to transfer responsibility to a single legislative body because agriculture was regarded a service which was particularly disadvantaged by partition. In the event, however, whatever practical advantages there may have been in maintaining a single agricultural administration were over-ridden by wider political imperatives, particularly the accommodation reached with the Ulster Unionists. Agriculture was, therefore, one of the key matters transferred to the new parliament in Northern Ireland.

For most of the 75 years since partition, particularly during the Stormont period, agriculture in the north and south of Ireland followed largely separate paths of development and were exposed to differing market experiences. Although initially the south retained Commonwealth status and availed of the free flow of agricultural goods within the United Kingdom, the protectionist approach of the 1930s resulted in the imposition of trade barriers. During the period 1926-60 'the economic environment in the North and South diverged and agriculture in the two regions developed very differently' (Sheehy, O'Brien and McClelland, 1981, p. 63). These differences were manifest in terms of performance and policy framework. For example whereas the south relied on protection for the home market and subsidies for exports, the north participated in the United Kingdom system of deficiency payments which helped give its farmers higher and more assured prices. In the 1960s, however, this gap narrowed as a result of the 1965 Anglo-Irish Trade Agreement and the participation of southern farmers in the British price system, especially in respect of cattle and beef. From the 1970s, under the influence of EC membership, southern farmers experienced 'much more rapid price increases than their Northern colleagues who were operating under the UK regime which tended to minimise price increases under the CAP' (Sheehy, O'Brien and McClelland, 1981, p. 64).

These general trends were reflected in patterns of north-south cooperation. For most of the Stormont period significant cross border cooperation between both governments and the representatives of farmers, either formally or informally, was rare. In Northern Ireland the Ministry of Agriculture and the UFU regarded agriculture as an integral component of a United Kingdom industry and saw London not Dublin as the natural point of contact and focus, not least because Britain was the destination for most of the surplus agricultural production. It was not until the 1960s that any regular cross border contacts developed under the impetus of the general thaw in north-south relations. Since then direct rule and EC membership, combined with the need to find an agreed political solution to the Northern Ireland problem, has provided an important dynamic towards increased cross border cooperation in agriculture.

The impact of partition

In the home rule debates in the late nineteenth century there was a general assumption that responsibility for agriculture and rural development would be one of the most important functions of a devolved Irish parliament. Irish control over Irish agriculture was the basic assumption which underlay all the home rule schemes and agriculture was one of the first services pencilled in for legislative devolution. In 1920, for example, Lloyd-George justified the creation of parliaments for Belfast and Dublin on the grounds that they could 'deal exclusively with the problems of agriculture and agricultural development in all its forms, legislatively as well as administratively' (HC Deb 127, c. 1326). That Irish agriculture, north and south, differed in certain important respects from that in Great Britain was an often repeated truism which was used to support the argument that the Irish should control their own agricultural industry. Even before the Government of Ireland Act had reached the statute book, however, events had amply illustrated the different perceptions within Ireland about what constitutional mechanisms would be best for agriculture. For example, whereas some Irish peers successfully objected to the inclusion of Ireland in the 1920 Agriculture Bill on the grounds that the formulation of Irish agricultural policy should be left to the new parliaments, Unionists generally favoured inclusion, consistent with the overall demand for equal treatment with Great Britain (HL Deb 43, c. 555, HC Deb 136, c. 1929).

The controversies arising from partition set the tone for north-south relations for most of the devolution period. The defining characteristic of the relationship was not cooperation but hostility and mutual suspicion. Firstly, the whole process of dividing up the extant administration gave rise to tensions. The Northern Ireland Government complained of obstructionist tactics by the southern administration which declined to cooperate with partition in an effort to keep Northern Ireland as weak as possible. Indeed the Free State Government made clear its intention to operate in the north, particularly in the field of agriculture. Thus it refused a request from Archdale, the Northern Ireland Minister, for a meeting to discuss the transfer of agricultural services, withheld records dealing with a great variety of agricultural issues, and obstructed the transfer of personnel (McColgan, 1983, ch. 6).

Secondly, north-south disputes were exacerbated by the indecision of the British authorities on the administration of reserved matters. The debate about the nature and scope of all Ireland arrangements in agriculture focused on the prevention of plant and animal disease. This was perhaps the most important function of government in the agricultural sphere before 1914 and the administration of the relevant legislation in Ireland, principally the Diseases of Animals Acts, was the responsibility of the DATII. During the negotiations on the 1920 Act several proposals were made for the transfer of responsibility for animal disease to the Council of Ireland, for example by Sir Henry Robinson (President of the Local Government Board for Ireland) and the Veterinary Medical Association of Ireland (McColgan, 1983, ch. 3). These were initially rejected as a possible contravention of the pledge that Ulster could decide on its own relationship with the rest of the country. Pressure eventually persuaded the Government to accept a House of Lords amendment that there should be a unified regime for protection against animal disease in Ireland. It is notable that the impetus for the change came from the British agricultural establishment which was concerned that only a single Irish administration could ensure that animals sent to Britain from Ireland were completely free from disease (HL Deb 43, c. 50-52). The Government pointed to the practical reality that under the new political arrangements there would be two separate departments of agriculture and 'no central machinery sufficient for a really effective all-Ireland agricultural administration' but decided not to oppose the amendment (McColgan, 1983, p. 48).

The Ulster Unionists strongly opposed the administration of any services by the Council of Ireland and pressed for the transfer to the regional Parliament of responsibility for reserved matters such as animal health legislation. The Free State Government tried to exploit the situation and maintained control of a number of veterinary inspectors. In Derry a Mr McCloskey granted export certificates on behalf of the Free State Government supported by local cattle dealers who would not recognize the appointee of the Northern Ireland Government. Moreover the English Ministry of Agriculture accepted the certificates of both inspectors despite the fact that the Northern Ireland Government had ordered that those of the southern inspector be refused (McColgan, 1983, pp. 112-3).

The Free State contended that reserved matters in Northern Ireland should be administered by the British Government in consultation with the south. This incensed the Ministry of Agriculture in Northern Ireland which wanted an agency agreement in order to permit it to administer the relevant legislation. In October 1922 a compromise was reached whereby an Imperial Secretary's Office was created in Belfast to administer the Council of Ireland services. As this was under the authority of the Home Office and not the unpopular Irish Office, it was acceptable to the Ulster Unionists. The Northern Ireland Government eventually achieved its aim in April 1926 when as a result of the Ireland (Confirmation of Agreement) Act 1925 the Council of Ireland powers, including diseases of animals, were transferred to Northern Ireland thus finally ensuring the complete division of agricultural matters between north and south.

The parity imperative and north-south relations

Agriculture could not be isolated from the general hostility which characterized Belfast-Dublin relations and such early disputes merely reinforced mutual distrust. From the outset, moreover, the Northern Ireland Government was primarily concerned to obtain parity within the United Kingdom. Loyalty to the Empire and recognition of Northern Ireland as an integral part of the United Kingdom was of great importance on a wider political level for it was not just a statement of constitutional fact but the foundation of the claim for parity. It also had the great advantage for the Unionist Government of accentuating the differences between Northern Ireland and the Irish Free State. The parity imperative was regarded by the Ministry of Agriculture as the best riposte to anti Northern Ireland propaganda. British public and private opinion was frequently reminded that Northern Ireland remained an integral part of the United Kingdom whereas the Free State had opted for independence. This approach met with only mixed success. In the inter war period, for example, the essential unity of Ireland and the homogeneity of Irish agriculture was still deeply ingrained in the British psyche. This perception was reinforced by the fact that prior to partition Ulster farmers had frequently joined with those in the rest of Ireland to argue the case for the island as a whole.

For example when the British Government decided again to allow the importation of live cattle from Canada which had been prohibited since 1892, it standardized animal health procedures through the introduction of a six day quarantine period for all cattle sent to Britain, including those from Ireland, north and south. For MAF constitutional formalities took second place to the administrative need to ensure the protection of British herds. On the question of animal disease Ireland had to be treated as a single unit. There was no way in which the Northern Ireland Government could stop cattle crossing the border from the south and until such a difficulty could be overcome no change of policy could be contemplated (HL Deb 53, c. 125-130). The ban had been resented by the Canadian Government and sections of British agriculture, but strongly supported by British cattle breeders and Irish farmers for whom the store cattle trade with Britain was vital. For farmers in the south, an appeal for preferential treatment was obviously weakened by the constitutional settlement which gave Ireland the same dominion status as Canada. On the other hand, farmers in Northern Ireland strongly objected to the decision, not simply because of the potentially severe economic repercussions but because it effectively treated Northern Ireland as a dominion. For the UFU the British Government had

> no right to make any differentiation between cattle from Antrim or Down, and cattle from Forfar and Yorkshire. We are still assessed for Imperial taxation; we still have to pay a substantial Imperial contribution, but apparently these do not carry with them the right to be treated on the same lines and on a parity with the other parts of the United Kingdom (Farmers' Journal, January 1923, p. 1079).

The parity argument was rehearsed time and time again. Northern Ireland was part of the United Kingdom and any attempt to disadvantage its farmers by putting southern farmers on an equal footing was strongly resisted by the agricultural network and the Government. The Ministry of Agriculture often had to try to alleviate the adverse impact of British policy decisions on Northern Ireland in respect of the south. For example the reversal of the decision to place an import duty on maize in 1932 was received by the UFU as a great victory which had prevented a 'burden being placed upon the farmers of Ulster which would have placed them in an invidious position compared with the farmers of the Irish Free State' (Farmers' Journal, March 1932, p. 3714). Chamberlain admitted that he had been

> very much impressed by representations which I have received from Northern Ireland as to the special difficulties which would arise there if this 10 per cent. duty were imposed...the idea that the inhabitants of Northern Ireland, who will stand favourable comparison in their loyalty to the British connection with any part of the Empire should, as it were, be made to suffer for that connection in any way, in comparison with others, goes very much against the grain (HC Deb 262, c. 329).

This attitude was reinforced by the contribution made by Northern Ireland farmers during the Second World War. The loyalty shown by many farmers made it politically and morally difficult to refuse them similar benefits to those in Great

Britain in the post war period. To have done so would have put them on the same basis as farmers in the south who had not participated in the war effort. In the negotiations on the 1947 Agriculture Act, the parity imperative was partly informed by the intention of the British Agricultural Departments and the Ministry of Food to pay lower prices to Éire farmers because they would not be subject to the corresponding controls to ensure efficiency. It was a political imperative for the regional Government that Northern Ireland prices could not be allowed to fall below those prevailing for Éire products. Moore was 'naturally anxious to ensure that our agriculture is in the same position in this respect as agriculture in Great Britain and that we are not relegated to the same category as Eire' (AG16/26/1). The same consideration underlay the Ministry of Agriculture's initial enthusiasm for national marketing schemes and its unease about the effects of decontrol and deficiency payments. This was reflected in concern that the Northern Ireland Government would be 'faced with serious political repercussions if we were to find ourselves relegated to a position economically the same as the Irish Republic simply because we are at such a long distance from our market and have a very high percentage of produce surplus to home needs' (CAB9E/57/4).

Domestic policy developments often had important north-south implications, particularly in those sectors such as milk and pigs where there was significant cross border trade. One isolated example of cooperation, for example, was the conference on pigs marketing held in Belfast in October 1929 between the Ministry of Agriculture and its southern counterpart following complaints from Scotland about the poor condition of Irish pork (AG16/9/2). In the milk sector trade restrictions were more common. On several occasions in the 1930s, for example, the regional Government urged the British Government to curtail subsidized butter imports from the Free State which often caused a collapse in the price of Northern Ireland butter and of milk for manufacture. The Treasury hoped that the British Government could 'reduce its liabilities on a subsidised Milk Scheme in Northern Ireland by controlling imports of Free State butter' and suggested a voluntary arrangement whereby all imports into Northern Ireland from the south would be stopped by mutual agreement (CAB9E/122/2). This was acceptable to the Northern Ireland Government provided it was made fully effective but this proved to be impossible in practice. The necessary action to ensure that Irish butter sent to Britain would not then be 're-exported' to Northern Ireland could not be taken because interference in the trade from one part of the United Kingdom to another was unconstitutional. As a result the Treasury provided a subsidy for Northern Ireland milk producers.

Under the pre war regional milk marketing scheme, Free State milk for liquid consumption in Northern Ireland was banned because this could undermine the scheme. This had serious consequences for a number of Unionists in Donegal who had traditionally supplied liquid milk for the Derry market. Many resolutions were sent to the Government from Unionist circles pressing the case for these 'good loyal men' to be allowed to continue to sell their milk in Derry (CAB9E/122/2). One of the affected producers, a Mr Gallagher, complained to the Dominions

Office about persecution by both the northern and southern Governments. The British Government was very sympathetic to the difficulties of these Donegal producers and urged north-south cooperation to guarantee the purity of the milk. The regional Government was reluctant to take joint action. In any case it was felt to be both administratively impracticable and injurious to public health to allow Free State liquid milk into Northern Ireland. Furthermore the Government was under pressure from its own milk producers to protect their position in Derry and to prohibit liquid milk supplies from Donegal. Faced with this point blank refusal to reconsider the position the Donegal producers instituted legal proceedings to compel the Northern Ireland Government to admit their milk. The Courts, however, all the way up to the House of Lords, (Gallagher vs Lynn, 1937) found in favour of the Ministry of Agriculture and accepted its argument that it could not licence the production of milk in the Free State for sale in liquid form in Northern Ireland as this would contravene the Government of Ireland Act. Moreover the claim that the Ministry's action contravened the Act by unlawfully interfering with trade outside of Northern Ireland was rejected on the grounds that the Act was not trade legislation but was designed to improve public health.

Anglo-Irish trade agreements

International commitments entered into by the United Kingdom had considerable relevance for agriculture in Northern Ireland, particularly when British policy moved in the direction of import control during the 1930s and 1960s. For the Northern Ireland Government, the perennially thorny issue was that of Anglo-Irish trade, a matter which had fundamental political implications. It was always a particular worry of the Government in Belfast that concessions for British manufactured goods by the Irish Government would be reciprocated by concessions for Irish agriculture which would adversely affect the position of Northern Ireland produce on the British market. The first priority of the Northern Ireland Government was usually the removal of protectionist barriers on certain exports to the Free State. Prior to the Ottawa Conference in 1932, for example, the Northern Ireland Government argued that unless the existing Free State duties on United Kingdom goods were abolished or substantially reduced then the exemption of Free State produce from the Import Duties Act should be discontinued. No preference 'should be afforded to that country in connection with any quota arrangements or other quantitative control of imports which may subsequently be introduced in regard to bacon, pig products, meat or other commodities' (AG16/11/2).

Most controversy, however, surrounded the Anglo-Irish Trade Agreements of 1938 and 1965. Under the terms of the outline 1938 agreement the United Kingdom granted Irish goods free entry in return for the creation of a tariff commission to review Irish duties on United Kingdom goods. This was greeted with hostility by the Northern Ireland Government because 'as long as the southern government continued its protective system the Northern Ireland government saw no reasons why reductions in duty should be conceded to Irish exports' (McMahon, 1984, p. 252). Some limited concessions by the Free State, made after the British Cabinet had tried to meet the objections of Northern Ireland, were instantly rejected. However when informed that it was most unlikely that the Free State would make any more concessions and that the British Government felt the deal the best possible under the circumstances, Craig unilaterally indicated his willingness to accept a bribe in the form of financial assistance. This came as a complete shock to Brooke and Andrews, however, who had been assured that under no conditions would the agreement be accepted.

Although totally opposed to the proposed agreement which was deemed to be the 'means of bringing further economic pressure on Northern Ireland to throw in her lot with Eire' the Northern Ireland Government considered how best to alleviate the detrimental effects of this 'inequitable and indefensible agreement' and how to persuade its supporters to accept it (CAB4/397). The Cabinet warned the British Government that if the Treaty was adopted the outcry would 'be such as to render the position of our Government impossible, unless concessions can be made to us which will put our Government in a position to alleviate, to some extent, the special disabilities under which our industry and agriculture will be labouring' (CAB4/397). It was suggested that the very minimum required to satisfy the Northern Ireland House of Commons was an annual industrial development grant, a grant towards any future budget deficit, a larger share of rearmament work, and the acceptance of the parity principle in Exchequer assistance for agriculture (CAB4/397). For the Treasury this was tantamount to blackmail but nevertheless it agreed to make some adjustments in the financial relations between Northern Ireland and the rest of the United Kingdom. In the area of agricultural subsidies it was agreed that where agricultural subsidies were granted to British farmers no objections would be raised to similar expenditure in Northern Ireland being borne on United Kingdom votes.

There was also hostility to the 1965 Anglo-Irish Trade Agreement. For the regional agricultural policy network this was designed to benefit British manufacturing and southern Irish agriculture at the expense of farmers in Northern Ireland. The UFU was appalled that the British Government was a party to the Agreement because it had a duty to safeguard the interests of all farmers in the United Kingdom. To 'grant additional assistance to farmers in the South even before it had done anything to reassure home farmers as to its intentions and to recreate the confidence which the last Price Review did so much to destroy is, quite simply, outrageous' (Farmers' Journal, January 1966, p. 47). Furthermore the UFU President stated that the Agreement had dealt a damaging blow to the local agricultural industry because producers feared 'that much of the value of the selective expansion which is referred to in the National Plan is being lost to foreign suppliers' (Farmers' Journal, March 1966, p. 13). The decision to bring producers in the Republic of Ireland into the beef and lamb guarantee arrangements caused particular anxiety because it threatened the fledgling dead meat industry in Northern Ireland. As the Agreement was strictly a matter for the British and Irish Governments there was little that the Northern Ireland Government could do directly to mitigate any adverse effects on the meat export industry. The Northern Ireland Government was faced with very hostile criticism in the House of Commons but could do nothing more than make representations 'at the highest level both at the Ministry of Agriculture across the water and indeed at the Home Office to have this matter satisfactorily resolved' (NIHC Deb 63, c. 334). The Ministry, however, was unable to convince Whitehall that the Agreement was the major cause of the difficulties experienced by Northern Ireland meat plants. The Northern Ireland Government was nonetheless able to use the transferred powers available to it to good effect - an all too rare occurrence - and provided direct financial assistance for the dead meat industry out of its own funds. Inter-governmental discussions continued periodically in an effort to arrive at a long term solution to the problem but in the absence of agreement the British departments fully supported the steps taken to ensure the viability of the Northern Ireland meat plants.

The development of north-south cooperation

Partition directly influenced the development of farmers' unions in Ireland and the scope for cross border cooperation. When the President and General Secretary of the Irish Farmers' Union (IFU) attended the first annual meeting of the UFU in Belfast in 1919 they expressed the hope that some sort of organizational arrangement or merger would allow cooperation in the interests of Irish agriculture. However there was rivalry and friction on both organizational and policy matters. The formation of an Irish Farmers' Council was suggested which would meet alternately in Belfast and Dublin, to which the UFU would appoint one third of the members. In organizational terms the UFU would deal exclusively with the whole of Ulster and the IFU with the rest of Ireland. This confederation arrangement, however, was rejected by the IFU who wanted four provincial unions, each of which would send members to a national council based in Dublin. This in turn was not acceptable to the UFU.

Despite the failure to agree on structures, there was some cooperation on policy issues. Nonetheless even here there was a tendency to split on north-south lines which reflected general attitudes on the constitutional position as well as agricultural policy. For instance, the UFU supported the inclusion of Ireland within the remit of the 1920 United Kingdom Agriculture Bill but lobbied (unsuccessfully) to have guaranteed minimum prices extended to all the main agricultural commodities. On the other hand, the IFU felt that the acceptance of state control was too high a price to pay for guaranteed prices for wheat and oats and campaigned for the exclusion of Ireland from the Bill.

It was hoped that north-south links could be maintained even after partition and the establishment of two separate parliaments in Ireland. Practical and political considerations militated against this, however. In Northern Ireland the UFU was closely linked to the Unionist governing elite and was far more concerned with devoting its energies to developing contacts with farmers' unions in Britain. There was little merit in allocating very scarce resources to promoting cross border contacts when the focus of efforts in influencing policy had to be the responsible authorities in Belfast and London. Also important was the much weaker and fragmented nature of the agricultural lobby in the south. The IFU's decision to put up candidates in Dáil elections rather than concentrating on lobbying government led to its demise. The Irish Department of Agriculture also refused to grant consultative status to farmers' organizations until the mid 1960s. Such factors, allied to more general socio-economic and political considerations, presented an obstacle to the development strong representative farmers' organization in the south with which the UFU could develop close contacts.

It was not until the establishment of the National Farmers' Association (later Irish Farmers' Association) in 1955 that significant cross border links developed between the representatives of farmers, north and south. In 1961 the UFU Council unanimously agreed to create machinery to permit consultation and the regular exchange of views with the NFA (Farmers' Journal, 6 October 1961, p. 19). Since then meetings between both organizations have been held on a regular basis, usually at commodity committee level and on specific matters such as the prevention of animal disease and the full range of issues which arose from common membership of the EC. Farmweek commented that there was 'close co-operation and consultation of mutual benefit to the farming communities of both areas. Leaders of the Ulster Farmers' Union and the National Farmers' Association meet regularly, alternately in Dublin and Belfast' (Farmweek, 19 January 1965) On the Anglo-Irish Trade Agreement, for example, the UFU and the NFA met in July 1966 and again in August 1968. On both occasions it was agreed that it was in the mutual interest of farmers in both areas that the subsidy paid on southern beef should go directly to producers not to meat plants. The effect of EC entry on cross border trade also stimulated north-south cooperation. In May 1973 the IFA President T.J. Maher addressed the UFU dinner and argued for closer cooperation within the EC. Throughout the 1970s and 1980s cooperation continued and deepened through regular meetings between commodity and other committees, facilitated by common membership of COPA. For example in September 1978 the UFU and IFA agreed a six point plan for the beef sector and in October 1983 their committees concerned with sheep and cattle met to find common ground on CAP reform. Meetings also took place at a leadership level on the more general problems faced by farmers in both parts of Ireland. In September 1976 both organizations met and agreed to convene a special meeting of border farmers on the general issue of regional development; in 1982 the leaders of the UFU and IFA met for talks on farm policy and developments affecting the members of both organizations. It was agreed that talks on areas of common interest would be continued at committee level. In 1989 the UFU and IFA embarked on a jointly funded major cross border study into low farm incomes.

Nevertheless there was still some criticism of the lack of an organized forum for Irish agriculture. For example Belfast Telegraph agriculture correspondent Michael Drake commented in January 1984 that although meetings between representatives of the major farming organizations in Ireland were not a new development

> such meetings only occur when the spirit moves either party or, more likely, when some crisis, which might have been prevented if the machinery for regular dialogue involving all appropriate organisations had been in existence, is about to loom. Perhaps the next time reasonable men and women meet to discuss Irish agriculture it will be with a prepared agenda and with a mandate from their respective organisations. Then they can really discuss the problems and expose the difficulties that lie in the path of economic progress and the achievement of a better living from the land (Belfast Telegraph, 19 January 1984).

However whilst the UFU's relations with the south were 'frequent, friendly and pragmatic' there was a limit to the extent of cooperative activity as 'public links with the Republic are open to misinterpretation by UFU members and could cause embarrassment' (Collins, 1993, p. 34). The UFU had to strike a balance between cross border cooperation in the best interests of regional agriculture and the need not to alienate its many Unionist members. This manifested itself in timid decisions not to participate in north-south conferences. In 1984 Co-operation North organized conferences in Drogheda and Belfast which were stimulated by the work of the New Ireland Forum on cross border cooperation in agriculture. Both conferences brought together several of the most important agricultural organizations in Ireland to discuss the prospects for and possible mutual benefits of closer north-south cooperation. However whilst the IFA, UAOS and NIAPA sent representatives, the UFU considered them 'too politically sensitive' and refused to attend (Belfast Telegraph, 30 October 1984). Michael Drake lamented that the UFU had not 'sent even a lone representative to keep a watching brief at this meeting on the green grassy slopes of the Boyne' (Belfast Telegraph, 19 January 1984). By 1995, however, in the context of the peace process the UFU agreed to combine with the IFU to make a joint submission on to the Forum for Peace and Reconciliation in Dublin on the future development of agriculture in Ireland.

NIAPA had no such reservations about cross border links. According to Collins, for NIAPA 'public and frequent contact with counterparts in the Republic helps it to define its position both with its predominantly nationalist membership and the wider coalition of radical "farm family" orientated unions with which it is associated' (Collins, 1993, p. 34). NIAPA actively pursued organizational links, even merger, with southern based organizations. In 1984 attempts were made to set up new body to represent the interests of farmers in border areas and there were preliminary discussions with the IFA about the possibility of establishing a cross border committee. NIAPA felt not enough was done for border farmers and body to look after the interests of those working within 20 miles of each side of the border. We want this body to have a strong voice in Brussels where it counts and with the Westminster and Dublin governments...It is essential that it is brought home to the powers that be that the border has been a hindrance to the development of these areas (Belfast Telegraph, 5 June 1984).

Little materialized in this respect but in 1993 NIAPA began merger discussions with the southern based United Farmers' Association (UFA). If successful this would establish a single organization for small to medium farmers in Ireland with a combined strength of almost 16,000, 9,000 of which would be based in Ulster as UFA has 3,000 members in Cavan, Donegal and Monaghan. Part of the rationale was to pool resources to be better able to meet the expenses of lobbying in the EC. According to UFA chairman Bertie Wall there was 'great strength in unity' because the 'problems for small, low income farmers on both sides of the border are almost identical. They are equally affected by such measures as CAP Reforms and could be equally represented on a European level' (Irish News, 10 July 1993). The necessity 'for a strong unified voice to represent small farmers in Ireland has never been greater, and the current initiative between ourselves and NIAPA offers real opportunities for better representation' (Irish News, 10 July 1993).

In the area of agricultural cooperation the Irish Co-operative Organisation Society (ICOS) and the UAOS shared common roots in Horace Plunkett's cooperative movement but went their separate ways after partition. Both organizations 'maintained a continuing dialogue down the years. This has now become more formal and provision has been made for the attendance of observers at each others meetings' (Belfast Telegraph, 1 March 1984). The wider implications were not lost on both which believed that the study of cooperation 'could be developed to good effect in the search for reconciliation between the two communities in Northern Ireland and between them and the people of the Republic' through a programme of education including residential courses with participants drawn from both jurisdictions (Belfast Telegraph, 1 March 1984).

Cooperation between farmers facilitated formal contacts at the governmental level. These developed significantly in the early 1960s in the context of the thaw in Belfast-Dublin relations attendant on O'Neill's liberalisation policy and under the impetus of increased international cooperation. Meetings between the Northern Ireland Minister of Agriculture, Harry West, and his opposite number Charles Haughey paralleled those at prime ministerial level between O'Neill and Lemass. For example, West travelled to Dublin with a UFU delegation in March 1965 to address a meeting of the NFA. Farmweek expressed the hope that the '"hands across the border" spirit of cooperation which has already been realistically demonstrated in the realm of agriculture will, it is hoped, be given even greater impetus by last weeks meeting between the two Irish Prime Ministers' (Farmweek, 19 January 1965). It was argued that friendly and informal talks between farming people was the best basis for negotiations; much had already been achieved but there was still great scope for translating the evident goodwill into practical and beneficial cooperation to mutual benefit outside political and constitutional differences. Low level official contacts had developed in the post war period, especially on animal disease which posed a common problem and benefitted from a common approach. Thus according to West there was

> undoubtedly the closest possible consultation with the Department of Agriculture in Eire on animal disease generally. We keep very close contact and this is one of the things in which we have complete co-operation with that Department. Animal disease is a problem that is common to both of us. Both countries are situated on an island and it is our ambition and earnest endeavour to keep this country free from animal disease (NIHC Deb 66, c. 432).

Political realities, however, placed a limit on the extent and nature of cross border cooperation. The issue at root reflected fundamental constitutional and political cleavages in Northern Ireland between Unionists and Nationalists. Cross border contacts were welcome to Nationalist critics of the regional Government's parity approach and anything which strengthened links with Britain. In the 1960s the rash of discussions on wider European cooperation, particularly concerning EC entry, encouraged Nationalists to urge the Northern Ireland Government to develop closer ties with the Irish Republic. For example Healy thought it desirable for both Irish governments to reconsider the resuscitation of the Council of Ireland to help, at least in an advisory capacity, formulate policies in those areas such as agriculture where the conditions in both countries were very similar and different to those prevailing in Great Britain (NIHC Deb 46, c. 231).

For the Unionist Government good relations with the Republic on matters of common interest did not mean any fundamental change in agricultural policy where the parity principle was still paramount. The Government rejected Healy's suggestion for institutionalized north-south arrangements and reiterated its commitment to the union with Britain. When in 1963 Patrick Gormley had urged a north-south exchange of visits West refused on the grounds that the 'problems and needs of the agricultural industry in Northern Ireland have a great deal in common with those of Great Britain. We propose to continue exclusively our association with the other areas in the United Kingdom in an effort to find solutions' (NIHC Deb 54, c 730). So although cross border contacts increased in the 1960s the Northern Ireland Government remained totally committed to the link with Britain. Agricultural development could not be considered 'in isolation from that of the United Kingdom as a whole. Developments in Northern Ireland agriculture must depend largely on the agricultural policy planned for the entire United Kingdom' (NIHC Deb 56, c. 953).

After the prorogation of Stormont cooperation continued at both ministerial and official level, particularly on issues arising from common membership of the EC. Obviously the Council of Agriculture Ministers provided an opportunity for the

British and Irish Governments to raise matters of mutual interest and NIO ministers also met their Dublin counterparts on several occasions. However although social and business relations were good at senior level, most civil servants had 'very little contact with any part of the agricultural network in the Republic. The links with MAFF are the most important outside Northern Ireland although informal direct links with DG VI are increasing' (Collins, 1993, p. 34).

An all Ireland agricultural policy?

Membership of the EC and the application of a common agricultural policy gave renewed impetus to cross border cooperation. According to the Belfast Telegraph the 'two parts of Ireland have been known to make combined approaches to Europe, and the EEC - with UK blessing - has occasionally regarded Northern Ireland as a special case, to avoid border complications' (Belfast Telegraph, 18 January 1985). For example, Northern Ireland was established as a separate region within the EC common sheepmeat regime in 1982 and later was incorporated into an all Ireland region for the transition period to a new support policy. This was reinforced by the increasing convergence of general trends in the agricultural industries in the north and south. According to a report in 1981 there had been 'a remarkable tendency for the two industries, which were already very similar in 1912, to become even more alike' (Sheehy, O'Brien and McClelland, 1981, p. 29). Also significant was the much better performance and expansion of agriculture in the Republic after EC entry compared with the relative decline in the north. Whereas farmers incomes in the north had been better throughout most of the Stormont period, after EC entry the income of farmers in south increased at a much faster rate. Moreover during the 1970s incomes rose in real terms in the south but fell in the north. Part of the explanation for the relatively poor performance of Northern Ireland agriculture in the EC was the different policies adopted by the Irish and British Governments towards the support and agri-monetary systems. As a substantial food exporter the south sought devaluation of the green pound to obtain the maximum possible price increases whereas the United Kingdom, as a food importer, was reluctant to penalize consumers through devaluation. The less rapid devaluation of the green pound in the United Kingdom resulted in southern farmers receiving higher prices for their produce than those in the north and schemes such as the Meat Industry Export Scheme (MIES) had to be introduced to prevent distortions of cross border trade.

The better performance of southern agriculture in the EC, coupled with the much more sensitive agricultural and rural policy followed by the Irish Government, only served to deepen the dissatisfaction which northern farmers felt about British policy and the level of farming incomes. A report prepared for the New Ireland Forum provided an analysis of agricultural development on both sides of the border and of the effects of integrated policy and planning on the agricultural industry in Ireland. According to the Report the position adopted by Irish Ministers for Agriculture in relation to improved support prices under the CAP has been more helpful to farmers in Ireland, North and South, than the position adopted by the UK Ministers, who have been more concerned with the effects of price increases on the EEC budget and on U.K. consumers than on the farming sector (New Ireland Forum, 1983, p. 67).

The joint submission to the Forum of ICOS and the UAOS also claimed that the 'policy adopted by the Republic in many instances when dealing with the EEC in Brussels has been more appropriate to the needs of Northern Ireland farmers where the agricultural industry represents a much larger proportion of GNP than elsewhere in the United Kingdom' (Belfast Telegraph, 1 March 1984). However it was also strongly emphasized that the submission was 'economic and social in its content and should not be interpreted as having any political implications regarding the constitutional position of either Northern Ireland or the Irish Republic' (Belfast Telegraph, 1 March 1984).

In relation to proposals for CAP reform, particularly for milk quotas, the 'position strongly advocated by Irish Ministers was of far greater value to farmers, North and South, than the position of the UK which, although expressing a less forceful degree of opposition to the superlevy, has in general welcomed the Commission's proposals to reduce sharply expenditure under the CAP' (New Ireland Forum, 1983, p. 67). Certainly the generous treatment won by the Irish Government for its milk producers at the 1984 summit was the cause of much soul searching and recrimination within the agricultural network in Northern Ireland. Before the summit Nationalist sources argued that the Irish Government was more likely to protect the interests of farmers in Northern Ireland than the British and urged a campaign for an all Ireland derogation. For the Irish News Garret FitzGerald's demand for special treatment was made 'on behalf of Northern farmers as well as Southern ones. Unionist MP's enthusiasm for Mrs Thatcher's strong stand at the summit has been rather misplaced. Mrs Thatcher has signally failed to put the case for the North's dairy farmers and it is Dr FitzGerald rather than Mrs Thatcher that they should be praising' (Irish News, 22 March 1984). SDLP agriculture spokesman Denis Haughey also found it significant that the hopes of all Irish farmers rested on the shoulders of the Irish Taoiseach. It was Mrs Thatcher, with her demands for cuts in the agriculture budget, who was the main opponent of the case for Irish farmers north and south: 'What a pity that in these negotiations which are vital for NI...we are misrepresented in Brussels by Mrs Thatcher...It is only in the context of the European Community that Irish agriculture can escape the stranglehold of Britain' (Irish News, 22 March 1984).

The general perception that the interests of Northern Ireland farmers were not properly protected by the British Government gave greater credence to Nationalist arguments for the development of an all Ireland agricultural policy. In the 1980s the issue of a single all Ireland CAP regime was increasingly debated in agricultural circles and beyond. This development occurred within the context of the greater focus on north-south relations, stimulated by the New Ireland Forum and developments in Anglo-Irish relations generally. A Co-operation North report in 1981 argued that the measures taken to maintain equilibrium in the beef and cattle trade such as MIES 'highlight the underlying unity of the agricultural industry throughout the whole island of Ireland and point to the use of common "green" exchange rates as a possible area for co-operation' (Sheehy, O'Brien and McClelland, 1981, p. 28). A report of the New Ireland Forum recommended that an all Ireland agricultural area be created and that a variable premium price support system would 'best serve the interests of producers and processors north and south' (Belfast Telegraph, 19 January 1984). It was also suggested that 'greater integration of effort by farm organisations would contribute possibly to achieving the common interests of their members' and that joint ventures between firms and marketing organizations north and south would lead to greater overall efficiency in agriculture throughout the entire country (Belfast Telegraph, 17 May 1984). Moreover greater 'integration of development programmes in under-developed regions which are contiguous on both sides of the border would enhance the results from development expenditure' (Belfast Telegraph, 17 May 1984).

Addressing the UFU annual dinner in April 1984 the IFA President proposed 'an examination by both our associations of the pluses and minuses of Ireland being treated as one unit for the purposes of the operation of the Common Agricultural Policy' (Belfast Telegraph, 20 April 1984). According to Joe Rea the priority for both the IFA and UFU was better farming and improved living conditions for farmers. It was essential to acknowledge the fundamental political differences in Ireland but have enough commonsense to ensure that good farming and good business were not impeded because of the diversity of political traditions. These sentiments were shared by NIAPA which during the quota controversy argued that 'all public representatives in the North and South should have fully supported the derogation of the super levy in the whole of Ireland. The problems of the farmers in the Republic of Ireland, which have received the sympathy of the European Council of Ministers, are the problems of the farmers in Northern Ireland' (NIA 136, p 32).

John Hume also believed that there was 'a remarkable and growing unanimity across party lines in the North that the same agricultural arrangements should apply North and South' (Belfast Telegraph, 3 April 1984). All agricultural interests in the island of Ireland should aim to establish 'a common agricultural regime for farmers in Ireland within the overall framework of European agricultural policy' (Belfast Telegraph, 3 April 1984). His colleague Denis Haughey stressed the similarities of the agricultural sectors north and south and pointed to the fact that all British Governments had 'uniformly been on a different side of the debate in Brussels on all agricultural matters from the side on which instinct and interests would place both parts of Ireland' (Belfast Telegraph, 17 January 1985). The central problem was the misrepresentation of Northern Ireland farmers' interests by the British Government. The arguments were 'overwhelming and compelling for a common agricultural regime for the whole of Ireland and I am calling on both Governments, in Dublin and in London, to set up a joint North-South commission to work out how it might be achieved' (Belfast Telegraph, 17 January 1985). Haughey claimed that his proposed north-south commission was politically neutral and the reaction of the British Government and the Unionist parties would be a litmus test of their willingness to reach an agreed settlement to the political and constitutional problems of Northern Ireland. If the British Government could not 'co-operate with us in a matter which involves no potential economic disadvantage to them and which need not prejudice political relationships, then of what value are the British Government's statements about closer co-operation with the Republic in matters of common interest?' (Belfast Telegraph, 17 January 1985).

The justifiable claim that the interests of Northern Ireland farmers could be better protected by the Irish Government created difficulties for Unionists who could less easily point to benefits of the parity approach and the link with Britain. This was only exacerbated by the better performance of southern farmers as a result of EC membership. The general Unionist approach, however, was to argue alongside the other British farmers' unions for a more sympathetic agricultural policy for the United Kingdom as a whole. In 1978, for example, the UFU emphatically rejected suggestions for an all Ireland green pound on the grounds that the best solution to the problems of regional agriculture and cross border difficulties lay in the devaluation of the green pound by the British Government. The difficulties faced by Unionists were apparent in the run up to the 1984 European summit. Instead of supporting the idea that farmers throughout Ireland should receive special treatment on the matter of quotas the Ulster Unionist Party supported Thatcher's strong stand against concessions to the Republic. The News Letter congratulated Thatcher on her refusal 'to accord to Eire special treatment which would have unfavourable repercussions for Ulster' (Belfast News Letter, 22 March 1984). On the other hand when it became apparent that the farmers of the Republic would be granted concessions, Unionists demanded equal treatment because special treatment for the Republic would create unfair competition across the border and damage the Ulster milk industry.

During the milk quotas controversy Jim Nicholson warned that an all Ireland agricultural economy would have serious ramifications for the constitutional position of Northern Ireland and accused John Hume, the Dublin Government and the IFA of attempting to make political capital out of the difficulties of Northern Ireland producers. Europe was no friend of Northern Ireland and the only solution to farmers' problems was to press the Secretary of State and British Government to ensure that the region's dependency on agriculture received special recognition (Belfast Telegraph, 24 April 1984). Haughey's proposal for a joint north-south commission was criticized for putting agriculture into the political arena and for showing scant regard for the future of the industry in Northern Ireland. The 'vast majority of Northern Ireland farmers and those engaged in the industry will be horrified at the thought of having their present standard of living lowered and being deprived of the few advantages they enjoy' (Belfast Telegraph, 18 January 1985). Whilst the Ulster Unionist Party recognized the advantages of cross border cooperation they would not countenance any attempt to evolve an all Ireland system. Roy Thompson of the DUP also strongly condemned the suggestion: 'It is nothing new, but Denis Haughey's purpose in resurrecting it now has nothing to do with the best interests of the farmers of Northern Ireland. He is out to promote wherever possible the merger of North and South for purely political motives' (Belfast Telegraph, 24 January 1985). The fact that north and south shared certain interests in agriculture was 'an entirely different thing from saying that North and South should always been treated as one unit for agriculture' (Belfast Telegraph, 24 January 1985).

The reaction of the Alliance Party was more measured. For Addie Morrow, Haughey had

> related the undoubted benefits of a common agricultural regime but has not pointed out the vast difficulties such a change would create unless, of course, we all suddenly agree to a united Ireland as Mr. Haughey would like...Let us by all means continue to work towards closer co-operation for the benefit of the agricultural community, but with a realistic appreciation of the problems (Belfast Telegraph, 24 January 1985).

This view echoed that of the Co-operation North report which stated that although considerable benefits would 'flow from a uniform implementation of the CAP on both sides of the border' the problems which would arise 'in respect of the North's trade with Great Britain would have to be resolved in any such arrangement and these problems could be so complex that a mutually acceptable solution might be very difficult to achieve' (Sheehy, O'Brien and McClelland, 1981, p. 69). For the Belfast Telegraph, Haughey's suggestion was 'perfectly logical. North and South have much more in common, agriculturally, than Northern Ireland and, say, East Anglia. But, of course, politics is unavoidable, and the climate is far from favourable' (Belfast Telegraph, 18 January 1985). The proposal that common agricultural interests should be given formal expression in a policy for an all Ireland region, separate from that of Britain, had

> some initial attraction, but the farmers of Northern Ireland - big and small, unionist and nationalist - would have to be convinced that what would be gained on the one hand would not be lost on the other. Some UK policies have benefited Ulster agriculture, and it could be a risky proposition to detach from the mainland - and perhaps lose out in the long term - for short term gains' (Belfast Telegraph, 18 January 1985).

The British Government refused to consider the development of an all Ireland agricultural policy. In 1984 Labour spokesman Clive Soley argued that Northern Ireland was caught between British and Irish policies and that 'the only solution is to make common representations to the European Community...on behalf of Northern Ireland and the Republic of Ireland' (HC Deb 58, c. 876). Adam Butler clearly iterated the British Government's stance when he replied that 'Northern Ireland receives special benefits from European funds and national Exchequer funds because of our recognition of the Province's special problems. A common agricultural policy for the whole of Ireland...would not be acceptable to the people of Northern Ireland, let alone to the Government' (HC Deb 58, c. 876).

Agriculture, the peace process, and the parity principle

The development of a bipartisan inter-governmental approach to the general political and constitutional problems of Northern Ireland altered the context in which the future of regional agriculture has been considered. The Anglo-Irish Joint Studies and Intergovernmental Council (initiated after the summit in 1981), and the Anglo-Irish Agreement, created the conditions for increased cross border cooperation in agriculture. The Council of Ireland proposed at the Sunningdale Conference in 1973 would inevitably have been concerned with agricultural matters had it been established. The Anglo-Irish Agreement committed both the British and Irish Governments to the promotion of cross border cooperation in economic and social development. Under Article 10 arrangements would be made to permit cross border cooperation between the relevant north and south authorities if a devolved assembly was established in Northern Ireland. In the absence of devolution the Intergovernmental Conference would provide the necessary framework for cross border economic development. In addition the International Fund for Ireland was established in 1986 to promote economic and social advance, and to encourage reconciliation between the two communities in Northern Ireland and throughout Ireland generally.

The Maher Report in 1986 noted that the Anglo-Irish Agreement 'increases opportunities for mutual advantageous co-operation between the population of all Ireland and in particular the two communities in Northern Ireland' (Farmweek, 6 June 1986). Collins, moreover, has noted that for senior civil servants 'the conventions of interaction with Dublin are straightforward, cooperative and cordial. Since the Anglo-Irish Agreement, all-Ireland considerations have formed a required part of all briefing papers, even if generally the response is perfunctory' (Collins, 1993, p. 34). However although Anglo-Irish developments regularized contacts at official and ministerial level, there was little detail about how political and administrative structures for agriculture might develop in the overall context of political agreement between the parties in Northern Ireland.

In the framework documents drawn up in 1995 the British and Irish Governments agreed on the need to establish 'new institutions and structures to take account of the totality of relationships and to enable the people of Ireland to work together in all areas of common interest while fully respecting their diversity' (Frameworks for the Future Part II, 1995, para. 5). A comprehensive accommodation would include interlocking and mutually supportive institutions across three strands: devolved structures within Northern Ireland, north-south institutions, and east-west structures to enhance cooperation between the British and Irish Governments. Agriculture has been explicitly identified as one of the likeliest candidates for future cross border cooperation or all Ireland arrangements. Cross border institutions are proposed to 'cater adequately for present and future political, social and economic inter-connections on the island of Ireland, enabling representatives of the main traditions, North and South, to enter agreed dynamic, new, co-operative and constructive relationships' (Frameworks for the Future Part II, 1995, para. 24). The pivotal role would be assumed by a North-South Body (NSB) drawn from the Irish Government and new democratic institutions in Northern Ireland which would carry out delegated functions over a range of designated matters (perhaps operating through subsidiary bodies organized on a functional basis, for example for aspects of agriculture). Both Governments would designate initial functions to the NSB after discussion with the political parties in Northern Ireland. Subsequently the NSB itself could recommend to the Irish Government and the Northern Ireland administration that additional functions be designated. In principle any responsibilities transferred to a new devolved assembly in Northern Ireland could be designated to the NSB. Moreover any EC matter relevant to the competence of either administration could be raised for consideration in the NSB which would also have an important role in developing 'an agreed approach for the whole island in respect of the challenges and opportunities of the European Union' (Frameworks for the Future Part II, 1995, para. 26).

Clearly on these criteria the agricultural sector is a prime candidate for designation to the NSB in some form, particularly given that it has always been one of the most significant transferred powers and that it is a sector with substantial EC input via the implementation of the CAP. This contention is explicitly supported by the exposition in the document of the three broad categories of designated functions.

On a range of "executive" matters the NSB would be directly responsible for the establishment of an agreed policy and for its implementation on a joint basis. Such executive level functions would come from several broad categories including sectors involving a natural or physical all Ireland framework, and overseas marketing and promotional activities. Specifically the NSB would be responsible for the management of all EC programmes and initiatives to be implemented on a cross border or island wide basis in Ireland. This would include the preparation of joint submissions under EC programmes and initiatives, in consultation with the two Governments under the aegis of the standing British-Irish Intergovernmental Conference. Although individual projects could be implemented either jointly or separately, this clearly opens the way for the joint implementation of a CAP regime for Ireland.

"Harmonising" responsibilities would involve consultation on the formulation of policy and the exchange of information. Both sides would be obliged to seek agreement on a common policy although implementation might be undertaken separately. The document explicitly identifies aspects of agriculture and fisheries such as research, training and advisory services, and animal welfare as likely candidates for harmonising.

Thirdly the NSB would be a "consultative" forum on any aspect of designated matters on the initiative of either side. There would be a duty to consult about policy and exchange information but no formal requirement for agreement, policy harmonisation or joint implementation. Here again agricultural matters might be prime candidates for consideration but as most of these issues will have executive or harmonising status there will be little of importance left on which to consult.

A further important recommendation is that designated matters could be moved on the scale between consultation, harmonisation and executive action. This opens the possibility that harmonising functions such as agricultural research and animal welfare could be upgraded to executive status. It is unlikely that 'downgrading' is envisaged given the express intention that the 'remit of the body should be dynamic, enabling progressive extension by agreement of its functions to new areas. Its role should develop to keep pace with the growth of harmonisation and with greater integration between the two economies' (Frameworks for the Future, 1995, para. 38). Indeed both Governments 'expect that significant responsibilities, including meaningful functions at executive level' will be a feature of any final agreement (Frameworks for the Future, 1995, para. 28).

The operation of the NSB would be subject to regular scrutiny in new agreed political institutions in Northern Ireland and in the Oireachtas, for example by the Northern Ireland Assembly Departmental Committee which would be established to oversee and scrutinize the work of the Department of Agriculture. Matters transferred to new political institutions in Northern Ireland will generally be excluded from consideration in the standing British-Irish Intergovernmental Conference maintained to deal with east-west issues. In the event of a breakdown of the agreement and the reintroduction of direct rule from Westminster, however, arrangements would be made to implement the commitment, to promote cooperation at all levels and to ensure that the cooperation developed through the NSB would be maintained.

Cross border cooperation in the agricultural sector in Ireland will form a significant part of any overall political settlement of the Northern Ireland problem. Agriculture is certain to be an important aspect of the remit of future north-south or all island institutional arrangements, perhaps akin to the Foyle Fisheries Commission jointly established by the Dáil and Northern Ireland Parliament in 1952. However history shows that this process will not be politically uncontroversial as only too clearly demonstrated by the breakdown of previous constitutional initiatives. The initial hostile reaction of the Unionist parties to the framework documents demonstrates that one of the main obstacles to be overcome in the search for general agreement will be the nature, scope and extent of institutional arrangements to link the two jurisdictions in Ireland. The historical precedents are not all unfavourable, however. A century earlier in 1895 Horace Plunkett, Unionist MP for Dublin South, initiated all party negotiations which eventually resulted in the creation of DATII in 1900.

In a sense the wheel has turned full circle since partition. In 1920 the British Government hoped that north-south cooperation in agriculture would be fostered by the proposed Council of Ireland which would act as a bridge between the two parliaments and in turn facilitate reunification. In an uncanny echo of contemporary developments, the Council of Ireland, which had no executive powers unlike the body envisaged in the framework documents, would have been able to discuss matters of mutual interest and consider what services ought to be administered on an all Ireland basis. For Macpherson, the Chief Secretary for Ireland, as 'a matter of practical business it would, of course, be in the interests of administration and of economy to transfer many Irish services to the Council, such as the Department of Agriculture' (HC Deb 127, c. 929). Then the balance of political forces enabled the Unionists to frustrate this intention and instead to use the powers transferred to the regional Parliament to develop an agricultural policy based on parity with Great Britain. Seventy five years on, the changed socio-economic and political conditions in Northern Ireland and the emasculation of Ulster Unionist power will mean that unlike in the 1920s cross border institutions can no longer be resisted. The parity imperative will remain at the heart of agricultural policy but the dynamic has been reversed. In the future it will not be parity with Great Britain which provides the guiding principle of agricultural policy but parity conceived in terms of Ireland as a whole.

Bibliography

Books and articles

Addison, P. (1977), *The Road To 1945*, Quartet, London.

Lord Astor and Rowntree, S. (1935), *The Agricultural Dilemma*, P.S. King, London.

Lord Astor and Rowntree, S. (1939), *British Agriculture*, Penguin, Harmondsworth.

Barton, B. (1988), *Brookeborough: The Making of a Prime Minister*, Institute of Irish Studies, Queen's University, Belfast.

Beer, S.H. (1969), *Modern British Politics*, Faber and Faber, London.

Bew, P., Gibbon, P. and Patterson, H. (1979), *The State in Northern Ireland 1921-72*, Manchester University Press, Manchester.

Birrell, D. and Murie, A. (1980), *Policy and Government in Northern Ireland: Lessons of Devolution*, Gill and Macmillan, Dublin.

Blake, J.W. (1956), *Northern Ireland in the Second World War*, HMSO, Belfast.

Bogdanor, V. (1979), *Devolution*, Oxford University Press, Oxford.

The British Association (1935), *Britain In Depression*, Pitman, London.

The British Association (1938), *Britain In Recovery*, Pitman, London.

Buckland, P. (1979), *The Factory of Grievances: Devolved Government in Northern Ireland 1921-39*, Gill and Macmillan, Dublin.

Chester, D.N. (ed.)(1951), *Lessons of the British War Economy*, Cambridge University Press, Cambridge.

Collins, N. (1993), 'Agricultural policy networks in Northern Ireland and the Republic of Ireland', Paper presented to *CAMAR Competitiveness Project Conference*, Belfast, October.

Collins, N. and Mack, N. (1995), 'Farm household participation in agricultural policy decision making', *Irish Political Studies*, Vol. 10, pp. 1-26.

Cox, G., Lowe, P. and Winter, M. (1986), 'From state direction to self regulation: the historical development of corporatism in British agriculture', *Policy and Politics*, Vol. 14, pp. 475-90.

Cruickshank, J.G. and Wilcock, D.N. (eds.)(1982), *Northern Ireland: Environment and Natural Resources*, Queen's University and New University of Ulster, Belfast and Coleraine.

Ditch, J.S. (1988), *Social Policy in Northern Ireland between 1939-1950*, Avebury, Aldershot.

Lord Ernle (1961), *English Farming: Past and Present*, Heinemann, London.

Grant, W. (1983), 'The National Farmers Union: The Classic Case of Incorporation?' in Marsh, D. (ed.), *Pressure Politics*, Junction Books, London.

Grant, W. (1991), *The Dairy Industry: an International Comparison*, Dartmouth, Aldershot.

Grant, W. (1992), 'Models of interest intermediation and policy formation applied to an internationally comparative study of the dairy industry', *European Journal of Political Research*, Vol. 21, pp. 53-68.

Greer A.J. (1994), 'Policy networks and state-farmer relations in Northern Ireland, 1921-72', *Political Studies*, Vol. 42, pp. 396-412.

Greer, J. and Murray, M. (1993), 'Rural Ireland - Personality and Policy Context' in Murray, M. and Greer, J. (eds.), *Rural Development in Ireland*, Avebury, Aldershot.

Hammond, R.J. (1951), *Food, Vol. I: The Growth of Policy*, HMSO, London, United Kingdom History of the Second World War.

Hancock, W.K. and Gowing, M.M. (1949), *The British War Economy*, HMSO, London, United Kingdom History of the Second World War.

Harbinson, J. (1973), *The Ulster Unionist Party, 1882-1973*, Blackstaff Press, Belfast.

Harkness, D.A.E. (1935), 'The Evolution of Agricultural Policy' in *The Ulster Year Book 1935*, HMSO, Belfast.

Isles, K.S. and Cuthbert, N. (1957), *An Economic Survey of Northern Ireland*, HMSO, Belfast.

Johnson, N. (1975), 'Editorial: The Royal Commission on the Constitution', *Public Administration*, Vol. 52, pp. 1-12.

Jordan, A.G., Maloney, W.A. and McLaughlin, A.M. (1992a), *Assumptions About the Role of Groups in the Policy Process: The British Policy Community Approach*, British Interest Group Project Working Paper No. 4, University of Aberdeen.

Jordan, A.G., Maloney, W.A. and McLaughlin, A.M. (1992b), *Policy Making in Agriculture: 'Primary' Policy Community or Specialist Policy Communities*, British Interest Group Project Working Paper No. 5, University of Aberdeen.

Jordan, A.G. and Schubert, K. (1992), 'A Preliminary Ordering of Policy Network Labels', *European Journal of Political Research*, Vol. 21, pp. 7-27.

La Palombara, J. (1964), *Interest Groups in Italian Politics*, Princeton, New Jersey.

Katzenstein, P.J. (1985), *Small States in World Markets*, Cornell University Press, Ithaca.

Lawrence, R.J. (1965), *The Government of Northern Ireland: Public Finance and Public Services, 1921-64*, Oxford University Press, Oxford.

Lee, J. (1973), *The Modernisation of Irish Society, 1848-1918*, Gill and Macmillan, Dublin.

McColgan, J. (1983), *British Policy and Irish Administration 1920-22*, George Allen and Unwin, London.

McMahon, D. (1984), *Republicans and Imperialists: Anglo-Irish Relations in the 1930s*, Yale University Press, Yale.

Middlemass, K. (1979), *Politics in Industrial Society*, Deutsch, London.

Mowat, C.L. (1955), *Britain Between The Wars, 1918-1940*, Methuen, London.

Murray, K.A.H. (1955), *Agriculture*, HMSO, London, United Kingdom History of the Second World War.

New Ireland Forum (1983), *A Comparative Description of the Economic Structure and Situation, North and South*, New Ireland Forum, Dublin.

O'Leary, C., Elliott. S. and Wilford, R. (1988), *The Northern Ireland Assembly 1982-1986: A Constitutional Experiment*, C Hurst and Queen's University Bookshop, London and Belfast.

Open University (1975), *Agriculture, D203, Decision making in Britain, Block III*, Open University Press, Milton Keynes.

Pelling, H. (1970), *Britain and the Second World War*, Collins, London.

Peters, B.G. (1989), *The Politics of Bureaucracy*, Longman, London.

Pollard, S. (1962), *The Development of the British Economy 1914-1950*, Edward Arnold, London.

Purdie, R. (1983), 'The Friends of Ireland' in Gallagher, T. and O'Connell, J. (eds.), *Contemporary Irish Studies*, Manchester University Press, Manchester.

Rhodes, R.A.W. (1988), *Beyond Westminster and Whitehall: the Sub-Central Governments of Britain*, Unwin Hyman, London.

Rhodes, R.A.W. and Marsh, D. (1992a), 'Policy Networks in British Politics: a Critique of Existing Approaches', in Marsh, D. and Rhodes, R.A.W. (eds.), *Policy Networks in British Government*, Clarendon Press, Oxford.

Rhodes, R.A.W. and Marsh, D. (1992b), 'New directions in the study of policy networks', *European Journal of Political Research*, Vol. 21, pp. 181-205.

Richardson, J.H. (1936), *British Economic Foreign Policy*, George Allen & Unwin, London.

Rose, R. (1982), *Understanding the United Kingdom: The Territorial Dimension in Government*, Longman, London.

Sayers, R.S. (1956), *Financial Policy*, HMSO, London, United Kingdom History of the Second World War.

Seaman, L.C.B. (1967), *Post-Victorian Britain 1902-1951*, University Paperbacks/Methuen, London.

Self, P. and Storing, H.J. (1962), *The State and the Farmer*, George Allen and Unwin, London.

Sheehy, S.J., O'Brien, J.T. and McClelland, S.D. (1981), *Agriculture in the Republic of Ireland and Northern Ireland*, Co-operation North, Dublin and Belfast.

Skidelsky, R. (1970), *Politicians and the Slump*, Pelican, Harmondsworth.

Smith, M.J. (1989), 'The Annual Review: the emergence of a corporatist institution?', *Political Studies*, Vol. 37, pp. 81-96.

Smith, M.J. (1990), *The Politics of Agricultural Support in Britain: the Development of the Agricultural Policy Community*, Dartmouth, Aldershot.

Stainer, T.F. (1985), *An analysis of Economic Trends in Northern Ireland Agriculture since 1970*, Department of Agriculture for Northern Ireland, Belfast.

Symons, L. (ed.)(1963), *Land Use in Northern Ireland*, London University Press, London.

Tracy, M. (1989), *Government and Agriculture in Western Europe 1880-1988*, Harvester Wheatsheaf, London.

Trimble, M.J. (1984), 'The impact of the European Community Policy on Northern Ireland Agriculture' in Simpson, J.V. (ed.), *European Community Policy in Northern Ireland*, Queen's University, Belfast.

Whetham, E.H. (1974), 'The Agriculture Act, 1920 and its repeal - The "Great Betrayal"', *Agricultural History Review*, Vol. 22, pp. 36-49.

Whetham, E.H. (1978), *The Agrarian History of England and Wales, Vol. VIII 1914-39*, Cambridge University Press, Cambridge.

Whyte, J. (1983), 'Discrimination under the Unionist regime', in Gallagher, T. and O'Connell, J. (eds.), *Contemporary Irish Studies*, Manchester University Press, Manchester.

Wilson, G.K. (1977), *Special Interests and Policy Making*, John Wiley & Sons, London.

Winch, D. (1969), *Economics And Policy*, Hodder and Stoughton, London.

Northern Ireland House of Commons debates

NIHC Deb 2, 25 May 1922
NIHC Deb 4, 27 March 1924
NIHC Deb 4, 13 May 1924
NIHC Deb 6, 7 September 1925
NIHC Deb 7, 20 April 1926
NIHC Deb 7, 20 August 1926
NIHC Deb 8, 15 March 1927
NIHC Deb 8, 21 March 1927
NIHC Deb 8, 11 May 1927
NIHC Deb 8, 27 October 1927
NIHC Deb 9, 10 May 1928
NIHC Deb 9, 21 May 1928

NIHC Deb 9, 23 May 1928
NIHC Deb 12, 11 March 1930
NIHC Deb 12, 13 March 1930
NIHC Deb 12, 7 October 1930
NIHC Deb 14, 14 April 1932
NIHC Deb 18, 6 May 1936
NIHC Deb 19, 12 October 1937
NIHC Deb 21, 23 March 1938
NIHC Deb 21, 26 April 1938
NIHC Deb 21, 20 October 1938
NIHC Deb 21, 26 October 1938
NIHC Deb 22, 9 May 1939
NIHC Deb 22, 4 September 1939
NIHC Deb 22, 19 September 1939
NIHC Deb 23, 6 February 1940
NIHC Deb 23, 1 May 1940
NIHC Deb 25, 28 October 1942
NIHC Deb 26, 22 July 1943
NIHC Deb 26, 5 October 1943
NIHC Deb 27, 28 March 1944
NIHC Deb 31, 21 May 1947
NIHC Deb 31, 4 June 1947
NIHC Deb 32, 17 February 1948
NIHC Deb 32, 8 December 1948
NIHC Deb 32, 9 December 1948
NIHC Deb 33, 10 May 1949
NIHC Deb 34, 29 June 1950
NIHC Deb 35, 25 April 1951
NIHC Deb 37, 24 February 1953
NIHC Deb 37, 25 February 1953
NIHC Deb 37, 8 April 1953
NIHC Deb 38, 10 November 1953
NIHC Deb 38, 18 February 1954
NIHC Deb 38, 2 March 1954
NIHC Deb 38, 25 May 1954
NIHC Deb 38, 17 November 1954
NIHC Deb 38, 23 November 1954
NIHC Deb 39, 11 May 1955
NIHC Deb 40, 2 May 1956
NIHC Deb 40, 6 November 1956
NIHC Deb 41, 12 March 1957
NIHC Deb 44, 16 April 1959
NIHC Deb 45, 28 October 1959
NIHC Deb 46, 17 February 1960

NIHC Deb 48, 6 June 1961
NIHC Deb 49, 24 October 1961
NIHC Deb 51, 26 April 1962
NIHC Deb 54, 2 May 1963
NIHC Deb 54, 15 May 1963
NIHC Deb 54, 11 June 1963
NIHC Deb 56, 21 January 1964
NIHC Deb 56, 25 February 1964
NIHC Deb 59, 17 February 1965
NIHC Deb 60, 12 May 1965
NIHC Deb 61, 29 June 1965
NIHC Deb 62, 4 December 1965
NIHC Deb 63, 26 April 1966
NIHC Deb 63, 18 May 1966
NIHC Deb 63, 2 June 1966
NIHC Deb 64, 14 June 1966
NIHC Deb 64, 26 October 1966
NIHC Deb 64, 23 November 1966
NIHC Deb 65, 1 February 1967
NIHC Deb 66, 18 April 1967
NIHC Deb 69, 25 April 1968
NIHC Deb 70, 2 July 1968
NIHC Deb 74, 20 November 1969
NIHC Deb 78, 16 December 1970

Northern Ireland Assembly debates

NIA Deb, 1 May 1984, p. 44.
NIA Deb, 11 June 1985, p. 121
NIA Deb, 5 July 1984, p. 898.
NIA Deb, 3 October 1984, p. 89.
NIA Deb, 27 November 1984, p. 289.

Northern Ireland Assembly reports

NIA 81, Draft Agriculture Order 1983
NIA 136 (ii), EEC 1984-85 Farm Price Agreement
NIA 161, Report of the Pigs Marketing Service Scheme and the Agricultural Marketing (NI) Order 1982
NIA 162, Promotion and Marketing of Seed Potatoes
NIA 165, Seed Potato Levy
NIA 195 (i), Milk Quotas

Public Record Office of Northern Ireland (PRONI)

CAB3A/116   Speeches by Craig, Brooke etc.

Cabinet conclusions

CAB4/324, 22 May 1934
CAB4/397, 25 March 1938
CAB4/401, 15 September 1938
CAB4/403, 16 November 1938
CAB4/513, 19 June 1942
CAB4/524, 17 September 1942
CAB4/696, 9 January 1947
CAB4/697, 13 January 1947
CAB4/735, 10 November 1947
CAB4/739, 11 December 1947
CAB4/836, 15 January 1951
CAB4/836, 2 February 1951

Cabinet Secretariat papers relating to agriculture

CAB9E/8/1	Rate relief
CAB9E/23/1-2	Agricultural development
CAB9E/34/1	Experimental farm
CAB9E/47/1	Rate relief
CAB9E/57/1-7	Agricultural marketing
CAB9E/69/1	General agricultural questions
CAB9E/75/1-2	Marketing of fruit
CAB9E/111/1	Milk dispute 1931
CAB9E/122/1-2	Milk marketing
CAB9E/134/1	Mechanization of farming
CAB9E/150/1	1947 Agriculture Act

Ministry of Agriculture policy papers

AG16/9/2	Marketing of meat 1929
AG16/11/2	Ottawa Conference
AG16/11/4	Pigs marketing
AG16/13/15	Pigs marketing
AG16/16/10	UFU grant
AG16/18/16	War plans
AG16/26/1	Agriculture Act 1949
AG16/26/17	Hill Farming Act 1946
AG18/11/4	Acreage payments policy

Department of Agriculture and Technical Instruction for Ireland

Cd 838 (1901), First Annual General Report, HMSO, Dublin.

Ministry/Department of Agriculture for Northern Ireland

General reports

Second General Report, 1922-23 (1924), HMSO, Belfast.
Cmd 129 (1930), Ninth General Report, HMSO, Belfast.
Cmd 180 (1937), Eleventh General Report, HMSO, Belfast.
Cmd 295 (1951), Twelfth General Report, HMSO, Belfast.
Cmd 577 (1973), Thirty Second General Report, HMSO, Belfast.
Cmd 588 (1975), Thirty Fourth General Report, HMSO, Belfast.
Thirty Seventh General Report (1978), HMSO, Belfast.
Forty Fourth General Report 1984-85 (1985), HMSO, Belfast.
Forty Fifth General Report 1985-86 (1986), HMSO, Belfast.
Forty Sixth General Report 1986-87 (1987), HMSO, Belfast.
Forty Ninth General Report 1989-90 (1990), HMSO, Belfast.
Fiftieth General Report 1990-91 (1991), HMSO, Belfast.
Fifty First General Report, 1991-92 (1992), HMSO, Belfast.
Fifty Second General Report, 1992-93 (1993), HMSO, Belfast.

Reports on agricultural statistics

Eighth Report on the Agricultural Statistics of Northern Ireland, 1961/62 to 1966/67 (1970), HMSO, Belfast.
Ninth Report on the Agricultural Statistics of Northern Ireland, 1966-67 to 1973-74 (1977), HMSO, Belfast.
Statistical Review of Northern Ireland Agriculture 1991 (1992b), HMSO, Belfast.

Northern Ireland Command Papers

Cmd 17 (1923) Report of the Agricultural Aid Committee, HMSO, Belfast.
Cmd 27 (1924) The Commission on the Natural and Industrial Resources of Northern Ireland Report on the Northern Ireland Egg Industry, HMSO, Belfast.
Cmd 75 (1927) Report of the Departmental Committee on the Transit, Prices and Marketing of Agricultural Produce, HMSO, Belfast.
Cmd 249 (1947) Reports of the Agricultural Enquiry Committee, HMSO, Belfast.
Cmd 479 (1965) Economic Development: Government Statement and the Wilson Report, HMSO, Belfast.
Cmd 500 (1966) Fatstock Marketing in Northern Ireland, HMSO, Belfast.

Cmd 545 (1970) Report of a Committee of Inquiry set up to examine the Marketing of Pigs in Northern Ireland, HMSO, Belfast.

Other government publications

Northern Ireland Digest of Statistics (10) September 1958.
Northern Ireland Digest of Statistics (41) March 1974.
Department of Manpower Services Gazette, No. 3, 1979.
Frameworks for the Future, Part II, 'A New Framework for Agreement', February 1995.

United Kingdom House of Commons debates

5th series

HC Deb 127, 29 March 1920
HC Deb 127, 31 March 1920
HC Deb 136, 22 December 1920
HC Deb 262, 23 February 1932
HC Deb 324, 27 May 1937
HC Deb 355, 14 December 1939
HC Deb 367, 26 November 1940
HC Deb 415, 15 November 1945
HC Deb 432, 27 January 1947
HC Deb 482, 11 December 1950
HC Deb 496, 27 February 1952
HC Deb 523, 18 February 1954
HC Deb 656, 30 March 1962
HC Deb 682, 1 August 1963
HC Deb 725, 4 March 1966

6th series

HC Deb 56, 22 March 1984
HC Deb 58, 26 April 1984
HC Deb 58, 26 April 1984
HC Deb 59, 4 May 1984
HC Deb 61, 7 June 1984
HC Deb 63, 3 July 1984

House of Lords debates

HL Deb 43, 13 December 1920
HL Deb 43, 17 December 1920
HL Deb 53, 22 February 1923

United Kingdom parliamentary papers

Cmd 2581 (1926) Agricultural Policy, HMSO, London.
Cmd 4519 (1934) Milk Policy, HMSO, London.
Cmd 4651 (1934) The Livestock Situation, HMSO, London.
Cmd 4828 (1935) Imports of Meat into the United Kingdom, HMSO, London.
Cmd 5533 (1937) Milk Policy, HMSO, London.
Cmd 8989 (1953) Decontrol of Food and Marketing of Agricultural Produce, HMSO, London.
Cmnd 390 (1958) Annual Review and Determination of Guarantees, HMSO, London.
Cmnd 553 (1958) Assistance for Small Farmers, HMSO, London.
Cmnd 2282 (1964) Report of the Committee of Inquiry into Fatstock and Carcase Meat Marketing and Distribution, HMSO, London.
Cmnd 2315 (1964) Annual Review and Determination of Guarantees, HMSO, London.
Cmnd 2621 (1965) Annual Review and Determination of Guarantees, HMSO, London.
Cmnd 2737 (1965) Marketing of Meat and Livestock, HMSO, London.
Cmnd 2738 (1965) Development of Agriculture, HMSO, London.
Cmnd 3669 (1968) Report of the United Kingdom Re-organisation Commission for Eggs, HMSO, London.
Cmnd 5460 (1973) Report of the Royal Commission on the Constitution 1969-73, HMSO, London.
Cmnd 6020 (1975) Food From Our Own Resources, HMSO, London.
Cmnd 7458 (1979) Farming and the Nation, HMSO, London.

HC 14 (1984-85), Dairy Quotas, First Report from the Agriculture Committee of the House of Commons, HMSO, London.
HC 274 (1984-85), comment on the Minister's response to the Committee's report on the implementation of dairy quotas, HMSO, London.

Journals and newspapers

The Belfast News Letter
The Belfast Telegraph
Farmweek
The Irish News
The Northern Whig
The Times
Ulster Farmers' Journal

Name index